Mathematics

for
NTSE, Olympiads & Competitive Exams

Jaya Ghosh
B.Sc. (Maths), MCA, MBA (HR)

Published by:

F-2/16, Ansari road, Daryaganj, New Delhi-110002
☎ 23240026, 23240027 • *Fax:* 011-23240028
Email: info@vspublishers.com • *Website:* www.vspublishers.com

Regional Office : Hyderabad
5-1-707/1, Brij Bhawan (Beside Central Bank of India Lane)
Bank Street, Koti, Hyderabad - 500 095
☎ 040-24737290
E-mail: vspublishershyd@gmail.com

Branch Office : Mumbai
Jaywant Industrial Estate, 1st Floor–108, Tardeo Road
Opposite Sobo Central Mall, Mumbai – 400 034
☎ 022-23510736
E-mail: vspublishersmum@gmail.com

Follow us on:

© **Copyright:** V&S PUBLISHERS
Edition 2018

DISCLAIMER

While every attempt has been made to provide accurate and timely information in this book, neither the author nor the publisher assumes any responsibility for errors, unintended omissions or commissions detected therein. The author and publisher makes no representation or warranty with respect to the comprehensiveness or completeness of the contents provided.

All matters included have been simplified under professional guidance for general information only, without any warranty for applicability on an individual. Any mention of an organization or a website in the book, by way of citation or as a source of additional information, doesn't imply the endorsement of the content either by the author or the publisher. It is possible that websites cited may have changed or removed between the time of editing and publishing the book.

Results from using the expert opinion in this book will be totally dependent on individual circumstances and factors beyond the control of the author and the publisher.

It makes sense to elicit advice from well informed sources before implementing the ideas given in the book. The reader assumes full responsibility for the consequences arising out from reading this book.

For proper guidance, it is advisable to read the book under the watchful eyes of parents/guardian. The buyer of this book assumes all responsibility for the use of given materials and information.

The copyright of the entire content of this book rests with the author/publisher. Any infringement/transmission of the cover design, text or illustrations, in any form, by any means, by any entity will invite legal action and be responsible for consequences thereon.

Publisher's Note

With a view to strengthen the career aspirations of student community, V&S Publishers has published this book **MATHEMATICS for NTSE, Olympiads & Competitive Exams** under its Gen X Series (Generating Xcellence in Generation X). While the books under Gen X Series are published to propel school students into higher learning orbit, this particular book is intended to boost the success rate of school students appearing or intending to write these research-based and other competitive examinations for higher studies or jobs. The importance of NTSE and Olympiad examinations lies in the fact that on the basis of its result, a student can win scholarship for five years or more years and succeed in building a bright career. And hence we are giving details of this examination right at the start of the book.

The MATHEMATICS forms part of the SAT (Scholastic Aptitude Test) question paper, one of the three papers which the students write in each of the Stages-I and II of the National Talent Search Examination (NTSE). Stage-I is conducted by States and Union Territories whereas NCERT conducts Stage-II examination.

This examination is organised to award scholarship to students currently studying at the Class X level. Scholarships are awarded up to Ph.D. in Sciences, Social Sciences, Humanities, Languages, Commerce, Vocational Studies and Fine arts. And up to second degree level for professional courses in medicines, engineering, technology, management and law. NTSE consists of Mental Ability Test (MAT), Language Test (LT) and Scholastic Aptitude Test (SAT) having multiple choice questions. Every year about **1000** scholarships are awarded - Rs.1250/- per month for Class XI & XII and Rs.2000/- at Graduation and Post-graduation level. Scholarship at Ph.D. level is governed by UGC norms.

All students studying in Class X in any recognized school are eligible to appear in Stage-I exam. For Stage-II, there is a quota for each State and Union Territory based on Student enrollment at secondary level. There are 3 papers in both stages–

1. Mental Ability Test (MAT)
2. Language Test (LT) and
3. Scholastic Ability Test (SAT).

Questions are in the form of multiple choices with negative marking deducting 1/3 marks only at the Stage II (National level). The tests are conducted in Asamiya, Bangla, English, Gujarati, Hindi, Kannada, Marathi, Malyalam, Odia, Punjabi, Tamil, Telugu and Urdu. However, language test is available in two languages – English & Hindi.

Test	No. of Questions	Maximum Marks	Time
Mental Ability Test (MAT)	50	50	45 minutes
Language Test	50	50	45 minutes
Scholastic Ability Test (SAT)	100	100	90 minutes

The concepts have been explained through various solved examples and multiple choice questions with answer key besides hints for solving the problems and use of everyday language hopefully enable students to master the subject with relative ease.

V&S Publishers has your welfare in mind, be assured!

Preface

To go through the NTSE examination a student must have a dedicated and serious approach. Students are often misled by the casual approach and the wrong notion that Objective Type Questions are easy to solve but in fact they require an extensive understanding of each prescribed subject or topic. Therefore, only hard work and diligent study can help the candidates crack the exam successfully.

This book provides a brief **Theory** on each topic, **Solved Examples** followed by **Fully Solved Exercises**.

The book contains questions very similar to what have been asked in the previous NTSE examinations of class 10th. I ask students *Do all the Exercises*, not missing even one of them. Make an attempt to answer the question first, and then read the given answer. I hope, on second reading, students would be able to do that on their own, without looking at the answers. In short, the condidates have to make an honest effort to achieve the goal.

Wish you a grand success in your examination, and a very bright future. I am sure the students will find this book most useful. I will be happy to receive constructive feedback and suggestions.

How to Read This Book

- The book in your hand is a unidirectional effort to guide and prepare students for NTSE/Olympiad examinations.

- The book covers. It consists of *Key Concepts* followed by *Solved Examples, Multiple Choice Questions* and *Answer Key and Hints and Solution*. The solutions to the MCQ's are provided at the end of each chapter.

- This book will really prove to be an asset for Class 7th, 8th, 9th and 10th students as they hardly find any material which can help them in building a strong foundation.

- The contents of this book have been developed as per the needs of the students *i.e.* the simple approach, conceptual clarity and exhaustive coverage in each section. Questions incorporated in the book conform to the latest pattern of NTSE making this book an exhaustive study material.

- *Previous Years Questions* have been given at the end of each chapter for clear cut understanding of the papers. Hint and Explanations of most of the questions have been provided so that the students could know how the correct answer has been reached at.

- A unique approach has been adopted to explain and illustrate methodology in Mathematics and Logical Reasoning, which is considered to be the key chapter to get an overall good score.

- Last, but not the least, four Mock Test Papers and two Solved Papers have been incorporated for the real exam – time feel.

Happy Reading.......

NTSE : An Introduction

The National Talent Search Examination for students studying in Class X is meant to identify and nurture talent. The examination is conducted every year at two levels: Stage – I (State Level) and Stage – II (National Level). National Talent Search Examination (NTSE) is an annual examination conducted by NCERT at national level. It is one of the most reputed talent search exams in India. It was started in the year 1963 and has grown in prestige and scope ever since. The objective of the exam is to identify students who have potential to excel in Science, Social Science, Engineering, Medicine, Management and Law. The successful students, called NTSE Scholars, receive financial support / scholarships from NCERT till the time they continue to study.

The NTSE not only provides scholarship to the good students but also highlights the students with good aptitude and knowledge.

Scholarships: About One thousand scholarships are awarded for different stages of education as follows:
(a) Scholarship of Rs. 1250/- per month for Class-XI to XII.
(b) Scholarship of Rs. 2000/- per month for Undergraduates and Post-graduates.
(c) Amount of Scholarship for Ph.D. be fixed in accordance with the UGC norms.

Reservation: 15% for students belonging to the SC category, 7.5% for students belonging to the ST category and 3% for Physically Challenged Group of Students.

Selection: Stage-I, selection will be done by States/UTs and those who qualify Stage- I, will be eligible to appear for Stage-II examination, conducted by NCERT.

Qualifying Marks: Qualifying marks for candidates from General category is 40% in each paper and for candidates from SC, ST, PH is 35% in each paper.

Language Test Qualifying in nature and marks obtained for Language Test will not be counted for final merit.

Important Dates: Dates for submission of application form and conduct of examination, are given below:

Stage	Area	Tentative Dates
Stage-I (State)	Last Date for Submission of Application Form	To be notified by the respective State and it may vary from state to state
	Examination in Mizoram, Meghalaya, Nagaland and Andaman and Nicobar Islands	7th November, 2015 (Saturday)
	Examination in All other States and Union Territories	8th November, 2015 (Sunday)
Stage-II (National)	Examination in All States and Union Territories	8th May, 2016 (Sunday)

Eligibility: All students of Class X studying in recognized schools are eligible to appear for the Stage -I examination, conducted by the States/UTs, in which the schools are located. There will be no domicile restriction.

Students registered under Open Distance Learning (ODL) will also be eligible for scholarship, provided the student is below the age of 18 years (as on 1st July of the particular year), the student is not employed and s/he is appearing in class X examination for the first time.

Examination: The pattern of written examination will be as follows:
♦ Stage I examination at the State/UT level will comprise three parts, namely (a) Mental Ability Test (MAT) (b) Language Test (LT) and (c) Scholastic Aptitude Test (SAT).
♦ **Qualifying Marks:** Qualifying marks for candidates from General category is 40% in each paper and for candidates from SC, ST, PH is 35% in each paper.
♦ **Lanuage Test** Qualifying in nature and marks obtained for Language Test will not be counted for final merit.

- The pattern of stage I will be as under:

Test		No. of Questions	No. of Marks	Duration (in minutes)
Mental Ability Test (MAT)		50	50	50
Scholastic Test	Language Comprehensive Test	40	40	40
	Aptitude Test	90	90	90
Total		180	180	180

- The pattern of stage II will be as under:

Test	No. of Questions	No. of Marks	Duration (in minutes)
(i) Mental Ability Test (MAT)	50	50	45
(ii) Language Test (LT) English/Hindi	50	50	45
(iii) Scholastic Aptitude Test (SAT)	100	100	90

At Stage – II (National Level), there will be negative marking in each paper. For each wrong answer 1/3 marks will be deducted. No marks will be deducted for unattempted questions.

Application Form: You may contact the State/UT Liaison officer for procuring application form.

The completed application form should be signed by the Principal of the school much before the last date of submission. The candidate as well as the Principal of the school must adhere to the last date for submission of the Application Form. **Different states may have different last dates for submission. Please confirm from the liaison officer of your state, the address at which the completed forms are to be submitted.** The State-wise contacts of the liaison officers are given in the CD and are also available on the NCERT website www.ncert.nic.in. **All queries related to application form should be directed to the State Liaison Officers (LOs). No application should be sent to NCERT.**

Fees: States and Union Territories may notify the fee required which will be paid for the Stage-I examination. Therefore, before submitting the application form, you may find out the fees charged for Stage-I Examination and also the mode of payment from the respective State"Liaison Officers (LOs). However, NCERT does not charge any fee for Stage-II examination.

Indian Students Studying Abroad in Class X can appear directly for Stage II NTS Examination under conditions prescribed in the NTS brochure which is available on the NCERT website. Candidates may fill up the Application Form, available on the NCERT website and send to the undersigned along with a photocopy of the mark sheet of previous examination, **latest by February 28th, 2016. Application Form for students study abroad will be uploaded on NCERT website in the month of October, 2015. Announcement for Indian Students Studying Abroad will be announced separately.**

How to Prepare for NTSE

Here are some tips on how to prepare for NTSE :

- **Start your preparation with last year's NTSE papers:** The objective is understood the type of questions asked and your current level. You should take last year's paper or NTSE sample questions and just write the exam once with all seriousness. It does not matter if you have not prepared or never heard of it before. Just sit down and write the test. This will help you gain a knowledge of NTSE and also give you a fair idea of the exam.

- **Analyze your performance:** Make sure to minutely assess what you could do and what you had a hard time with. Is it the knowledge of subject matter that you lacked? Or did you miss out because you made some silly mistakes? Or is it that mental ability questions that took a long time for you to crack? Whatever it is, just analyze your performance very minutely and critically

- **Make a plan:** Once you know your weak points, make a plan. You will definitely need to study and revise the subject matter. That is required not just for NTSE but also for your school. So there is no letting up on that front. You will also need to practice more mental ability questions. But the allocation of time will depend upon your analysis of how weak or strong you are in that particular aspect

- **Practice, practice and practice:** These are the only 3 steps that can lead to success. Get exposed to more questions of mental ability so that you are not shocked on the exam day, solve more papers and then analyze each one in detail. Take help from seniors. As you practice, you can also get confident of your speed, subject knowledge and accuracy.

Tips on How to Write Examination

The written examination (NTSE II stage) comprises two tests namely, MAT (Mental Ability Test) and SAT (Scholastic Ability Test). Each test comprises 100 multiple choice type questions which are attempted in 90 minutes. Thus on an average, the examinee will get around 54 seconds to answer a question. Therefore, both speed and accuracy are essential.

- In the MAT section, questions of the same type are grouped together. Since the instructions for all these questions are the same, read them carefully and answer all the questions.

- Use your time wisely. If you are doubtful at a particular question, omit it and move ahead without wasting much time on it. Do not let yourself get stuck on a tough question and lose time. You can always return to questions that you have omitted before the time is up.

- Do easy questions first because you earn as much credit for correctly answering those questions as you do for correctly answering a difficult question.

Do's for Answering Multiple Choice Questions in NTSE

- If the question is 'conceptual', i.e., if the answer it seeks is a statement, begin by covering the alternatives with a ruler or piece of paper. Then, carefully read and understand the stem of the question before looking at the alternatives.

- Circle or underline key words in the stem, paying special attention to qualifying words such as 'always,' 'major,' 'increase,' etc.

- Use your knowledge of headings from where lecture notes, lab, etc. is drawn. Recall a few salient points about the information. If necessary, jot down any relevant facts you need to process the alternatives. This does not have to take much time but this recall is an essential step.

- Predict an answer, if possible.

- Think over all of the alternatives and check the format of the question. Is only one of the alternatives correct, or can several or all of the alternatives be correct?

- If you know the answer, carefully mark the correct answer on your answer sheet.
- If you do not know the answer, re-check the question. Narrow your choices by eliminating any alternative that you know is incorrect. If two options still look equally appealing, compare each to the stem of the question, making sure that the one you eventually choose answers what is asked.
- If you are unable to make a choice and need to spend more time with the question, put a big question mark beside that question, and move on to the next.
- Don't stick to one question in the exam. It is much better to move on and finish all of those questions that you can answer and then to come back to the problematic questions.
- If the answer that you have calculated, is not one of the given options, check your procedure again, making any necessary changes, and recalculate your answer.
- If you still do not arrive at one of the given options, put a big question mark on that question, and go on to the next. When you get to the end of the exam, go back to any questions that you did not answer the first time.

Don'ts for Answering Multiple-Choice Questions

- Don't guess any choice as the correct answer because there is negative marking.
- Don't select an alternative just because you remember learning the information in the course; it may be a 'true' statement in its own right, but you have to make sure that it is the 'correct' answer to the question.
- Don't pick an answer just because it seems to make sense. You must answer from your knowledge of the course content, not just from your general knowledge and logic.
- Don't dismiss an alternative because it seems too obvious and simple. If you are well prepared for the exam, some of the questions will appear very straight forward to you.

CONTENTS

Publisher's Note *3*
Perface *4*
NTSE : An Introduction *7*
How to Prepare for NTSE *9*

Mathematics

1.	Number System	13
2.	Polynomials	26
3.	Pair of Linear Equations in Two Variables	34
4.	Quadratic Equations	42
5.	Arithmetic Progressions	50
6.	Trigonometry	57
7.	Height and Distance	65
8.	Co-ordinate Geometry	70
9.	Triangles and Quadrilaterals	78
10.	Circles	88
11.	Mensuration	98
12.	Statistics	113
13.	Probability	122
14.	Logarithm	129
15.	Surds and Indices	133
16.	Simplification	136
17.	Commercial Mathematics	139

Mathematics

- ✓ Number System
- ✓ Pair of Linear Equations in Two Variables
- ✓ Arithmetic Progressions
- ✓ Height and Distance
- ✓ Triangles and Quadrilaterals
- ✓ Mensuration
- ✓ Probability
- ✓ Surds and Indices
- ✓ Commercial Mathematics
- ✓ Polynomials
- ✓ Quadratic Equations
- ✓ Trigonometry
- ✓ Co-ordinate Geometry
- ✓ Circles
- ✓ Statistics
- ✓ Logarithm
- ✓ Simplification

UNIT 1
Number System

- **Number System**
  Quantitative aptitude deals mainly with different topics in arithmetic, which is the science that deals with the relations of numbers to one another. It includes all the methods that are applicable to numbers.

  I. Complex Numbers
  A complex number is a number that can be put in the form $a + bi$, where a and b are real numbers and i is called the imaginary unit, where $i^2 = 1$.

  II. Real Numbers
  In mathematics, a real number is a value that represents a quantity along a continuous line. The real numbers include all the rational numbers such as the integer 5 and the fraction 4/3, and all the irrational numbers such as $\sqrt{2}$ (1.41421356... the square root of two, an irrational algebraic number) and π (3.14159265..., a transcendental number). Real numbers can be thought of as points on an infinitely long line called the number line or real line, where the points corresponding to integers are equally spaced.

- **The Real Number Line**
  The Real Number Line is like an actual geometric line. A point is chosen on the line to be the 'origin', the points to the right are positive, and points to the left are negative.

  Now real number line can be divided into two categories rational numbers and irrational numbers.

- **Rational Numbers**
  A rational number of the form $\frac{p}{q}$ or a number which can be expressed in the form of $\frac{p}{q}$, where p and q are integers and $q \neq 0$ is called a Rational Number.

  $\frac{1}{2}, \frac{-2}{5}$ are example of rational numbers.

  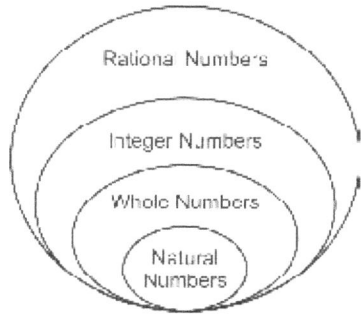

- **Irrational Numbers**
  A number which cannot be put in the form $\frac{p}{q}$, where p and q are integers and $q \neq 0$ is called an irrational number.

  OR

  A number whose decimal expression is non-terminating and non recurring is called an irrational number.

  $\sqrt{2}, \sqrt{-3}, \sqrt{-5}$ π (Pi) are irrational numbers.

  Rational numbers can be further sub divided into integers and fractions.

  Integers (Z) : There are different types of numbers, natural numbers, whole numbers, fractions, decimals etc.

  Natural Numbers = 1, 2, 3, 4, 5...

  Whole Numbers = 0, 1, 2, 3, 4...

  Fractions = 1/2, 1/3, 1/4 ... These numbers lie between the two whole numbers.

  Decimals = 0.1, 0.2, 0.3 ... These numbers also lie between the two whole numbers.

  Whole numbers along with negative numbers are called **Integers.**

  The numbers ..., -4, -3, -2, -1, 0, 1, 2, 3, 4 ... etc. are called integer.

  1, 2, 3, 4... are **Positive integer.**

  -1, -2, -3... are **Negative numbers.**

- **Fractions:**
  A fraction includes two parts, numerator and denominator $-\frac{3}{7}, \frac{9}{5}, \frac{11}{7}$ etc.

  Fractions are primarily of five types:
  (a) Proper Fraction
  (b) Improper Fraction
  (c) Mixed Fraction
  (d) Compound Fraction
  (e) Complex Fraction

- **Concept of Unit Digits**

  For the concept of identifying the unit digit, we have to first familiarize with the concept of cyclicity. Cyclicity of any number is about the last digit and how they appear in a certain defined manner. Let's take an example to clear this concept.

  The cyclicity chart of 2 is:
  $$2^1 = 2$$
  $$2^2 = 4$$
  $$2^3 = 8$$
  $$2^4 = 16$$
  $$2^5 = 32$$

  Have a close look at the above. You would see that as 2 is multiplied every time with its own self, the last digit changes. On the 4th multiplication, 2^5 has the same unit digit as 2^1. This shows us the cyclicity of 2 is 4, that is after every fourth multiplication, the unit digit will be two.

- **Cyclicity Table**

  The cyclicity table for numbers is given below:

Number	Cyclicity
1	1
2	4
3	4
4	2
5	1
6	1
7	4
8	4
9	2
10	1

  How did we figure out the above? Multiply and see for yourself. It's good practice.

  Now let us use the concept of cyclicity to calculate the Unit digit of a number.

  What is the unit digit of the expression 4^{45}?

  Now we have two methods to solve this but we choose the best way to solve it i.e. through cyclicity

  We know the cyclicity of 4 is 2
  Have a look:
  $$4^1 = 4$$
  $$4^2 = 16$$
  $$4^3 = 64$$

  Here the 4 comes again to the end when the 4 raised to the power of 3 so it is clear that the cyclicity of 4 is 2. Now with the cyclicity number 2, divide the given power i.e. 45/2. In this case remainder the remainder will be 1 i.e. $4^1 = 4$

  So the unit digit in this case is 4.

- **Rules of Divisibility**

  A divisibility rule is a shorthand way of discovering whether a given number is divisible by a fixed divisor without performing the division, usually by examining its digits.

  ➢ **Divisibility by 2**
  A number is divisible by 2, if its last digit (unit's place) is either 0, 2, 4, 6 or 8.
  We note that all even numbers are divisible by 2.

  ➢ **Divisibility by 3**
  A number is divisible by 3 if the sum of its digits is divisible by 3.

  ➢ **Divisibility by 4**
  A number is divisible by 4, if the number formed by the last two digits is divisible by 4.

  ➢ **Divisibility by 5**
  A number is divisible by 5, if the last digit is either 0 or 5. For example: 2635, 12970, 38525,...

  ➢ **Divisibility by 6**
  A number is divisible by 6, if it is divisible by 2 and 3 both.

  ➢ **Divisibility by 8**
  A number is divisible by 8, if the last three digits taken together is divisible by 8.

  ➢ **Divisibility by 9**
  A number is divisible by 9, if the sum of the digits of the given number is divisible by 9.

  ➢ **Divisibility by 11**
  A number is divisible by 11, if the difference of the sum of its digits at odd place and the sum of its digits at even places, is either 0 or a number is divisible by 11.

- **Number Series**

  Arithmetic Progression (A.P.) : A sequence is said to be in Arithmetic Progression when it is increased or decreased by a constant number. This constant number is called the common difference (c.d) of the arithmetic progression.

  Examples :
  - 1, 3, 5, 7...   c.d. = 2
  - −7, −3, 1, 5, 9 ...   c.d. = 4

- N^{th} term of an A.P.

  $(t_n) = a + (n-1)d$

- Sum of the first n term of an A.P.

  $(S_n) = \{2a + (n-1)d\}$

Geometric Progression : A sequence is said to be in Geometric Progression, if the ratio between any two adjacent numbers in the sequence is constant (non zero). This constant is said to be common ratio (c.r.)

Examples :
- 1, 2, 4, 8 ....c.r. = 2
- 1, 1/2, 1/4, 1/8..............c.r. =1/2
- The Nth term of G.P. (t_n) = ar^{n-1}

■ **Factorization**

It is the process of splitting any number into the form of its basic prime factors.

For example : $24 = 2 \times 2 \times 2 \times 3 = 2^3 \times 3$

24 is expressed in the factorised form in terms of its basic prime factors. This is the factorisation form of 24.

Important Formulas

- Sum of all the first 'n' natural numbers

  $= \dfrac{n(n+1)}{2}$

- Sum of first 'n' odd numbers = n^2
- Sum of first 'n' even numbers = $n(n+1)$
- Sum of squares of first 'n' natural numbers

  $= \dfrac{n(n+1)(n+2)}{6}$

- Sum of cubes of first 'n' natural numbers

  $= \left[\dfrac{n(n+1)}{2}\right]^2$

- $(a+b)(a-b) = (a^2 - b^2)$
- $(a+b)^2 = (a^2 + b^2 + 2ab)$
- $(a-b)^2 = (a^2 + b^2 - 2ab)$
- $(a+b+c)^2 = a^2 + b^2 + c^2 + 2(ab + bc + ca)$
- $(a^3 + b^3) = (a+b)(a^2 - ab + b^2)$
- $(a^3 - b^3) = (a-b)(a^2 + ab + b^2)$
- $(a^3 + b^3 + c^3 - 3abc)$

  $= (a+b+c)(a^2 + b^2 + c^2 - ab - bc - ac)$;

  when $a + b + c = 0$, then $a^3 + b^3 + c^3 = 3abc$

Ratio and Proportion

Ratio is a way of comparing two or more quantities. If x and y are two quantities of the same kind and in the same units, then the fraction $\dfrac{x}{y}(y \neq 0)$ is called the ratio of x to y. It is written as $x : y$

- Ratio between the two numbers say 2 and 3 may be written as a:

  (i) Fraction, $\dfrac{2}{3}$

  (ii) Division, $2 \div 3$

  (iii) With the ratio sign (:), 2:3

- A comparison by division is called ratio.
- Ratio is a pure number with no unit.
- The symbol ':' is read as 'is to'
- For comparison by ratio, the two quantities must be in the same units.
- Two ratios are equivalent if the fractions corresponding to them are equivalent.
- Usually ratio is expressed in its simplest form, i.e. the form in which their terms have no common factor expect 1 e.g. 3:6 is expressed as 1:2.
- Multiplying or dividing both terms of a ratio by the same number does not change the value of the ratio

  e.g. $\dfrac{5}{9} = \dfrac{5}{9} \times \dfrac{2}{2} = \dfrac{10}{18}$

- The order of the ratio is very important, e.g. the ratio 3:7 is different from the ratio 7:3.

Comparison of Ratio

Ratios can be compared in the same way as fractions. To compare two ratios, convert them into like fraction.

Ratio of Three Quantities

The ratio of three quantities can be simplified:

- By converting all quantities of different units to the same unit
- If some or all quantities are fraction, multiply all of them by the L.C.M. of the denominators of the fraction. If any of them is a mixed number like $3\dfrac{1}{2}$, change it to an improper fraction first.
- If the quantities have a common factor, divide all of them by the common factor.
- If some or all the quantities are decimals, convert all of them to whole numbers by multiplying all of them by a suitable power of 10, i.e. 10,100,1000 etc.

Proportions

The relationship between two ratios, where the first ratio is always equal to the second, is called a proportion. Proportion can be written in two ways:

- by using a double colon, a:b::c:d
- as to equivalent fractions, $\dfrac{a}{b} = \dfrac{c}{d}$

Continued Proportion

A continued proportion is one in which the ratio between the first and the second term is equal to the ratio between the second and the third term

Mean Proportion

If the middle terms are repeated, then each of the middle terms is the mean proportion.

Solved Examples

1. The digit in the unit place of the number $7^{95} \times 3^{58}$ is:
   (a) 7   (b) 2
   (c) 6   (d) 4

   Solution:
   The Cyclicity table for 7 is as follows:
   $7^1 = 7$
   $7^2 = 49$
   $7^3 = 343$
   $7^4 = 2401$
   $7^5 = 16807$
   Let's divide 95 by 4: the remainder is 3.
   Thus, the last digit of 7^{95} is equal to the last digit of 7^3 i.e. 3.
   The Cyclicity table for 3 is as follows:
   $3^1 = 3$
   $3^2 = 9$
   $3^3 = 27$
   $3^4 = 81$
   $3^5 = 243$
   Let's divide 58 by 4, the remainder is 2. Hence the last digit will be 9.
   Therefore, unit's digit of ($7^{95} \times 3^{58}$) is unit's digit of product of digit at unit's place of 7^{95} and $3^{58} = 3 \times 9 = 27$. Hence option (a) is the answer.

2. What is the unit digit in $\{(6374)^{1793} \times (625)^{317} \times (341^{491})\}$?
   (a) 0   (b) 2
   (c) 3   (d) 5

   Solution: Option (a) is correct.
   Explanation:
   Unit digit in $(6374)^{1793}$ = Unit digit in $(4)^{1793}$
        = Unit digit in $[(4^2)^{896} \times 4]$
        = Unit digit in $(6 \times 4) = 4$
   Unit digit in $(625)^{317}$ = Unit digit in $(5)^{317} = 5$
   Unit digit in $(341)^{491}$ = Unit digit in $(1)^{491} = 1$
        Required digit = Unit digit in $(4 \times 5 \times 1)$
        = 0

3. Evaluate: $(2^2 + 4^2 + 6^2 + ... + 20^2) = ?$
   (a) 770   (b) 1155
   (c) 1540   (d) 385 × 385

   Solution: Option (c) is correct.
   Explanation:
   $(2^2 + 4^2 + 6^2 + ... + 20^2)$
   $= (1 \times 2)^2 + (2 \times 2)^2 + (2 \times 3)^2 + ... + (2 \times 10)^2$
   $= (2^2 \times 1^2) + (2^2 \times 2^2) + (2^2 \times 3^2) + ... + (2^2 \times 10^2)$
   $= 2^2 \times [1^2 + 2^2 + 3^2 + ... + 10^2]$
   [Ref: $(1^2 + 2^2 + ... + n^2) = 1/6\, n(n+1)(2n+1)$]
   $= 4 \times 1/6 \times 10 \times 11 \times 21$
   $= (4 \times 5 \times 77) = 1540$

4. Which one of the following can't be the square of natural number?
   (a) 30976   (b) 75625
   (c) 28561   (d) 143642

   Solution: Option (d) is correct.
   Explanation: The square of a natural number never ends in 2.
   ∴ 143642 is not the square of a natural number.

5. The least six-digit number completely divisible by 111 is:
   (a) 100000   (b) 110000
   (c) 100011   (d) 111000

   Solution: Option (c) is correct.
   Explanation: The least Six-digit number is 100000.
   When 100000 ÷ 111, Quotient 990 and Remainder = 100
   Therefore required number
        = 100000 + (111 − 100)
        = 100000 + 11
        = 100011

6. It is being given that $(2^{32} + 1)$ is completely divisible by a whole number. Which of the following numbers is completely divisible by this number?
   (a) $(2^{16} + 1)$ (b) $(2^{16} - 1)$
   (c) (7×2^{23}) (d) $(2^{96} + 1)$

   Solution: Option d) is correct.
   Explanation:
   Let $2^{32} = x$. Then, $(2^{32} + 1) = (x + 1)$
   Let $(x + 1)$ be completely divisible by the natural number N. Then,
   $(2^{96} + 1) = [(2^{32})^3 + 1] = (x^3 + 1) = (x + 1)(x^2 - x + 1)$, which is completely divisible by N, since $(x + 1)$ is divisible by N.

7. $\dfrac{854 \times 854 \times 854 - 276 \times 276 \times 276}{854 \times 854 + 854 \times 276 + 276 \times 276} = ?$
   (a) 1130   (b) 578
   (c) 565   (d) 1156

   Solution: Option (b) is correct.
   Explanation: Given Exp.
   $= \dfrac{(a^3 - b^3)}{(a^2 + ab + b^2)} = (a - b)$
   $= (854 - 276) = 578$

8. The sum of first 45 natural numbers is:
   (a) 1035   (b) 1280
   (c) 2070   (d) 2140

   Solution: Option (a) is correct.
   Explanation:
   Let $S_n = (1 + 2 + 3 + ... + 45)$
   This is an A.P. in which
        $a = 1, d = 1, n$

Number System

$= 45$ and $l = 45$
∴ $S_n = n/2 (a + l)$
$= 45/2 \times (1 + 45)$
$= (45 \times 23) = 1035$
Required sum $= 1035$

9. Find the mean proportion between 8 and 242.
   (a) 44 (b) 22
   (c) 56 (d) 16
   Solution: Option (a) is correct.
   Explanation: Let the mean proportion be represented by x
   We have $8 : x : 242$
   or $8 : x :: x : 242$
   ⇒ $x^2 = 242 \times 8 = 1936$
   $x = \sqrt{1936} = 44$
   Thus the continued proportion is 8:44:242 or the mean proportion between 8 and 242 is 44.

10. What is the value of $\dfrac{P+Q}{P-Q}$ if $\dfrac{P}{Q}$?
    (a) 4/3 (b) 2/3
    (c) 2/6 (d) 7/8
    Solution: Option (a) is correct.
    Explanation:
    $\dfrac{P+Q}{P-Q} = \dfrac{\dfrac{P}{Q}+1}{\dfrac{P}{Q}-1} = \dfrac{7+1}{7-1} = \dfrac{8}{6} = \dfrac{4}{3}$

11. If two numbers are in the ratio 6:13 and their least common multiple is 312, then the sum of number is:
    (a) 75 (b) 57
    (c) 76 (d) 67
    Solution: Option (c) is correct.
    Explanation:
    Let the given number be $6x$ and $13x$.
    Given, LCM $= 3 \times 6 \times x = 312$
    ⇒ $x = \dfrac{312}{13 \times 6} = 4$
    Sum of numbers $= 6x + 13x$
    $19 \times 4 = 76$

12. A mixture (40 L) contains conic and water in the ratio 3 :1. To make the ratio 5:2, how much additional amount of water is required?
    (a) 5 L (b) 1 L
    (c) 3 L (d) 2 L
    Solution: Option (d) is correct.
    Explanation:
    In 40 L mixture, conic $= 30$ and water $= 10$
    Now $\dfrac{30}{10+x} = \dfrac{5}{2}$
    ⇒ $60 = 50 + 5x$
    ⇒ $x = 2$ L

Multiple Choice Questions

1. What is the unit digit in the product
   $(3^{65} \times 6^{59} \times 7^{71})$?
   (a) 1 (b) 2
   (c) 4 (d) 6

2. On dividing a number by 68, we get 269 as quotient and 0 as remainder. On dividing the same number by 67, what will be the remainder?
   (a) 0 (b) 1
   (c) 2 (d) 3

3. On multiplying a number by 7, the product is a number each of whose digits is 3. The smallest such number is:
   (a) 47619 (b) 47719
   (c) 48619 (d) 47649

4. If x and y are the two digits of the number $653xy$ such that this number is divisible by 80, then $x + y = ?$
   (a) 2 or 6 (b) 4
   (c) 4 or 8 (d) 8

5. How many terms are there in the G.P. 3, 6, 12, 24, ... , 384?
   (a) 8 (b) 9
   (c) 10 (d) 11

6. If x and y are positive integers such that $(3x + 7y)$ is a multiple of 11, then which of the following will be divisible by 11?
   (a) $4x + 6y$ (b) $x + y + 4$
   (c) $9x + 4y$ (d) $4x - 9y$

7. In a division sum, the remainder is 0. A student mistook the divisor by 12 instead of 21 and obtained 35 as quotient. What is the correct quotient?
   (a) 0 (b) 12
   (c) 13 (d) 20

8. Find the value of :
   $2 + 2^2 + 2^3 + ... + 2^9 = ?$
   (a) 2044 (b) 1022
   (c) 1056 (d) None of these

9. The sum of how may terms of the series $6 + 12 + 18 + 24 + ...$ is 1800?
   (a) 16 (b) 24
   (c) 20 (d) 18

10. What is the unit digit in $(7^{95} - 3^{58})$?
    (a) 0 (b) 4
    (c) 6 (d) 7

11. $(x^n - a^n)$ is completely divisible by $(x - a)$, when
    (a) n is any natural number
    (b) n is an even natural number
    (c) n is an odd natural number
    (d) n is prime

12. Which of the following numbers will completely divide $(3^{25} + 3^{26} + 3^{27} + 3^{28})$?
    (a) 11 (b) 16
    (c) 25 (d) 30

13. n is a whole number which when divided by 4 gives 3 as remainder. What will be the remainder when $2n$ is divided by 4?
    (a) 3 (b) 2
    (c) 1 (d) 0

14. 476 ** 0 is divisible by both 3 and 11. The non-zero digits in the hundred's and ten's places are respectively:
    (a) 7 and 4 (b) 7 and 5
    (c) 8 and 5 (d) None of these

15. Evaluate:
$$9 + \frac{3}{4} + 7 + \frac{2}{17} - (9 + \frac{1}{15}) = ?$$
    (a) $7 + \frac{719}{1020}$ (b) $9 + \frac{817}{1020}$
    (c) $9 + \frac{719}{1020}$ (d) $7 + \frac{817}{1020}$

16. On dividing 2272 as well as 875 by 3-digit number N, we get the same remainder. The sum of the digits of N is:
    (a) 10 (b) 11
    (c) 12 (d) 13

17. A boy multiplied 987 by a certain number and obtained 559981 as his answer. If in the answer both 98 are wrong and the other digits are correct, then the correct answer would be:
    (a) 553681 (b) 555181
    (c) 555681 (d) 556581

18. Which one of the following is the common factor of $(47^{43} + 43^{43})$ and $(47^{47} + 43^{47})$?
    (a) $(47 - 43)$ (b) $(47 + 43)$
    (c) $(47^{43} + 43^{43})$ (d) None of these

19. In a division sum, the divisor is 10 times the quotient and 5 times the remainder. If the remainder is 46, what is the dividend?
    (a) 4236 (b) 4306
    (c) 4336 (d) 5336

20. Evaluate:
    $\{(476 + 424)^2 - 4 \times 476 \times 424\} = ?$
    (a) 2906 (b) 3116
    (c) 2704 (d) 2904

21. Which of the following numbers will completely divide $(4^{61} + 4^{62} + 4^{63} + 4^{64})$?
    (a) 3 (b) 10
    (c) 11 (d) 13

22. $(1^2 + 2^2 + 3^2 + ... + 10^2) = ?$
    (a) 330 (b) 345
    (c) 365 (d) 385

23. The difference of the squares of two consecutive even integers is divisible by which of the following integers?
    (a) 3 (b) 4
    (c) 6 (d) 7

24. If the number 91876 * 2 is completely divisible by 8, then the smallest whole number in place of * will be:
    (a) 1 (b) 2
    (c) 3 (d) 4

25. If 60% of 3/5 of a number is 36, then the number is:
    (a) 80 (b) 100
    (c) 75 (d) 90

26. A and B together have Rs. 1210. If 4/15 of A's amount is equal to 2/5 of B's amount, how much amount does B have?
    (a) Rs. 460 (b) Rs. 484
    (c) Rs. 550 (d) Rs. 664

27. Two numbers are respectively 20% and 50% more than a third number. The ratio of the two numbers is:
    (a) 2 : 5 (b) 3 : 5
    (c) 4 : 5 (d) 6 : 7

28. A sum of money is to be distributed among A, B, C, D in the proportion of 5 : 2 : 4 : 3. If C gets Rs. 1000 more than D, what is B's share?
    (a) Rs. 500 (b) Rs. 1500
    (c) Rs. 2000 (d) None of these

29. Seats for Mathematics, Physics and Biology in a school are in the ratio 5 : 7 : 8. There is a proposal to increase these seats by 40%, 50% and 75% respectively. What will be the ratio of increased seats?
    (a) 2 : 3 : 4 (b) 6 : 7 : 8
    (c) 6 : 8 : 9 (d) None of these

30. In a mixture of 60 litres, the ratio of milk and water 2 : 1. If the this ratio is to be 1 : 2, then the quantity of water to be further added is:
    (a) 20 litres (b) 30 litres
    (c) 40 litres (d) 60 litres

31. The ratio of the number of boys and girls in a college is 7 : 8. If the percentage increase in the number of boys and girls be 20% and 10% respectively, what will be the new ratio?
    (a) 8 : 9 (b) 17 : 18
    (c) 21 : 22 (d) Cannot be determined

32. Salaries of Ravi and Sumit are in the ratio 2 : 3. If the salary of each is increased by Rs. 4000, the new ratio becomes 40 : 57. What is Sumit's salary?
    (a) Rs. 17,000 (b) Rs. 20,000
    (c) Rs. 25,500 (d) Rs. 38,000

33. If $0.75 : x :: 5 : 8$, then x is equal to:
    (a) 1.12 (b) 1.2
    (c) 1.25 (d) 1.30

34. The sum of three numbers is 98. If the ratio of the first to second is 2 : 3 and that of the second to the third is 5 : 8, then the second number is:
    (a) 20 (b) 30
    (c) 48 (d) 58

35. If Rs. 782 be divided into three parts, proportional to 1/2 : 2/3 : 3/4, then the first part is:
    (a) Rs. 182 (b) Rs. 190
    (c) Rs. 196 (d) Rs. 204

36. The salaries A, B, C are in the ratio 2 : 3 : 5. If the increments of 15%, 10% and 20% are allowed respectively in their salaries, then what will be new ratio of their salaries?
    (a) 3 : 3 : 10 (b) 10 : 11 : 20
    (c) 23 : 33 : 60 (d) Cannot be determined

37. If 40% of a number is equal to two-third of another number, what is the ratio of first number to the second number?
    (a) 2 : 5 (b) 3 : 7
    (c) 5 : 3 (d) 7 : 3

38. The fourth proportional to 5, 8, 15 is:
    (a) 18 (b) 24
    (c) 19 (d) 20

39. Two numbers are in the ratio 3:5. If 9 is subtracted from each, the new numbers are in the ratio 12 : 23. The smaller number is:
    (a) 27 (b) 33
    (c) 49 (d) 55

40. In a bag, there are coins of 25 p, 10 p and 5 p in the ratio of 1 : 2 : 3. If there is Rs. 30 in all, how many 5 p coins are there?
    (a) 50 (b) 100
    (c) 150 (d) 200

41. A and B invest in a business in the ratio 3 : 2. If 5% of the total profit goes to charity and A's share is Rs. 855, the total profit is:
    (a) Rs. 1425 (b) Rs. 1500
    (c) Rs. 1537.50 (d) Rs. 1576

42. A, B and C jointly thought of engaging themselves in a business venture. It was agreed that A would invest Rs. 6500 for 6 months, B, Rs. 8400 for 5 months and C, Rs. 10,000 for 3 months. A wants to be the working member for which, he was to receive 5% of the profits. The profit earned was Rs. 7400. Calculate the share of B in the profit.
    (a) Rs. 1900 (b) Rs. 2660
    (c) Rs. 2800 (d) Rs. 2840

43. A, B and C enter into a partnership in the ratio 7/2 : 4/3 : 6/5. After 4 months, A increases his share 50%. If the total profit at the end of one year be Rs. 21,600, then B's share in the profit is:
    (a) Rs. 2100 (b) Rs. 2400
    (c) Rs. 3600 (d) Rs. 4000

44. A, B, C subscribe Rs. 50,000 for a business. A subscribes Rs. 4000 more than B and B Rs. 5000 more than C. Out of a total profit of Rs. 35,000, A receives:
    (a) Rs. 8400 (b) Rs. 11,900
    (c) Rs. 13,600 (d) Rs. 14,700

45. Three partners shared the profit in a business in the ratio 5 : 7 : 8. They had partnered for 14 months, 8 months and 7 months respectively. What was the ratio of their investments?
    (a) 5 : 7 : 8 (b) 20 : 49 : 64
    (c) 38 : 28 : 21 (d) None of these

46. A starts business with Rs. 3500 and after 5 months, B joins with A as his partner. After a year, the profit is divided in the ratio 2 : 3. What is B's contribution in the capital?
    (a) Rs. 7500 (b) Rs. 8000
    (c) Rs. 8500 (d) Rs. 9000

47. A and B entered into partnership with capitals in the ratio 4 : 5. After 3 months, A withdrew 1/4 of his capital and B withdrew 1/5 of his capital. The gain at the end of 10 months was Rs. 760. A's share in this profit is:
    (a) Rs. 330 (b) Rs. 360
    (c) Rs. 380 (d) Rs. 430

48. A and B started a partnership business investing some amount in the ratio of 3 : 5. C joined them after six months with an amount equal to that of B. In what proportion should the profit at the end of one year be distributed among A, B and C?
    (a) 3 : 5 : 2 (b) 3 : 5 : 5
    (c) 6 : 10 : 5 (d) Data inadequate

49. A, B, C rent a pasture. A puts 10 oxen for 7 months, B puts 12 oxen for 5 months and C puts 15 oxen for 3 months for grazing. If the rent of the pasture is Rs. 175, how much must C pay as his share of rent?
    (a) Rs. 45 (b) Rs. 50
    (c) Rs. 55 (d) Rs. 60

50. A and B started a business in partnership investing Rs. 20,000 and Rs. 15,000 respectively. After six months, C joined them with Rs. 20,000. What will be B's share in total profit of Rs. 25,000 earned at the end of 2 years from the starting of the business?
    (a) Rs. 7500 (b) Rs. 9000
    (c) Rs. 9500 (d) Rs. 10,000

National Talent Search Examination (NTSE)-X

Answer Key

1. (c)	2. (b)	3. (a)	4. (a)	5. (a)	6. (d)	7. (d)	8. (b)	9. (b)	10. (b)
11. (a)	12. (d)	13. (b)	14. (c)	15. (d)	16. (a)	17. (c)	18. (b)	19. (d)	20. (c)
21. (b)	22. (d)	23. (b)	24. (c)	25. (b)	26. (b)	27. (c)	28. (c)	29. (a)	30. (d)
31. (c)	32. (d)	33. (b)	34. (b)	35. (d)	36. (c)	37. (c)	38. (b)	39. (b)	40. (c)
41. (b)	42. (b)	43. (d)	44. (d)	45. (b)	46. (d)	47. (a)	48. (c)	49. (a)	50. (a)

Explanatory Notes

1. (c)
   Unit digit in $3^4 = 1$
   $\Rightarrow$ Unit digit in $(3^4)^{16} = 1$
   Unit digit in 3^{65} = Unit digit in $[(3^4)^{16} \times 3]$
   $= (1 \times 3) = 3$
   Unit digit in $6^{59} = 6$
   Unit digit in 7^4 $\Rightarrow$ Unit digit in $(7^4)^{17}$ is 1.
   Unit digit in 7^{71} = Unit digit in $[(7^4)^{17} \times 7^3]$
   $= (1 \times 3) = 3$
   Required digit = Unit digit in $(3 \times 6 \times 3)$
   $= 4$.

2. (b)
   Number $= 269 \times 68 + 0 = 18292$

   ```
   67) 18292 (273
        134
        ---
         489
         469
        ---
         202
         201
        ---
          1
   ```

   Therefore, required remainder = 1

3. (a)
   By hit and trial, we find that
   $47619 \times 7 = 333333$

4. (a)
   $80 = 2 \times 5 \times 8$
   Since $653xy$ is divisible by 2 and 5 both, so $y = 0$
   Now, 653×0 is divisible by 8, so 3×0 should be divisible by 8.
   This happens when $x = 2$ or 6
   $x + y = (2 + 0) = 2$ [or] $x + y = (6 + 0) = 6$

5. (a)
   Here $a = 3$ and $r = 6/3 = 2$. Let the number of terms be n.
   Then, $t_n = 384 \Rightarrow ar^{n-1} = 384$
   $\Rightarrow 3 \times 2^{n-1} = 384$
   $\Rightarrow 2^{n-1} = 128 = 2^7$
   $\Rightarrow n - 1 = 7$
   $\Rightarrow n = 8$
   Number of terms = 8

6. (d)
   By hit and trial, we put $x = 5$ and $y = 1$ so that $(3x + 7y) = (3 \times 5 + 7 \times 1) = 22$, which is divisible by 11.
   $\therefore (4x + 6y) = (4 \times 5 + 6 \times 1) = 26$, which is not divisible by 11;
   $(x + y + 4) = (5 + 1 + 4) = 10$, which is not divisible by 11;
   $(9x + 4y) = (9 \times 5 + 4 \times 1) = 49$, which is not divisible by 11;
   $(4x - 9y) = (4 \times 5 - 9 \times 1) = 11$, which is divisible by 11.

7. (d)
   Number $= (12 \times 35)$
   Correct Quotient $= 420 \div 21 = 20$

8. (b)
   This is a G.P. in which
   $a = 2, r = \dfrac{2^2}{2} = 2$ and
   $n = 9$.
   $\therefore S_n = \dfrac{a(r^n - 1)}{(r-1)} = \dfrac{2 \times (2^9 - 1)}{(2-1)}$
   $= 2 \times (512 - 1) = 2 \times 511 = 1022$

9. (b)
   This is an A.P. in which
   $a = 6, d = 6$ and
   $S_n = 1800$
   Then, $n/2 [2a + (n-1)d] = 1800$
   $\Rightarrow n/2 [2 \times 6 + (n-1) \times 6] = 1800$
   $\Rightarrow 3n(n+1) = 1800$
   $\Rightarrow n(n+1) = 600$
   $\Rightarrow n^2 + n - 600 = 0$
   $\Rightarrow n^2 + 25n - 24n - 600 = 0$
   $\Rightarrow n(n + 25) - 24(n + 25) = 0$
   $\Rightarrow (n + 25)(n - 24) = 0$
   $\Rightarrow n = 24$
   Number of terms = 24

10. (b)
    Unit digit in 7^{95} = Unit digit in $[(7^4)^{23} \times 7^3]$
    = Unit digit in $[($Unit digit in $(2401))^{23} \times (343)]$
    = Unit digit in $(1^{23} \times 343)$
    = Unit digit in $(343) = 3$

Unit digit in 3^{58} = Unit digit in $[(3^4)^{14} \times 3^2]$
$\qquad$ = Unit digit in [Unit digit in $(81)^{14} \times 3^2$]
$\qquad$ = Unit digit in $[(1)^{14} \times 3^2]$
$\qquad$ = Unit digit in (1×9)
$\qquad$ = Unit digit in $(9) = 9$
Unit digit in $(7^{95} - 3^{58})$
$\qquad$ = Unit digit in $(343 - 9)$
$\qquad$ = Unit digit in $(334) = 4$

11. (a)
For every natural number n, (x^n / a^n) is completely divisible by $(x - a)$.

12. (d)
$(3^{25} + 3^{26} + 3^{27} + 3^{28}) = 3^{25} \times (1 + 3 + 3^2 + 3^3)$
$\qquad = 3^{25} \times 40$
$\qquad = 3^{24} \times 3 \times 4 \times 10$
$\qquad = (3^{24} \times 4 \times 30)$,
which is divisible by 30.

13. (b)
$\qquad$ Let $n = 4q + 3$
Then $\qquad 2n = 8q + 6$
$\qquad\qquad = 4(2q + 1) + 2$
Thus, when 2n is divided by 4, the remainder is 2.

14. (c)
Let the given number be 476 xy 0.
Then $(4 + 7 + 6 + x + y + 0) = (17 + x + y)$ must be divisible by 3.
And, $(0 + x + 7) - (y + 6 + 4) = (x - y - 3)$ must be either 0 or 11.
$\qquad x - y - 3 = 0 \Rightarrow y = x - 3$
$\qquad (17 + x + y) = (17 + x + x - 3)$
$\qquad\qquad = (2x + 14)$
$\Rightarrow \qquad x = 2$ or $x = 8$
$\qquad x = 8$ and $y = 5$

15. (d)
Given sum $= 9 + \dfrac{3}{4} + 7 + \dfrac{2}{17} - \left(9 + \dfrac{1}{15}\right)$
$\qquad = (9 + 7 - 9) + \left(\dfrac{3}{4} + \dfrac{2}{17} - \dfrac{1}{15}\right)$
$\qquad = 7 + \dfrac{765 + 120 - 68}{1020}$
$\qquad = 7 + \dfrac{817}{1020}$

16. (a)
Clearly, $2272 - 875 = 1397$, is exactly divisible by N.
Now, $1397 = 11 \times 127$
The required 3-digit number is 127, the sum of whose digits is 10.

17. (c)
$987 = 3 \times 7 \times 47$
So, the required number must be divisible by each one of 3, 7, 47
553681 → (Sum of digits = 28, not divisible by 3)
555181 → (Sum of digits = 25, not divisible by 3)
555681 is divisible by 3, 7, 47

18. (b)
When n is odd, $(x^n + a^n)$ is always divisible by $(x + a)$.
Each one of $(47^{43} + 43^{43})$ and $(47^{47} + 43^{43})$ is divisible by $(47 + 43)$.

19. (d)
$\qquad$ Divisor $= (5 \times 46) = 230$
$\therefore \quad 10 \times$ Quotient $= 230$
$\Rightarrow \qquad$ Quotient $= 230/10 = 23$
$\qquad$ Dividend = (Divisor × Quotient) + Remainder
$\qquad = (230 \times 23) + 46$
$\qquad = 5290 + 46$
$\qquad = 5336$

20. (c)
Given Exp. $= [(a + b)^2 - 4ab]$,
where $\quad a = 476$ and $b = 424$
$\qquad = [(476 + 424)^2 - 4 \times 476 \times 424]$
$\qquad = [(900)^2 - 807296]$
$\qquad = 810000 - 807296$
$\qquad = 2704$.

21. (b)
$(4^{61} + 4^{62} + 4^{63} + 4^{64}) = 4^{61} \times (1 + 4 + 4^2 + 4^3)$
$\qquad = 4^{61} \times 85$
$\qquad = 4^{60} \times (4 \times 85)$
$\qquad = (4^{60} \times 340)$
which is divisible by 10

22. (d)
We know that $(1^2 + 2^2 + 3^2 + ... + n^2)$
$\qquad = 1/6 \, n(n + 1)(2n + 1)$
Putting $\quad n = 10$, required sum
$\qquad = 1/6 \times 10 \times 11 \times 21$
$\qquad = 385$

23. (b)
Let the two consecutive even integers be 2n and (2n + 2). Then,
$\qquad (2n + 2)^2 = (2n + 2 + 2n)(2n + 2 - 2n)$
$\qquad = 2(4n + 2)$
$\qquad = 4(2n + 1)$,
which is divisible by 4

24. (c)
Then number 6 × 2 must be divisible by 8.
$\therefore \, x = 3$, as 632 is divisible 8

25. (b)
   Let the number be X. Then
   $$60\% \text{ of } 3/5 \text{ of } X = 36$$
   $\Rightarrow (60/100) \times (3/5) \times X = 36$
   $\Rightarrow X = (36 \times 25)/9 = 100$
   Required number = 100

26. (b)
   $(4/15)A = (2/5)B$
   $A = [(2/5) \times (15/4)]B$
   $A = 3B/2$
   $A/B = 3/2$
   $A : B = 3 : 2$
   B's share = Rs. $1210 \times 2/5$
   = Rs. 484

27. (c)
   Let the third number be x
   Then, first number = 120% of x
   = $(120/100)x = 6x/5$
   Second number = 150% of x
   = $(150/100)x = 3x/2$
   Ratio of first two numbers
   = $6x/5 : 3x/2$
   = $12x : 15x = 4 : 5$

28. (c)
   Let the shares of A, B, C and D be Rs. $5x$, Rs. $2x$, Rs. $4x$ and Rs. $3x$ respectively.
   Then, $4x - 3x = 1000$
   $\Rightarrow x = 1000$
   $\therefore$ B's share = Rs. $2x$
   = Rs. (2×1000)
   = Rs. 2000

29. (a)
   Originally, let the number of seats for Mathematics, Physics and Biology be $5x$, $7x$ and $8x$ respectively.
   Number of increased seats are (140% of $5x$), (150% of $7x$) and (175% of $8x$).
   $[(140/100) \times 5x], [(150/100) \times 7x]$
   and $[(175/100) \times 8x]$
   $\Rightarrow 7x, 21x/2$ and $14x$.
   $\therefore$ The required ratio = $7x : 21x/2 : 14x$
   $\Rightarrow 14x : 21x : 28x \Rightarrow 2 : 3 : 4$

30. (d)
   Quantity of milk = $(60 \times 2/3)$ litres
   = 40 litres
   Quantity of water in it = $(60 - 40)$ litres
   = 20 litres.
   New ratio = 1 : 2
   Let quantity of water to be added further be x litres.
   Then, milk : water = $40/(20 + x)$
   Now, $40/(20 + x) = 1/2$
   $\Rightarrow 20 + x = 80$
   $\Rightarrow x = 60$
   Quantity of water to be added = 60 litres

31. (c)
   Originally, let the number of boys and girls in the college be $7x$ and $8x$ respectively.
   Their increased number is (120% of $7x$) and (110% of $8x$).
   $[(120/100) \times 7x]$ and $[(110/100) \times 8x]$
   $42x/5$ and $44x/5$
   The required ratio = $(42x/5 : 44x/5) = 21 : 22$

32. (d)
   Let the original salaries of Ravi and Sumit be Rs. $2x$ and Rs. $3x$ respectively.
   Then, $(2x + 4000) / (3x + 4000) = 40/57$
   $\Rightarrow 57(2x + 4000) = 40(3x + 4000)$
   $\Rightarrow 6x = 68,000$
   $\Rightarrow 3x = 34,000$
   Sumit's present salary = $(3x + 4000)$
   = Rs.(34000 + 4000)
   = Rs. 38,000

33. (b)
   $(x \times 5) = (0.75 \times 8)$
   $x = (0.75 \times 8)/5$
   = $6/5 = 1.20$

34. (b)
   Let the three parts be A, B, C. Then,
   A : B = 2 : 3 and
   B : C = 5 : 8 = $(5 \times 3/5) : (8 \times 3/5) = 3 : 24/5$
   A : B : C = 2 : 3 : 24/5 = 10 : 15 : 24
   Therefore B = $(98 \times 15/49) = 30$

35. (d)
   Given ratio = $1/2 : 2/3 : 3/4 = 6 : 8 : 9$.
   1st part = Rs. $(782 \times 6/23)$ = Rs. 204

36. (c)
   Let A = $2k$, B = $3k$ and C = $5k$
   A's new salary = 115/100 of $2k$ = $23k/10$
   B's new salary = 110/100 of $3k$ = $33k/10$
   C's new salary = 120/100 of $5k$ = $6k$
   New ratio = $(23k/10 : 33k/10 : 6k)$
   = 23 : 33 : 60

37. (c)
   Let 40% of A = $2B/3$
   Then, $40A/100 = 2B/3$
   $\Rightarrow 2A/5 = 2B/3$
   $\Rightarrow A/B = (2/3 \times 5/2) = 5/3$
   A : B = 5 : 3.

38. (b)
   Let the fourth proportional to 5, 8, 15 be x.
   Then, $5 : 8 : 15 : x$
   $\Rightarrow 5x = (8 \times 15)$
   $x = (8 \times 15)/5 = 24$

39. (b)
   Let the numbers be $3x$ and $5x$
   Then, $(3x - 9)/(5x - 9) = 12/23$

⇒ $23(3x - 9) = 12(5x - 9)$
⇒ $9x = 99$
⇒ $x = 11$
The smaller number = $(3 \times 11) = 33$

40. (c)
Let the number of 25 p, 10 p and 5 p coins be x, $2x$, $3x$ respectively.
Then, sum of their values Rs. $[25x/100 + (10 \times 2x)/100 + (5 \times 3x)/100]$ = Rs. $60x/100$
$60x/100 = 30$
$x = (30 \times 100)/60 = 3000/50 = 50$
Hence, the number of 5 p coins = $(3 \times 50) = 150$

41. (b)
Let the total profit be Rs. 100.
After paying to charity, A's share
= Rs. $(95 \times 3/5)$ = Rs. 57
If A's share is Rs. 57, total profit
= Rs. 100
If A's share Rs. 855, total profit
= $(100/57 \times 855) = 1500$

42. (b)
For managing, A received
= 5% of Rs. 7400 = Rs. 370
Balance = Rs. $(7400 - 370)$ = Rs. 7030
Ratio of their investments
= $(6500 \times 6) : (8400 \times 5) : (10000 \times 3)$
= $39000 : 42000 : 30000$
= $13 : 14 : 10$
B's share = Rs. $(7030 \times 14/37)$ = Rs. 2660

43. (d)
Ratio of initial investments
= $(7/2 : 4/3 : 6/5)$
= $105 : 40 : 36$
Let the initial investments be $105x$, $40x$ and $36x$
∴ A : B : C = $(105x \times 4 + 150/100 \times 105x \times 8)$
: $(40x \times 12) : (36x \times 12)$
= $1680x : 480x : 432x$
= $35 : 10 : 9$.
Hence, B's share = Rs. $21600 \times 10/54$
= Rs. 4000

44. (d)
Let   C = x
Then, B = $x + 5000$ and
A = $x + 5000 + 4000 = x + 9000$

So, $x + x + 5000 + x + 9000 = 50000$
$3x = 36000$
⇒ $x = 12000$
∴ A : B : C = $21000 : 17000 : 12000 = 21 : 17 : 12$
A's share = Rs. $(35000 \times 21/50)$ = Rs. 14,700

45. (b)
Let their investments be Rs. x for 14 months, Rs. y for 8 months and Rs. z for 7 months respectively.
Then, $14x : 8y : 7z = 5 : 7 : 8$.
Now, $14x/8y = 5/7$
$98x = 40y$
$y = 98x/40 = 49x/20$
And $14x/7z = 5/8$
$112x = 35z$
$z = 112x/35 = 16x/5$
$x : y : z = x : 49x/20 : 16x/5$
= $20 : 49 : 64$

46. (d)
Let B's capital be Rs. x
Then, $(3500 \times 12)/7x = 2/3$
⇒ $14x = 126000$
⇒ $x = 9000$

47. (a)
A : B = $[4x \times 3 + (4x - ¼ \times 4x) \times 7]$:
= $[5x \times 3 + (5x - 1/5 \times 5x) \times 7]$
= $(12x + 21x) : (15x + 28x)$
= $33x : 43x$
= $33 : 43$.
A's share = Rs. $760 \times 33/76$
= Rs. 330

48. (c)
Let the initial investments of A and B be $3x$ and $5x$.
A : B : C = $(3x \times 12) : (5x \times 12) : (5x \times 6)$
= $36 : 60 : 30 = 6 : 10 : 5$

49. (a)
A : B : C = $(10 \times 7) : (12 \times 5) : (15 \times 3)$
= $70 : 60 : 45 = 14 : 12 : 9$
C's rent = Rs. $175 \times 9/35$ = Rs. 45

50. (a)
A : B : C = $(20,000 \times 24) : (15,000 \times 24) : (20,000 \times 18)$
= $4 : 3 : 3$
B's share = Rs. $25000 \times 3/10$
= Rs. 7,500

National Talent Search Examination (NTSE)-X

Previous Year Questions

1. What least value should be assigned to * so that the number 451*603 is exactly divisible by 9?
   [NTSE 2012 – Himachal Pradesh first stage paper]
   (a) 2 (b) 5
   (c) 8 (d) 7

2. How many three digit numbers are divisible by 6 in all?
   [NTSE 2002 – Assam second stage paper]
   (a) 149 (b) 150
   (c) 151 (d) 166

3. The largest natural number which exactly divides the product of any four consecutive natural numbers is:
   [NTSE 2000 – Goa second stage paper]
   (a) 6 (b) 12
   (c) 24 (d) 120

4. The sum of all two digit numbers divisible by 5 is:
   [NTSE 2005 – Gujarat second stage paper]
   (a) 1035 (b) 1245
   (c) 1230 (d) 945

5. If the number 653 xy is divisible by 90, then $(x + y) = $?
   [NTSE 2003 – Bihar second stage paper]
   (a) 2 (b) 3
   (c) 4 (d) 6

6. A began a business with Rs. 85,000. He was joined afterwards by B with Rs. 42,500. For how much period does B join, if the profits at the end of the year are divided in the ratio of 3 : 1?
   [NTSE 2004 – Tripura first stage paper]
   (a) 4 months (b) 5 months
   (c) 6 months (d) 8 months

7. Aman started a business investing Rs. 70,000. Rakhi joined him after six months with an amount of Rs. 1,05,000 and Sagar joined them with Rs. 1.4 lakhs after another six months. The amount of profit earned should be distributed in what ratio among Aman, Rakhi and Sagar respectively, 3 years after Aman started the business?
   [NTSE 2004 – Punjab first stage paper]
   (a) 7 : 6 : 10
   (b) 12 : 15 : 16
   (c) 42 : 45 : 56
   (d) Cannot be determined

8. Arun, Kamal and Vinay invested Rs. 8000, Rs. 4000 and Rs. 8000 respectively in a business. Arun left after six months. If after eight months, there was a gain of Rs. 4005, then what will be the share of Kamal?
   [NTSE 2005 – MP first stage paper]
   (a) Rs. 890 (b) Rs. 1335
   (c) Rs. 1602 (d) Rs. 1780

9. Simran started a software business by investing Rs. 50,000. After six months, Nanda joined her with a capital of Rs. 80,000. After 3 years, they earned a profit of Rs. 24,500. What was Simran's share in the profit?
   [NTSE 2004 – Karnataka second stage paper]
   (a) Rs. 9,423 (b) Rs. 10,250
   (c) Rs. 12,500 (d) Rs. 10,500

10. The ratio of the length of a ground to its width is 7:4. Find the length of the ground if the width is 100 m.
    [NTSE 2004 – Maharashtra first stage paper]
    (a) 175 m (b) 150 m
    (c) 200 m (d) 225 m

Number System

Answer Key

| 1. (c) | 2. (b) | 3. (c) | 4. (c) | 5. (c) | 6. (d) | 7. (b) | 8. (a) | 9. (d) | 10. (a) |

Explanatory Notes

1. **(c)**
   A number is divisible by 9, when the sum of digits is divisible by 9. Sum of digits in the number (451*603) is 19. Now next multiple of 9 after 18 is 27. Therefore value 8, (27 – 19) should be assigned to *.

2. **(b)**
   First three digit numbers divisible by 6 is 102. Each subsequent number with a difference of 6 is divisible by 6.
   Therefore required number are
   $$102, 108, 114 \ldots 996.$$
   This is an AP with $a = 102$ and $d = 6$
   $$996 = 102 + (n-1)6$$
   Thus, $n = 150$

3. **(c)**
   The required number is $1 \times 2 \times 3 \times 4 = 24$

4. **(d)**
   Required numbers are 10, 15, 20, 25, ..., 95
   This is an A.P. in which
   $$a = 10, d = 5 \text{ and } l = 95$$
   $\Rightarrow \quad t_n = 95\, a + (n-1)d = 95$
   $\Rightarrow \quad 10 + (n-1) \times 5 = 95$
   $\Rightarrow \quad (n-1) \times 5 = 85$
   $\Rightarrow \quad (n-1) = 17$
   $\Rightarrow \quad n = 18$
   $\therefore$ Required Sum $= n/2\,(a+l)$
   $\quad = 18/2x\,(10 + 95)$
   $\quad = (9 \times 105) = 945$

5. **(c)**
   $$90 = 10 \times 9$$
   Clearly, $653xy$ is divisible by 10, so $y = 0$
   Now, 653×0 is divisible by 9
   So, $(6 + 5 + 3 + x + 0) = (14 + x)$ is divisible by 9.
   So, $x = 4$
   Hence, $(x + y) = (4 + 0) = 4$

6. **(d)**
   Suppose B joined for x months.
   Then, $[(85000 \times 12)/(42500 \times x) = 3/1]$
   $x = [(85000 \times 12)/(42500 \times 3)] = 8$
   So, B joined for 8 months

7. **(b)**
   Aman : Rakhi : Sagar = $(70{,}000 \times 36) : (1{,}05{,}000 \times 30) : (1{,}40{,}000 \times 24)$
   $= 12 : 15 : 16$

8. **(a)**
   Arun : Kamal : Vinay
   $= (8{,}000 \times 6) : (4{,}000 \times 8) : (8{,}000 \times 8)$
   $= 48 : 32 : 64$
   $= 3 : 2 : 4$
   Kamal's share = Rs. $(4005 \times 2/9)$ = Rs. 890

9. **(d)**
   Simran : Nanda = $(50000 \times 36) : (80000 \times 30)$
   $= 3 : 4$
   Simran's share = Rs.$24500 \times 3/7$ = Rs. 10,500

10. **(a)**
    It is given that $4x = 100$
    $x = 100/4 = 25$m
    Therefore $7x = 7 \times 25 = 175$ m

UNIT 2
Polynomials

■ **Polynomial**

Polynomials are algebraic expressions that include real numbers and variables. Division and square roots cannot be involved in the variables. The variables can only include addition, subtraction and multiplication.

Let x be a variable, n be a positive integer and $a_0, a_1, a_2, ..., a_n$ be constants. Then,
$f(x) = a_n x^n + a_{n-1} x^{n-1} + ... + a_1 x + a_0$ is called a Polynomial in variable x.

Here, $a_n x^n, a_{n-1} x^{n-1}, ..., a_1 x, a_0$ are known as terms and $a_n, a_{n-1}, ..., a_1, a_0$ are coefficients.

Examples:
- $P(x) = 3x - 2 \rightarrow$ polynomial in variable x.
- $Q(y) = 3y^2 - 2y + 4 \rightarrow$ is a polynomial in y.
- $F(u) = 1/2\, u^3 - 3u^2 + 2u - 4 \rightarrow$ is a polynomial in variable u.

Examples:
- $2x^2 - 3\sqrt{x} + 5$

Solution:
It is not a polynomial because the exponent of one term is 1/2 which is less than 1.

- $1/(x^2 - 2x + 5)$

Solution:
It is not a polynomial because the exponent is negative.

- $2x^3 - 3/x + 4$

Solution: As the exponent of 2nd term is -1 so it is not a polynomial.

■ **Degree of Polynomial**

Degree of Polynomial is the exponent of the highest degree term in a polynomial.

A polynomial of degree 0 is called a Constant Polynomial. On the basis of Degree of Polynomial, there are different types of polynomial. They are as follows:

Degree	Name of Polynomial	Form of Polynomial	Example
0	Constant Polynomial	f(x) = a, a is a constant.	f(x) = 2
1	Linear Polynomial	f(x) = ax + b, a ≠ 0	f(x) = 3x + 4
2	Quadratic Polynomial	f(x) = ax² + bx + c, a ≠ 0	f(x) = 2x² + 4x - 4
3	Cubic Polynomial	f(x) = ax³ + bx² + cx + d, a ≠ 0	f(x) = 3x³ - x² + 4x + 5
4	Quadratic Polynomial	f(x) = ax⁴ + bx³ + cx² + dx + e, a ≠ 0	f(x) = - 4x⁴ + 3x³ - x² + 8x + 6

The graph of a polynomial $p(x)$ of degree n can intersect or touch the x axis at atmost n points.

■ **Zeros of Polynomial**

It is a solution to the polynomial equation, $P(x) = 0$. It is the value of x that makes the polynomial equal to 0.

The value of a polynomial f(x) at $x = a$ is obtained by substituting $x = a$ in the given polynomial and is denoted by $f(a)$ which is Zeros of Polynomial.

Relationship between the Zeroes and Coefficient of a Polynomial

Case 1: Quadratic Polynomial
$$ax^2 + bx + c$$

If α and β are the roots of the equation, then

$$\text{Sum of zeroes} = \alpha + \beta = -\frac{\text{Coefficient of } x}{\text{Coefficient of } x^2} = -\frac{b}{a}$$

$$\text{Product of zeroes} = \alpha\beta = \frac{\text{Coefficient term}}{\text{Coefficient of } x^2} = \frac{c}{a}$$

So, the equation of polynomial is given by
$$x^2 - (\alpha + \beta)x + \alpha\beta$$

Case 2: Cubic Polynomial
$$ax^3 + bx^2 + cx + d, a \neq 0$$
Sum of zeroes = $\alpha + \beta + \gamma = -b/a$
Sum of the product of zeroes taken two at a time
$$= \alpha\beta + \beta\gamma + \alpha\gamma = c/a$$
Product of zeroes = $\alpha\beta\gamma = -d/a$
The cubic polynomial can be written as
$$x^3 - (\alpha + \beta + \gamma)x^2 + (\alpha\beta + \beta\gamma + \alpha\gamma)x - \alpha\beta\gamma$$

■ **Remainder Theorem**
Remainder theorem: Let P(x) be any polynomial of degree greater than or equal to one and let 'a' be any real number. If P(x) is divided by the linear polynomial $x - x$, then the remainder is P(a).
If P(a) = 0, then $x - a$ is the factor of the given polynomial.

■ **Polynomial Identities**
An algebraic expression in which the variables involved have only non negative integral powers is called polynomial.
For factorization or for the expansion of polynomial we use the following identities.

■ **Some Polynomial Identities**
1. $(x + y)^2 = x^2 + 2xy + y^2$
2. $(x - y)^2 = x^2 - 2xy + y^2$
3. $(x + y)(x - y) = x^2 - y^2$
4. $(x + a)(x + b) = x^2 + (a + b)x + ab$
5. $(x + y)^3 = x^3 + 3x^2y + 3xy^2 + y^3$
   $= x^3 + y^3 + 3xy(x + y)$
6. $(x - y)^3 = x^3 - 3x^2y + 3xy^2 - y^3$
   $= x^3 + y^3 - 3xy(x - y)$
7. $(x + y + z)^2 = x^2 + y^2 + z^2 + 2xy + 2yz + 2zx$
8. $x^3 + y^3 = (x + y)(x^2 - xy + y^2)$
9. $x^3 - y^3 = (x - y)(x^2 + xy + y^2)$
10. $x^3 + y^3 + z^3 - 3xyz = (x + y + z)$
If $x + y + z = 0$, then $x^3 + y^3 + z^3 = 3xyz$

Solved Examples

1. Find the value of $f(x) = x^3 - 2x^2 + 2x - 4$ at $x = -1$
   Solution:
   $f(x) = x^3 - 2x^2 + 2x - 4$
   $f(-1) = (-1)^3 - 2(-1)^2 + 2(-1) - 4$
   $= -1 - 2 - 2 - 4$
   $= -9$
   Note: If $f(a) = 0$, then $x = a$ is the root of the polynomial $f(x)s$

2. Write the equation of polynomial, if sum of zeroes = -8 and product of zeroes is 15.
   Solution:
   As sum of zeroes = $\alpha + \beta = -8$
   Product of zeroes = $\alpha\beta = 15$
   Equation is $x^2 - (\alpha + \beta)x + \alpha\beta$
   $x^2 - (-8)x + 15$
   $x^2 + 8x + 15$

3. Find the cubic polynomial with the sum, sum of the product of zeroes taken two at a time, and product of its zeroes as 2, -7, -14 respectively.
   Solution:
   If α, β and γ are the zeroes of a cubic polynomial then
   $x^3 - (\alpha + \beta + \gamma)x^2 + (\alpha\beta + \beta\gamma + \alpha\gamma)x - \alpha\beta\gamma$
   $\alpha + \beta + \gamma = 2$
   $\alpha\beta + \beta\gamma + \alpha\gamma = -7$
   $\alpha\beta\gamma = -14$
   $x^3 - (2)x^2 + (-7)x - (-14)$

4. Find the remainder when $x^4 - x^3 - 3x^2 - 2x + 1$ is divided by $x - 1$.
   Solution:
   $P(x) = x^4 - x^3 - 3x^2 - 2x + 1$ and
   $x - 1 = 0$
   $x = 1$
   So put $x = 1$ in P(x)
   $P(1) = (1)^4 - (1)^3 - 3(1)^2 - 2(1) + 1$
   $= 1 - 1 - 3 - 2 + 1$
   $= -5 + 1$
   $= -4$
   So, by remainder theorem, -4 is the remainder when $x^4 - x^3 - 3x^2 - 2x + 1$ is divided by $x - 1$.

5. Find the remainder when $p(x) = 4x^3 - 12x^2 + 14x - 3$ is divided by $g(x) = x - 1/2$
   Solution: By remainder theorem,
   $g(x) = x - 1/2 \Rightarrow x = 1/2$
   Put $x = 1/2$ in the given polynomial
   $p(1/2) = 4(1/2)^3 - 12(1/2)^2 + 14(1/2) - 3$
   $= 4/8 - 12/4 + 7 - 3$
   $= 1/2 - 3 + 4$
   $= 1/2 + 1$
   $p(1/2) = 3/2$

6. Let R_1 and R_2 are the remainders of when the polynomials $x^3 + 2x^2 - 5ax - 7$ and $x^3 + ax^2 - 12x + 6$ are divided by $x + 1$ and $x - 2$ respectively. If $2R_1 + R_2 = 6$, find the value of a.

[27]

Solution:
Let $p(x) = x^3 + 2x^2 - 5ax - 7$ and $q(x)$
$= x^3 + ax^2 - 12x + 6$
$\Rightarrow \quad R_1 = p(-1)$
$\Rightarrow \quad R_1 = (-1)^3 + 2(-1)^2 - 5a(-1) - 7$
$\Rightarrow \quad R_1 = -1 + 2 + 5a - 7$
$\Rightarrow \quad R_1 = 5a - 6$

And,
$R_2 =$ Remainder when $q(x)$ is divided by $x - 2$
$\quad R_2 = q(2)$
$\Rightarrow \quad R_2 = (2)^3 + a(2)^2 - 12(2) + 6$
$\Rightarrow \quad R_2 = 8 + 4a - 24 + 6$
$\Rightarrow \quad R_2 = 4a - 10$
As $\quad 2R_1 + R_2 = 6$
Put the values of R_1 and R_2 in the above equation
$2(5a - 6) + 4a - 10 = 6$
$10a - 12 + 4a - 10 = 6$
$14a - 22 = 6$
$14a = 28$
$a = 28/14$
$a = 2$

7. Expand the following using Polynomial Identities.
$(2a + 5)^2$
Solution:
$(2x + 5)^2 = (2a)^2 + 2(2a)(5) + 5^2$
[using the identity $(x + y)^2 = x^2 + 2xy + y^2$]
$(2x + 5)^2 = 4a^2 + 20a + 25$

8. Expand the following using Polynomial Identities.
$(b + 6)(b - 6)$
Solution:
[using the identity $(x + y)(x - y) = x^2 - y^2$]
$(b + 6)(b - 6) = b^2 - 6^2$
$= b^2 - 36$

9. Factorize: $64a^3 - 27b^3 - 144a^2b + 108ab^2$
Solution:
$64a^3 - 27b^3 - 144a^2b + 108ab^2$
$= (4a)^3 - (3b)^3 - 36ab(4a - 3b)$
$= (4a)^3 - (3b)^3 - 3(4a)(3b)(4a - 3b)$
$= (4a - 3b)^3$ [using $x^3 + y^3 - 3xy(x - y)$]
$= (4a - 3b)(4a - 3b)(4a - 3b)$

10. Evaluate: $(104)^3$
Solution:
$(104)^3 = (100 + 4)^3$
$= (100)^3 + (4)^3 + 3(100)(4)(100 + 4)$
[Using $(x + y)^3 = x^3 + 3x^2y + 3xy^2 + y^3$
$= x^3 + y^3 + 3xy(x + y)$]
$= 1000000 + 64 + 124800$
$= 1124864$

11. Evaluate: $(-12)^3 + (7)^3 + (5)^3$
Solution:
$(-12)^3 + (7)^3 + (5)^3$
From the above we can see that
$-12 + 7 + 5 = 0$
$(-12)^3 + (7)^3 + (5)^3 = 3(-12)(7)(5)$
[Using identity 10]
$= -1260$

Multiple Choice Questions

1. How many polynomials are there having 4 and -2 as zeros?
   (a) One (b) Two
   (c) Three (d) More than three

2. The zeros of the quadratic polynomial $x^2 + 88x + 125$ are
   (a) both positive
   (b) both negative
   (c) one positive and one negative
   (d) both equal

3. If a and b are the zeros of $x^2 + 5x + 8$, then the value of $(a + b)$ is
   (a) 5 (b) -5
   (c) 8 (d) -8

4. If α and β are the zeros of $2x^2 + 5x + -9$, then the value of $\alpha\beta$ is
   (a) $-\dfrac{5}{2}$ (b) $\dfrac{5}{2}$
   (c) $-\dfrac{9}{2}$ (d) $\dfrac{9}{2}$

5. If one zero of the quadratic polynomial $kx^2 + 3x + k$ is 2, then the value of k is
   (a) $\dfrac{5}{6}$ (b) $-\dfrac{5}{6}$
   (c) $\dfrac{6}{5}$ (d) $-\dfrac{6}{5}$

6. If one zero of the quadratic polyminal $(k - 1)x^2 + kx + 1$ is -4, then the value of the k is
   (a) $-\dfrac{5}{4}$ (b) $\dfrac{5}{4}$
   (c) $-\dfrac{4}{3}$ (d) $\dfrac{4}{3}$

7. If 2 and 3 are the zeros of the quadratic polynomial $x^2 + (a + 1)x + b$, then
   (a) $a = -2, b = 6$ (b) $a = 2, b = -6$
   (c) $a = -2, b = -6$ (d) $a = 2, b = 6$

8. If one of the zeros of the quadratic polynomial $x^2 + bx + c$ is negative of the other, then
   (a) $b = 0$ and c is positive
   (b) $b = 0$ and c is negative
   (c) $b \neq 0$ and c is positive
   (d) $b \neq 0$ and c is negative

Polynomials

9. If the zeros of the quadratic polynomial $ax^2 + bx + c$, where $a \neq 0$ and $c \neq 0$, are equal then,
   (a) c and a have the same sign
   (b) c and a have opposite signs
   (c) c and b have the same sign
   (d) c and b have opposite signs

10. The zeros of the quadratic polynomial $x^2 + kx + k$, where $k > 0$
    (a) are both positive
    (b) are both negative
    (c) are always equal
    (d) are always unequal

11. If one zero of $3x^2 + 8x + k$ be the reciprocal of the other, then $k = ?$
    (a) 3
    (b) -3
    (c) $-\dfrac{1}{3}$
    (d) $\dfrac{1}{3}$

12. If the sum of zeros of quadratic polynomial $kx^2 + 2x + 3k$ is equal to the product of its zeros, then $k = ?$
    (a) $\dfrac{1}{3}$
    (b) $-\dfrac{1}{3}$
    (c) $\dfrac{2}{3}$
    (d) $-\dfrac{2}{3}$

13. If, α and β are the zeros of $f(x) = 2x^2 + 6x - 6$, then
    (a) $\alpha + \beta = \alpha\beta$
    (b) $\alpha + \beta = > \alpha\beta$
    (c) $\alpha + \beta < \alpha\beta$
    (d) $\alpha + \beta + \alpha\beta = 0$

14. If, α, β are the zeros of the polynomial $x^2 - 5x + c$ and $a - b = 1$, then $c = ?$
    (a) 0
    (b) 1
    (c) 4
    (d) 6

15. If a, b are the zeros of the polynomial $x^2 + 6x + 2$, then $\left(\dfrac{1}{\alpha}, \dfrac{1}{\beta}\right) = ?$
    (a) 3
    (b) -3
    (c) 12
    (d) -12

16. If one of the zeros of the cubic polynomial $ax^3 + bx^2 + cx + a$ is 0, then the product of the other two zeros is :
    (a) $-\dfrac{c}{a}$
    (b) $\dfrac{c}{a}$
    (c) 0
    (d) $-\dfrac{b}{a}$

17. If one of the zeros of the cubic polynomial $x^3 + ax^2 + bx + c$ is -1, then the product of the other two zeros is :
    (a) $a - b - 1$
    (b) $b - a - 1$
    (c) $1 - a + b$
    (d) $1 + a - b$

18. If the zeros of the polynomial $x^3 - 3x^2 x + 1$ are $a - b$, a and $a + b$, then $a + d$ is
    (a) a natural number
    (b) an integer
    (c) a rational number
    (d) an irrational number

19. If, a, b be the zeros of the polynomial $x^2 - 8x + k$ such that $a^2 + b^2 = 40$, then $k = ?$
    (a) 6
    (b) 9
    (c) 12
    (d) -12

20. Which of the following is a the statment ?
    (a) $x^2 + 5x - 3$ is a linear polynomial
    (b) $x^2 + 4x - 1$ is a binomial
    (c) $x + 1$ is monomial
    (d) $5x^3$ is a monomial

National Talent Search Examination (NTSE)-X

Answer Key

1. (d)	2. (b)	3. (b)	4. (c)	5. (d)	6. (b)	7. (c)	8. (b)	9. (a)	10. (b)
11. (a)	12. (d)	13. (a)	14. (d)	15. (b)	16. (b)	17. (c)	18. (d)	19. (c)	20. (d)

Explanatory Notes

1. (d)
Clearly, an infinite number of polynomials of the form $a(x - 4)(x + 2)$ or $a(x^2 - 2x - 8)$ for an arbitrary real number a, have 4 and -2 as zeros.

2. (b)
Let α and β be the zeros of $x^2 + 88x + 125$, then $\alpha + \beta = -88$ and $\alpha\beta = 125$. This happens when α and β are both negative

3. (b)
Clearly, $\alpha + \beta = -5$

4. (c)
Clearly, $\alpha\beta = -\dfrac{9}{2}$

5. (d)
Since z is zero of $kx^2 + 3x + k$, we have :
$k(2)^2 + 3x + k = 0$
$5k + 6 = 0$
$5k = -6$
$k = -\dfrac{6}{5}$

6. (b)
Since -4 is a zero of $(k-1)x^2 + kx + 1$, we have :
$(k-1)(-4)^2 + k(-4) + 1 = 0$
$12k - 15 = 0$
$12k = 15$
$k = \dfrac{15}{12} = \dfrac{5}{4}$

7. (c)
Since -2 and 3 are the zeros of $x^2 + (a + 1)x + b$, we have
$(-2)^2 + (a + 1)(-2) + b = 0$
$\Rightarrow \quad b - 2a = -2$ .... eq. (1)
and $3^2 + (a + 1) \times 3 + b = 0$
$\Rightarrow \quad b + 3a = -12$ .... eq. (2)
on solving (1) and (2), we get
$a = -2$ and $b = -6$

8. (b)
Let α and $-\alpha$ be the zeros of $x^2 + bx + c$, then
$\alpha + (-\alpha) = -b$
$-b = 0 \quad \Rightarrow b = 0$
and $\alpha \times (-\alpha) = c$
$\alpha^2 = -c$
$\Rightarrow c$ is negative, as $\alpha^2 > 0$
$\therefore \quad b = 0$ and c is negative

9. (b)
Let α and α be the zeros of $ax^2 + bx + c$
Then $\alpha + \alpha = -\dfrac{b}{a}$
$2\alpha = -\dfrac{b}{a} \quad \Rightarrow \alpha = -\dfrac{b}{2a}$
and $\alpha \times \alpha = \dfrac{c}{a} \quad \Rightarrow \alpha^2 = \dfrac{c}{a} > 0$
$\therefore$ c and a must have the same sign.

10. (b)
Let α and β be the zeros of $x^2 + kx + k$
Then, $\alpha + \beta - k$ and $\alpha\beta = k$
This is possible only when α and β are both negative.

11. (a)
Let α and $\dfrac{1}{\alpha}$ be the zeros of $3x^2 + 8x + k$.
Then product of roots $= \dfrac{k}{3}$
$\Rightarrow \alpha \times \dfrac{1}{\alpha} = \dfrac{k}{3} \quad \Rightarrow \dfrac{k}{3} = 1 \quad \Rightarrow k = 3$

12. (d)
Let α and β be the zeros of $kx^2 + 2x + 2k$.
Then, $\alpha + \beta = \dfrac{-2}{k}$ and $\alpha\beta = \dfrac{3k}{k} = 3$
Now $\alpha + \beta = \alpha\beta \Rightarrow \dfrac{-2}{k} = 3$
$\Rightarrow \quad k = \dfrac{-2}{3}$

13. (a)
Since α, β are the zeros of $2x^2 + 6x - 6$, we have
$\alpha + \beta = \dfrac{-6}{2} = -3$
and $\alpha\beta = \dfrac{-6}{2} = -3$
Hence $\alpha + \beta = \alpha\beta$

14. (d)
$(\alpha + \beta) =$ and $\alpha - \beta = 1)$
$\Rightarrow \quad \alpha = 3$ and $\beta = 2$
Since 3 is a zero of the polynomial

[30]

$x^2 - 5x + c$, we have
$$3^2 - 5 \times 3 + c = 0$$
$\Rightarrow \quad 9 - 15 + c = 0$
$\Rightarrow \quad c = 6$

15. (b)
Since, α and β are zeros of $x^2 + 6x + 2$, we have
$$\alpha + \beta = -6 \text{ and } \alpha\beta = 2$$
∴ $\left(\dfrac{1}{\alpha} + \dfrac{1}{\beta}\right) = \dfrac{\alpha + \beta}{\alpha\beta} = \dfrac{-6}{2} = -3$

16. (b)
Let α, β, 0 be the zeros of $ax^3 + bx^2 + cx + d$
Then, sum of the products of zeros, taken two at a time is given by
$$(\alpha\beta + \beta \times 0 + \alpha \times 0) = \dfrac{c}{a}$$
$\Rightarrow \quad \alpha\beta = \dfrac{c}{a}$
⇒ The product of the other two zeros is $\dfrac{c}{a}$

17. (c)
Since -1 is a zero of $x^3 + ax^2 + bx + c$, we have :
$$(-1)^3 + a \times (-1)^2 + b \times (-1) + c = 0$$
$\Rightarrow \quad a - b + c - 1 = 0$
$c = 1 - a + b$
Also, product of all zeros is given by
$$\alpha\beta \times (-1) = -c$$
$\Rightarrow \quad \alpha\beta = c$
$\Rightarrow \quad \alpha\beta = 1 - a + b$

18. (d)
Since $a - d$, a, $a + d$ are the zeros of $x^3 - 3x^2 + x + 1$, we have :
Sum of zeros = 3
$\Rightarrow \quad a + d + a - d = 3$
$3a = 3$
$\Rightarrow \quad a = 1$
So, the zeros are $(1 - d)$, 1, $(1 + d)$
Product of zeros = (-1)
$\Rightarrow (1 - d) \times 1 \times (1 + d)$
$\Rightarrow \quad 1 - d^2 = 1$
$\Rightarrow \quad d^2 = 2; d = \sqrt{2}$
∴ $a + d = \left(1 \pm \sqrt{2}\right)$, which is irrational

19. (c)
Since, α, β are the zeros of $x^2 - 8x + k$, we have :
$$\alpha + \beta = 8$$
and $\alpha\beta = k$
Also, it is given that $\alpha^2 + \beta^2 = 40$
Now, $(\alpha + \beta)^2 = (\alpha^2 + \beta^2) + 2\alpha\beta$
$\Rightarrow \quad 40 + 2k = 8^2$
∴ $2k = 64 - 40 = 24$
$\Rightarrow \quad k = 12$

20. (d)
$5x^3$ consist of one term only, so it is a monomial.

National Talent Search Examination (NTSE)-X

Previous Year Questions

1. Which is true
   [NTSE 2003 – Delhi first stage paper]
   (a) Degree of a zero polynomial is 'O'
   (b) Degree of a zero polynomial is not defined
   (c) Degree of a constant polynomial is not defined
   (d) A polynomial of degree n must have n zeros

2. Which of the following is a monomial ?
   [NTSE 2005 – Assam first stage paper]
   (a) $x + 2$ (b) $x^2 + 2x + 3$
   (c) $4x^2$ (d) $x^2 + 8$

3. If, a, b are the zeros of the quadratic polynomial $f(x) = x^2 - Px + q$, then $\dfrac{1}{\alpha} + \dfrac{1}{\beta} =$
   [NTSE 2012 – Punjab second stage paper]
   (a) $p - q$ (b) $p + q$
   (c) $\dfrac{p}{q}$ (d) $\dfrac{q}{p}$

4. If, a, b are the zeros of the quadratic polynomial $f(x) = x^2 - 5x + 4$, then $\dfrac{1}{\alpha} + \dfrac{1}{\beta} - 2ab =$
   [NTSE 2006 – Goa second stage paper]
   (a) $\dfrac{27}{4}$ (b) $\dfrac{-27}{4}$
   (c) $\dfrac{4}{27}$ (d) $\dfrac{-4}{27}$

5. A quadratic polynomial, whose zeros are – 3 and 4 is :
   [NTSE 2002 – Kerala first stage paper]
   (a) $x^2 - x + 12$ (b) $x^2 + x + 12$
   (c) $\dfrac{x^2}{2} - \dfrac{x}{2} - 6$ (d) $2x^2 + 2x - 24$

6. Which of the following is a polynomial
   [NTSE 2001 – Manipur second stage paper]
   (a) $x^2 - 5x + 6\sqrt{x} + 3$ (b) $x^{3/2} - x + x^{1/2} + 1$
   (c) $\sqrt{x} + \dfrac{1}{\sqrt{x}}$ (d) None of the these

7. The zeros of the polynomial $x^2 - 2x + 3$ are :
   [NTSE 2004 – Haryana first stage paper]
   (a) $-3, 1$ (b) $-3, -1$
   (c) $3, -1$ (d) $3, 1$

8. The zeros of the polynomial $4x^2 + 5\sqrt{2}x - 3$ are :
   [NTSE 2003 – Bihar first stage paper]
   (a) $-3\sqrt{2}, \sqrt{2}$ (b) $-3\sqrt{2}, \dfrac{\sqrt{2}}{2}$
   (c) $\dfrac{-3\sqrt{2}}{2}, \dfrac{\sqrt{2}}{4}$ (d) None of these

9. If, α, β are the zeros of the quadratic polynomial $ax^2 + bx + c$, then $(\alpha^2 + \beta^2) = ?$
   [NTSE 2012 – U.P. first stage paper]
   (a) $\dfrac{a^2 - 2bc}{b^2}$ (b) $\dfrac{b^2 - 2ac}{a^2}$
   (c) $\dfrac{a^2 - 2bc}{b^2}$ (d) $\dfrac{b^2 + 2ac}{a^2}$

10. If two of the zeros of the cubic polynomial $ax^3 + bx^2 + cx + d$ is 0, then the product of the other two zeros is :
    [NTSE 2005 – Tamilnadu second stage paper]
    (a) $\dfrac{-b}{a}$ (b) $\dfrac{b}{a}$
    (c) $\dfrac{c}{a}$ (d) $\dfrac{-d}{a}$

Polynomials

Answer Key

| 1. (b) | 2. (c) | 3. (c) | 4. (b) | 5. (c) | 6. (d) | 7. (c) | 8. (c) | 9. (b) | 10. (a) |

Explanatory Notes

1. (b)
   By definition, degree of a zero polynomial is not defined.

2. (c)
   $4x^2$ consists of one term only, so it is a monomial

3. (c)
   $$\alpha + \beta = P, \alpha\beta = q$$
   $$\therefore \quad \frac{1}{\alpha} + \frac{1}{\beta} = \frac{\alpha + \beta}{\alpha\beta} = \frac{P}{q}$$

4. (b)
   $$\alpha + \beta = 5, \alpha\beta = 4$$
   $$\therefore \quad \frac{1}{\alpha} + \frac{1}{\beta} - 2\alpha\beta = \frac{\alpha + \beta}{\alpha\beta} - 2\alpha\beta$$
   $$= \frac{5}{4} - 8 = \frac{-27}{4}$$

5. (c)
   Sum of the zeros $= -3 + 4 = 1$
   Product of the zeros $= -3(4) = -12$
   $\therefore$ Required polynomial $= x^2 - 1(x) - 12$
   $= x^2 - x - 12$
   i.e. $\frac{x^2}{2} - \frac{x}{2} - 6$

6. (d)
   Clearly, none of the given expressions is a polynomial.

7. (c)
   $$x^2 - 2x - 3 = 0$$
   $$\Rightarrow \quad x^2 - 3x + x - 3 = 0$$
   $$\Rightarrow \quad x(x-3)(x+3) = 0$$
   $$(x-3)(x+1) = 0$$
   $$x = 3, \text{ or } x = -1$$

8. (c)
   $$4x^2 + 5\sqrt{2}x - 3 = 0$$
   $$\Rightarrow \quad 4x^2 + 6\sqrt{2}x - \sqrt{2}x - 3 = 0$$
   $$\Rightarrow \quad 2x\left(2x + 3\sqrt{2}\right)\frac{-1}{\sqrt{2}}\left(2x + 3\sqrt{2}\right) = 0$$
   $$\Rightarrow \quad \left(2x + 3\sqrt{2}\right)\left(2x\frac{-1}{\sqrt{2}}\right) = 0$$
   $$\Rightarrow \quad x = \frac{-3\sqrt{2}}{2}$$
   or $\quad x = \frac{1}{2\sqrt{2}}$
   $$\Rightarrow \quad x = \frac{-3\sqrt{2}}{2}$$
   or $\quad x = \frac{1}{2\sqrt{2}} \times \frac{\sqrt{2}}{\sqrt{2}} = \frac{\sqrt{2}}{4}$

9. (b)
   $$\alpha + \beta = \frac{-b}{a} \text{ and } \alpha\beta = \frac{c}{a}$$
   $$\therefore \quad (\alpha^2 + \beta^2) = (\alpha + \beta)^2 - 2\alpha\beta$$
   $$= \frac{b^2}{a^2} - \frac{2c}{a} = \frac{b^2 - 2ac}{a^2}$$

10. (a)
    Let $\alpha, 0, 0$ be the zeros of $ax^3 + bx^2 + cx + d$
    Then, sum of zeros $= \frac{-b}{a}$
    $$\Rightarrow \quad \alpha + 0 + 0 = \frac{-b}{a}$$
    $$\alpha \quad \alpha = \frac{-b}{a}$$
    Hence the third zero is $\frac{-b}{a}$

UNIT 3
Pair of Linear Equations in Two Variables

1. A linear equation in two variables is represented geometrically by a straight line.
2. Each solution of a linear equation in two variables, $ax + by + c = 0$, corresponds to a point on the line representing the equation and vice versa.
3. The general form of a pair of linear equations in two variables is:
   $$a_1x + b_1y + c_1 = 0$$
   $$a_2x + b_2y + c_2 = 0$$
   where, $a_1, a_2, b_1, b_2, c_1, c_2$, are real number, such that $a_1^2, b_1^2 \neq 0, a_2^2, b_2^2 \neq 0$

   Example 1:
   $$2x + 3y - 4 = 0$$
   Here, $a = 2; b = 3$ and $c = -4$

   Example 2:
   $$-x + y = 0$$
   Here, $a = -1; b = 1$ and $c = 0$

4. A system of linear equations in two variables represents two lines in the plane. For two given lines there could be three possible cases:
   I. Intersecting lines, lines may intersect at a point
   II. Parallel lines
   III. Overlapping or coincidental to each other
5. If the lines intersect at a point, that point gives unique solution of the system of equations. In this case system of equations is said to be consistent.
6. If the lines coincide (overlap), the pair of equations will have infinitely many solutions. System of equations is said to be dependent and consistent.
7. If the lines are parallel, the pair of equations has no solution. In this case, the pair of equations is said to be inconsistent.
8. System of equations can be solved using Algebraic and graphical expressions.
9. Graphical method can be used to obtain the solution of a system of equations but it has its limitations in cases where the solution is non-integral.
10. Steps to be followed while using the method of substitution for solving linear equations in 2 variables:

Step 1: Find the value of one variable, say y in terms of the other variable i.e. x from either equation, whichever is convenient.

Step 2: Substitute this value of y in the other equation, and reduce it to an equation in one variable, i.e. in terms of x, which can be solved.

Step 3: Substitute the value of x (or y) obtained in step 2 in the equation used in step 1 to obtain the value of the other variable.

Step 4: The values of x and y so obtained are the coordinates of the solution of system of equations.

11. There could be three possibilities on substituting the variable in the other equation:
   I. Equation reduces to a linear equation in one variable x which can be solved to get the value of x and then y.
   II. Equation reduces to a true equation involving no variable, and then the given pair of equation has infinitely many solutions.
   III. Equation reduces to false equation involving no variable; then the given pair of equation has no solution.
12. Steps to be followed in the Elimination Method of solving simultaneous linear equations:

Step 1: First multiply both the equations by some suitable non-zero constants to make the coefficients of one variable (either x or y) numerically equal.

Step 2: Then add or subtract one equation from the other so that one variable gets eliminated. If you get an equation in one variable, go to step 3.

If in Step 2, we obtain a true statement involving no variable, then the original pair of equations has infinitely many solutions.

If in Step 2, we obtain a false statement involving no variable, then the original pair of equations has no solution, i.e. it is inconsistent.

Step 3: Solve the equation in one variable (x or y) so obtained to get its value.

Step 4: Substitute this value of x (or y) in either of the original equations to get the value of the other variable.

13. Steps to be followed in Cross Multiplication Method of solving simultaneous linear equations:

    Step 1: Write the equations in the general form
    $$a_1x + b_1y + c_1 = 0$$
    $$a_2x + b_2y + c_2 = 0$$

    Step 2: Arrange these in the following manner
    $$\frac{x}{\underset{b_2\quad c_2}{b_1\searrow\nearrow c_1}} = \frac{y}{\underset{c_2\quad a_2}{c_1\searrow\nearrow a_1}} = \frac{1}{\underset{a_2\quad b_2}{a_1\searrow\nearrow b_1}}$$

    Step 3: Cross multiplication
    $$\frac{x}{b_1c_2 - b_2c_1} = \frac{y}{a_2c_1 - a_1c_2} = \frac{1}{a_1b_2 - a_2b_1}$$
    $$(1) \qquad\qquad (2) \qquad\qquad (3)$$

    (a) Comparing (1) and (3), we get the value of x
    $$x = \frac{b_1c_2 - b_2c_1}{a_1b_2 - a_2b_1}$$

    (b) Comparing (2) and (3), we get the value of y
    $$y = \frac{a_2c_1 - a_1c_2}{a_1b_2 - a_2b_1}$$

14. Equations which are not linear but can be reduced to linear form by some suitable substitutions are called equations reducible to linear form.

15. The speed of the boat downstream is the sum of speed of boat in still water and speed of the stream.

16. The speed of the boat upstream is the difference of speed of boat in still water and speed of the stream.

17. Reduced equation can be solved by any of the algebraic method (substitution, elimination or cross multiplication) of solving linear equation.

Solved Examples

1. For what value of k will the equations $x + 2y + 7 = 0$; $2x + ky + 14 = 0$ represent the coincident line.

   Solution: For coincident lines we have,
   $$\frac{a_1}{a_2} = \frac{b_1}{b_2} = \frac{c_1}{c_2}$$
   $\Rightarrow \qquad 1/2 = 2/k = 7/14$
   $\Rightarrow \qquad 1/2 = 2/k$
   $\therefore \qquad k = 4$

   Graphical Method for Linear Equations
   Graphical method is used to find the solution of linear equations in two variables.

2. Solving equation by graphical method
   $$x - y = 1 \qquad \text{..........Equation (1)}$$
   $$2x + y = 8 \qquad \text{..........Equation (2)}$$

   Solution:
   First, solve each equation for 'y' or change each equation in $y = mx + b$ form
   For equation (1), $y = x - 1$
   Here, Slope $= m = 1$ and y intercept $= -1$
   For equation (2) $y = -2x + 8$
   Here, Slope $= m = -2$ and y intercept $= 8$
   After converting the equations in $y = mx + b$ form, prepare a function table. Take any values of x, put that value one by one in the given equation and find the value of y. From the following table we get (x, y) co-ordinates.

x	$y = x - 1$	(x, y)
	$y = -2x + 8$	(x, y)
0	$y = 0 - 1 = -1$	$(0, -1)$
	$y = -2(0) + 8 = 8$	$(0, 8)$
1	$y = 1 - 1 = 0$	$(1, 0)$
	$y = -2(1) + 8 = -2 + 8 = 6$	$(1, 6)$
-1	$y = -1 - 1 = -2$	$(-1, -2)$
	$y = -2(-1) + 8 = 2 + 8 = 10$	$(-1, 10)$
3	$y = 3 - 1 = 2$	$(3, 2)$
	$y = -2(3) + 8 = -6 + 8 = 2$	$(3, 2)$

Now, plot the points (x, y) for given lines and join them. The intersection point of these two lines will be the solution.

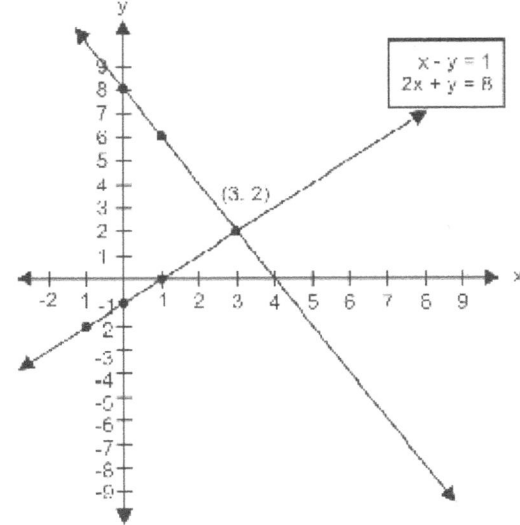

Note: Since the two lines cross at (3, 2), the solution is $x = 3$ and $y = 2$. Checking these value shows that this answer is correct. Plug these values into the original equations and get a true result.

$$x - y = 1 \qquad 2x + y = 8$$
$$(3) - 2 = 1 \qquad 2(3) + 2 = 8$$
$$1 = 1 \text{ (check)} \qquad 6 + 2 = 8$$
$$8 = 8 \text{ (check)}$$

Substitution Method

In the Substitution method, find the value of any one variable (x or y) from one equation and put it in other equation and then solve it like a simple equation.

3. **Solve the following using the Substitution method**
   Find the solution by the Substitution method
   $$2x + y = 6 \text{ and } 2x - y = -2$$
   Solution:
   $$2x + y = 6 \qquad ...(1)$$
   $$2x - y = -2 \qquad ...(2)$$
   $$y = -2x + 6$$
   Put $y = -2x + 6$ in equation (2)
   $$2x - (-2x + 6) = -2$$
   $$2x + 2x - 6 = -2 \text{ (use a distributive law)}$$
   $$4x - 6 = -2$$
   $$4x = -2 + 6$$
   $$4x = 4$$
   $$\boxed{x = 1}$$
   Now put $x = 1$ in any one of the given equations.
   Equation (1) $\Rightarrow 2(1) + y = 6$
   $$2 + y = 6$$
   $$y = 6 - 2$$
   $$y = 4$$
   Solution is $\boxed{(1, 4)}$

Solving Equation by Elimination Method

An equation can be solved by eliminating one of the variables without solving one variable in terms of the other. The method involves making the coefficients of one the variables the additive inverses **(equal but opposite in sign)**. The variable can then be eliminated by adding the two equations. This method is also called the Elimination method as it deals straight with getting rid of one of the variables.

4. Solving system of equation by elimination method/ Addition method:
   $$3x + 4y = -1 \qquad ...(1)$$
   $$6x - 2y = 3 \qquad ...(2)$$

Step 1: Decide on the variable to be eliminated	The variable x can be eliminated by adding the equations if the coefficient of x in equation (1) is changed to $-6x$.
Step 2: Eliminate the variable by suitably multiplying the equations and adding them. In the above problem the first equation is multiplied by -2.	Equation(1) x (-2) $-6x - 8y = +2$ $6x - 2y = 3$ $\overline{}$ $10y = 5$ $y = 5/-10$ (dividing both sides by -10) $y = -\frac{1}{2}$
Step 3: Plug in the value of y found in any one of the given equations and solve for x.	Plugging $y = -1/2$ in equation (1) $3x + 4(-1/2) = -1$ $3x + (-2) = -1$ $3x = +1$ Transposing -2 to the right side $x = $ '1/3' Dividing by 3 and simplifying
Check: Plug the values of x and y found in equation (2) and check whether the equation is satisfied.	$6x(1/3) - 2x(-1/2) = 3$ $\Rightarrow 2 + 1 = 3$ The equation is satisfied.

The solution is (1/3, –1/2)

5. At the first meeting of the Chess Club, 12 students were present. After efforts were made to increase interest in the club, twice as many girls and 3 times as many boys attended the second meeting compared to those that attended the first. If there were 29 students at the second meeting, how many boys and how many girls attended each meeting?

Solution:

Let the number of boys and girls in the first meeting be x and y respectively.
$$x + y = 12 \qquad ...(1)$$
No. of boys in the second meeting = $3x$
No. of girls in the second meeting = $2y$
Total number of students = 29
$$3x + 2y = 29 \qquad ...(2)$$
Equation (1) was multiplied by -2 to eliminate y
$$-2x - 2y = -24 \qquad ...(3)$$
adding the two equations
$$3x + 2y = 29$$
$$-2x - 2y = -24$$
$$x = 5$$

Plugging $x = 5$ in equation (1)
$$5 + y = 12 \Rightarrow y = 7$$
No. of boys who attended the first meeting = 5
No. of girls who attended the first meeting = 7
No. of boys who attended the second meeting = 15
No. of girls who attended the second meeting = 14

Cross Multiplication Method

In this section we will discuss cross multiplication method. It is also known as Cramer's rule.
Let the two equations be,
$$a_1x + b_1y + c_1 = 0$$
$$a_2x + b_2y + c_2 = 0$$
be a system of linear equations in two variables x and y such that:
$$\frac{a_1}{a_2} \neq \frac{b_1}{b_2}$$
i.e. $a_1b_2 - a_2b_1 \neq 0$

then the system has a unique solution given by:
$$x = \frac{b_1c_2 - b_2c_1}{a_1b_2 - a_2b_1} \text{ and } y = \frac{c_1a_2 - c_2a_1}{a_1b_2 - a_2b_1}$$

6. Find the solution of the given equations
   $2x + 3y = 17$ and $3x - 2y = 6$
   Solution:
   $a_1 = 2$, $b_1 = 3$, and $c_1 = -17$
   $a_2 = 3$, $b_2 = -2$ and $c_2 = -6$
   $$x = \frac{b_1c_2 - b_2c_1}{a_1b_2 - a_2b_1} \text{ and } y = \frac{c_1a_2 - c_2a_1}{a_1b_2 - a_2b_1}$$
   Thus,
   $$x = \frac{(3 \times -6) - (-2 \times -17)}{(2 \times -2) - (3 \times 3)} \quad\quad y = \frac{(-17 \times 3) - (-6 \times 2)}{(2 \times -2) - (3 \times 3)}$$
   $$x = \frac{-52}{-13} = 4 \quad\quad y = \frac{-39}{-13} = 3$$
   Hence, the solution is $x = 4$ and $y = 3$

Multiple Choice Questions

1. The pair of equations $5x - 15y = 8$ and $3x - 9y = \frac{24}{5}$ has
   (a) one solution
   (b) two solutions
   (c) infinity many solutions
   (d) no solution

2. The pair of equations $x + 2y + 5 = 0$ and $-3x - 6y + 1 = 0$ have
   (a) a unique solution
   (b) exactly two solutions
   (c) infinitely many solutions
   (d) no solution

3. Graphically, the pair of equations $6x - 3y + 10 = 0$, $2x - y + 9 = 0$ represents two lines which are
   (a) intresecting at exactly one point
   (b) intresecting at exactly two points
   (c) coincident
   (d) parallel

4. If a pair of linear equations is consitent, then the lines will be
   (a) parallel
   (b) always coincident
   (c) intersecting or coincident
   (d) always intersecting

5. The pair of equations $x = 0$ and $y = -7$ has
   (a) one solution
   (b) two solutions
   (c) infinitely many solutions
   (d) no solution

6. The pair of equations $x = a$ and $y = b$ graphically represents lines which are
   (a) parallel
   (b) intersecting at (b, a)
   (c) coincident
   (d) intersecting at (a, b)

7. How many solutions, a linear equation in two variables have ?
   (a) one solution
   (b) two solutions
   (c) no solution
   (d) infinite number of solutions

8. How many solutions do two linear equations in two vriables have, if their graph intersect in one point ?
   (a) one solution
   (b) two solutions
   (c) three solutions
   (d) infinite number of solutions

9. How many solutions do two linear equations in two variables representing coincident lines have?
   (a) one solution   (b) two solutions
   (c) three solutions   (d) infinite solutions

10. Which of the following is not a solution of the pair of equations $3x - 2y = 4$ and $9x - 6y = 12$
    (a) $x = 2, y = 1$ (b) $x = 4, y = 4$
    (c) $x = 6, y = 7$ (d) $x = 5, y = 3$

11. Which is solution of $x - 2y = 0$ and $3x + 4y = 10$
    (a) $x = 2, y = 1$ (b) $x = 1, y = 1$
    (c) $x = 2, y = 2$ (d) $x = 3, y = 1$

12. The solution of the equations $\frac{a}{x} - \frac{b}{y} = 0$ and $\frac{ab^2}{x} + \frac{a^2b}{y} = a^2 + b^2$ is
    (a) $x = a, y = b$ (b) $x = -a, y = b$
    (c) $x = a, y = -b$ (d) $x = -a, y = -b$

13. One equation of a pair of dependent liner equations is – $5x + 7y = 2$. The second equation can be
    (a) $10x + 14y + 4 = 0$
    (b) $-10x - 14y + 4 = 0$
    (c) $-10x + 14y + 4 = 0$
    (d) $10x - 14y = -4$

14. For what value of k, do the equations $3x - y + 8 = 0$ and $6x - ky = -16$ represent coincident lines ?
    (a) $\dfrac{1}{2}$
    (b) $-\dfrac{1}{2}$
    (c) 2
    (d) –2

15. If the lines given by $3x + 2ky = 2$ and $2x + 5y + 1 = 0$ are parallel, then the value of k is
    (a) $-\dfrac{5}{4}$
    (b) $\dfrac{2}{5}$
    (c) $\dfrac{15}{4}$
    (d) $\dfrac{3}{2}$

16. The value of c for which the pair of equations $cx - y = 2$ and $6x - 2y = 3$ will have infinitely many solutions is
    (a) 3
    (b) – 3
    (c) – 12
    (d) no value

17. If the sum of the ages of father and his son is 65 years and twice the difference of their ages is 50 years, then age of father is
    (a) 45
    (b) 40
    (c) 50
    (d) 155

18. Solution of $x + y = 6$ and $2x + 3y = 8$ is
    (a) $x = 8, y = 2$
    (b) $x = 10, y = -4$
    (c) $x = 2, y = -4$
    (d) $x = 2, y = \dfrac{4}{3}$

19. The sum of the digits of a two digit number is 9. If the digits are reversed, new number is 27 less than the given number. Then the number is
    (a) 72
    (b) 63
    (c) 81
    (d) 54

20. The sum of the digits of a two digit number is 9. If 27 is added to it, the digits of the number get reversed. The nuber is
    (a) 25
    (b) 72
    (c) 63
    (d) 36

Pair of Linear Equations in Two Variables

Answer Key

1. (c)	2. (d)	3. (d)	4. (c)	5. (a)	6. (d)	7. (d)	8. (a)	9. (d)	10. (d)
11. (a)	12. (a)	13. (d)	14. (c)	15. (c)	16. (d)	17. (a)	18. (b)	19. (b)	20. (d)

Explanatory Notes

1. (c)
$$\because \frac{5}{3} = \frac{-15}{-9} = \frac{8/24}{5}$$
$$\frac{5}{3} = \frac{5}{3} = \frac{40}{24}$$
$$\frac{5}{3} = \frac{5}{3} = \frac{5}{3}$$

2. (d)
$$\because \frac{1}{-3} = \frac{2}{-6} \neq \frac{5}{1}$$

3. (c)
Since $\frac{6}{2} = \frac{3}{1} \neq \frac{10}{9}$

4. (c)

5. (a) Unique solution is $x = 0, y = -7$

6. (d) $x = a, y = b$ means the point (a, b)

7. (d) A linear equation represents a line and every pint on it is its solution. There are infinite points on a line and hence infinite solutions.

8. (a) $\therefore$ the unique point of intersection is the solution
Thus, there is one solution.

9. (d) $\therefore$ two coincident lines meet in infinite points and hence there exist infinite solutions.

10. (d)
$\because 3(5) - 2(3) = 9 \neq 4$
$9(5) - 6(3) = 27 \neq 12$

11. (a)

12. (a) $x = a$ and $y = b$ satisfy both the equations

13. (a)
$$\frac{-5}{10} = \frac{7}{-14} = \frac{2}{-4}$$

14. (c) For coincident lines :
$$\frac{3}{6} = \frac{-1}{-k} = \frac{8}{16}$$
Since $6x - ky = -16$
$\Rightarrow 6x - ky + 16 = 0$
$\Rightarrow \frac{1}{2} = \frac{1}{k} \Rightarrow k = 2$

15. (c) Since given lines are parallel
$\therefore \frac{3}{2} = \frac{2k}{5} \neq \frac{-2}{1} \Rightarrow k = \frac{15}{4}$

16. (d) For infinitely many solutions, we have
$\frac{c}{6} = \frac{-1}{-2} = \frac{-2}{-3} = \frac{2}{3}$ i.e. $\frac{c}{6} = \frac{1}{2} = \frac{2}{3}$
Since $\frac{1}{2} \neq \frac{2}{3}$
$\therefore c$ has no value.

17. (a)
$x + y = 65$ and $2(x - y) = 50$
$\Rightarrow x - y = 25$
$\therefore 2x = 90; \quad x = 45$

18. (b)
$x + y = 6$
$2x + 2y = 12$ ....(1)
Also $2x + 3y = 8$ ....(2)
From eq. (1) and (2)
$-y = 4, \quad y = -4$
$\therefore x - 4 = 6, \quad x = 10$
Thus $x = 10$ and $y = -4$

19. (b) Let the given number be xy so that
$x + y = 9$ ...(1)
Again value of this digit $= 10x + y$
New digit $= yx$
Its value $10y + x$
$\therefore 10x + y - 10y - x = 27$
$\Rightarrow 9x - 9y = 27$
$\Rightarrow x - y = 3$ ...(2)
From equation (1) and (2)
$2x = 12, \Rightarrow x = 6, \therefore y = 3$
Thus required number is 63

20. (d) Let the digit be xy, $\therefore x + y = 9$
Its value is $10x + y$. When the digits are reversed, the new number is yx.
Its value $= 10y + x$
By the given condition,
$10x + y + 27 = 10y + y$
$\Rightarrow 9x - 9y + 27 = 0$
$x - y + 3 = 0$
Also $x + y - 9 = 0$
$\therefore 2x - 6 = 0$
$x = 3$
$\therefore y = 6$
Thus, required number is 36

National Talent Search Examination (NTSE)-X

Previous Year Questions

1. A pair of linear euqations which has a unique solution $x = 2, y = -3$ is

   [NTSE 2000 – Delhi first stage paper[
   (a) $x + y = -1, 2x - 3y = -5$
   (b) $2x + 5y = -11, 4x + 10y = -22$
   (c) $2x - y = 1, 3x + 2y = 0$
   (d) $x - 4y - 14 = 0, 5x - y - 13 = 0$

2. If $x = a$ and $y = b$ is the solution of the equations $x - y = 2$ and $x + y = 4$, then the value of a and b are repectively.

   [NTSE 2001 – MP first stage paper]
   (a) 3 and 5   (b) 5 and 3
   (c) 3 and 1   (d) – 1 and – 3

3. Aruna has only Re. 1 and Rs. 2 coins with her. If the total number of coins that she has is 50 and the amount of money with her is Rs. 75, then the number of Re. 1 and Rs. 2 coins are respectively.

   [NTSE 2012 – Goa second stage paper]
   (a) 35 and 15   (b) 35 and 20
   (c) 15 and 35   (d) 25 and 25

4. The father's age is six times his son's age. Four years hence, the age of the father will be four times his son's age. The presentage in years of the son and the father are respectively.

   [NTSE 2003 – WB second stage paper]
   (a) 4 and 24   (b) 5 and 30
   (c) 6 and 36   (d) 3 and 24

5. The value of x which satisfies the equations $px + qy = p - q, qx - py = p + q$ is

   [NTSE 2004 – Assam first stage paper]
   (a) – 1   (b) 1
   (c) 0   (d) 2

6. For what value $k : 4x + 6y = 1$ and $2x + ky = 7$ are inconsistent ?

   [NTSE 2002 – Punjab second stage paper]
   (a) $k = 2$ (b) $k = 3$
   (c) $k = 4$ (d) $k = -2$

7. If four angles of a cyclic quadrilaterals are $(2x + 1)°, (2x - 1)°, (y + 5)°$ and $(y - 5)°$, then

   [NTSE 2012 – Bihar first stage paper]
   (a) $x = 45°, y = 90°$ (b) $x = 90°, y = 45°$
   (c) $x = 60°, y = 80°$ (d) $x = 80°, y = 60°$

8. If the system of equations $3x + y = 1; (2k-1)x + (k-1)y = 2k + 1$ is inconsistent, then k is equal to

   [NTSE 2001 – Manipur first stage paper]
   (a) 1   (b) – 1
   (c) – 2   (d) 2

9. The value of k for which the system of euqations $kx - y = 2; 6x - 2y = 3$ has a unique solution is/are

   [NTSE 2005 – UP Second stage paper]
   (a) 2   (b) 1
   (c) 0   (d) All of these

10. The value of k for which $x + 2y + 7 = 0$ and $2x + ky + 14 = 0$ represent coincident lines is

    [NTSE 2006 – Haryana second stage paper]
    (a) 3   (b) 4
    (c) – 4   (d) – 3

Pair of Linear Equations in Two Variables

Answer Key

| 1. (d) | 2. (c) | 3. (d) | 4. (c) | 5. (b) | 6. (b) | 7. (a) | 8. (d) | 9. (d) | 10. (b) |

Explanatory Notes

1. (d)
   $\because \quad x - 4y - 14 = 0$
   and $\quad 5x - y - 13 = 0$
   $\Rightarrow \quad 5x - 20y - 70 = 0$
   and $\quad 5x - y - 13 = 0$
   $\therefore \quad -19y - 57 = 0, y = -3$
   $\therefore \quad x = -12 + 14 = 2$

2. (c)
   $\because \quad a - b = 2, a + b = 4$
   $\quad 2a = 6, \Rightarrow a = 3$
   and $\quad 2b = 2 \Rightarrow b = 1$

3. (d)
   $\quad x + y = 50, x + 2y = 75$
   $\Rightarrow \quad y = 25 \text{ and } x = 25$

4. (c)
   Let son's age $= x$
   $\therefore$ Father's age $= 6x$
   After four years, son's age $= x + 4$
   and father's age $= 6x + 4$
   $\therefore \quad 6x + 4 = 4(x + 4)$
   $\quad 6x + 4 = 4x + 16$
   $\quad 6x - 4x = 16 - 4$
   $\quad 2x = 12$
   $\Rightarrow \quad x = 6$
   $\therefore$ Son's age $= 6$
   and Father's age $= 36$

5. (c)
   $\quad px + qy = (p - q) \quad .... (1)$
   $\quad qx + py = (p + q) \quad .... (2)$
   Multiply (1) by p and (2) by 2 and then add; we get
   $\quad p^2x + q^2x = p^2 - pq + pq + q^2$
   $\Rightarrow \quad x(p^2 + q^2) = p^2 + q^2$
   $\quad x = \dfrac{(p^2 + q^2)}{(p^2 + q^2)}$
   $\Rightarrow \quad x = 1$

6. (d)
   Since given equations are inconsistent
   $\therefore \dfrac{4}{2} = \dfrac{6}{k} \neq \dfrac{11}{7} \quad \therefore k = 3$

7. (a)
   $(2x - 1)° + (2x + 1)° = 180°$
   $\Rightarrow \quad 4x° = 180° \Rightarrow x° = \dfrac{180°}{4} = 45°$
   and $(y - 5)° + (y + 5)° = 180°$
   $\quad 2y° = 180°, \quad y° = \dfrac{180°}{2} = 90°$

8. (d)
   The system of equation is inconsistent if
   $\dfrac{3}{2k-1} = \dfrac{1}{k-1} \neq \dfrac{1}{2k+1}$
   $\Rightarrow \quad 3k - 3 = 2k - 1$
   and $\quad 2k + 1 \neq k - 1$
   $\Rightarrow \quad k = 2$

9. (d)
   The given system will have a unique solution if
   $\dfrac{k}{6} \neq \dfrac{-1}{-2}$ i.e. $\dfrac{1}{2} \Rightarrow k \neq \dfrac{6}{2} = 3; 2 \neq 3, 1 \neq 3, 0 \neq 3$
   $\therefore$ Option (d) is correct.

10. (b)
    The given lines represent coincident lines if
    $\dfrac{1}{2} = \dfrac{2}{k} = \dfrac{7}{14}; \quad \dfrac{1}{2} = \dfrac{2}{k} = \dfrac{1}{2} \Rightarrow k = 4$

UNIT 4
Quadratic Equations

A quadratic equation is an equation of the second degree, i.e. it contains at least one term that is squared. The standard form is $ax^2 + bx + c = 0$ with a, b, and c being constants, or numerical coefficients, and x is an unknown variable. One absolute rule is that the first constant 'a' cannot be a zero.

Standard Forms of Equations

1. Examples of quadratic equations in the standard form ($ax^2 + bx + c = 0$) are:
   - $6x^2 + 11x - 35 = 0$
   - $2x^2 - 4x - 2 = 0$
   - $-4x^2 - 7x + 12 = 0$
2. Examples of quadratic equations lacking the linear coefficient or the 'bx':
   - $2x^2 - 64 = 0$
   - $x^2 - 16 = 0$
3. Examples of quadratic equations lacking the constant term or 'c' are:
   - $x^2 - 7x = 0$
   - $2x^2 + 8x = 0$
4. Examples of quadratic equation in factored form are:
   - $(x + 2)(x - 3) = 0$
     [on computing it becomes $x^2 - 1x - 6 = 0$]
   - $(x + 1)(x + 6) = 0$
     [on computing it becomes $x^2 + 7x + 6 = 0$]
   - $(x - 6)(x + 1) = 0$
     [on computing it becomes $x^2 - 5x - 6 = 0$
5. Examples of other forms of quadratic equations are:
   - $x(x - 2) = 4$
     [on multiplying and moving it becomes $x^2 - 2x - 4 = 0$]
   - $x(2x + 3) = 12$
     [on multiplying and moving it becomes $2x^2 - 3x - 12 = 0$]
   - $3x(x + 8) = -2$ [on multiplying and moving, it becomes $3x^2 + 24x + 2 = 0$]

Finding Roots of Quadratic Equations

a. The standard form of a quadratic equation is: $ax^2 + bx + c = 0$.
b. We can use the Quadratic Formula to solve equations in standard form:

$$x = \frac{-b \pm \sqrt{b^2 - 4ac}}{2a}$$

Discriminant: The radical portion of this formula $\sqrt{b^2 - 4ac}$ determines the nature of the roots. This quantity under the radical sign $b^2 - 4ac$, is called the discriminant.

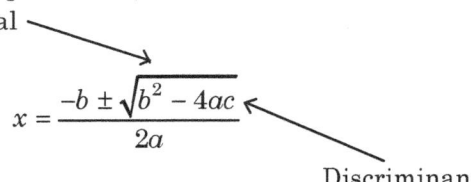

Three things may occur regarding the discriminant:

I. If $b^2 - 4ac > 0$

   We can take the square root of this positive amount and there will be two different real answers (or roots) to the equation.

II. If $b^2 - 4ac < 0$

   We cannot take the square root of a negative number, so there will be no real roots.

III. If $b^2 - 4ac = 0$

   The amount under the radical is zero and since the square root of zero is zero, we will get only 1 distinct real root.

Examples:

(a) $x^2 - 6x + 9 = 0$

$a = 1, b = -6, c = 9$

$$x = \frac{-b \pm \sqrt{b^2 - 4ac}}{2a}$$

$$x = \frac{+6 \pm \sqrt{(-6)^2 - 4(1)(9)}}{2(1)}$$

$$x = \frac{6 \pm \sqrt{36 - 36}}{2}$$

$$x = \frac{6 \pm \sqrt{0}}{2} \quad \text{← The discriminant is equal zero}$$

$$x = \frac{6 \pm 0}{2}$$

Quadratic Equations

$x = \dfrac{6}{2} = 3$ (There is only 1 real root.)

(b) $x^2 - 3x + 1 = 0$

$a = 1, b = 3, c = 1$

$x = \dfrac{-3 \pm \sqrt{9 - 4(1)(1)}}{2(1)}$ ← ┌ The discriminant is positive ┐

$x = \dfrac{-3 \pm \sqrt{5}}{2}$

$x = \dfrac{-3 + \sqrt{5}}{2}$

$x = \dfrac{-3 - \sqrt{5}}{2}$

Since the discriminant is positive (it equals + 5) there are two real roots.

(c) $x^2 + x + 3 = 0$

$a = 1, b = 1, c = 3$

$x = \dfrac{-1 \pm \sqrt{1 - 4(1)(3)}}{2(1)}$ ← ┌ The discriminant is negative ┐

$x = \dfrac{-1 \pm \sqrt{-11}}{2}$

The discriminant is –11. Since we cannot take the square root of a negative number, we have not real roots.

Quadratic Factorization using Splitting of Middle Term

The method of splitting the middle term is divided into three parts.
1. The given quadratic equation into the standard form if not already in the standard form is divided into three parts.
2. Split the middle term
3. Factor the quadratic equation

To factor the form: $ax^2 + bx + c$		Factor: $6x^2 + 19x + 10$
(1)	Find the product of 1st and last term ($a \times c$).	$6 \times 10 = 60$
(2)	Find the factors of 60 in such way that addition or subtraction of that factor is the middle term ($19x$) (Sp-litting of middle term) $15 \times 4 = 60$	$15 + 4 = 19$
(3)	Write the centre term using the sum of the two new factors, including the proper signs.	$6x^2 + 15x + 4x + 10$
(4)	Group the terms to form pairs - the first two terms and the last two terms. Factor each pair by finding com-mon factors.	$3x(2x + 5) + 2(2x + 5)$
(5)	Factor out the shared (common) binomial parenthesis.	$(3x + 2)(2x + 5)$

Examples on Quadratic Factorization using Splitting of Middle Term

Examples 1:

$$12x^2 - 15 = 11x$$

Solution:

$12x^2 - 15 = -11x$

$12x^2 - 15 + 11x = 0$ [add + $11x$]

$12x^2 + 11x - 15 = 0$

$12x^2 + 20x - 9x - 15 = 0$

$4x(3x + 5) - 3(3x + 5) = 0$

$(3x + 5)(4x - 3) = 0$

$3x + 5 = 0$ or $4x - 3 = 0$

$3x = -5$ or $4x = 3$

$x = -5/3$ or $x = 3/4$

Solution is $(-5/3, 3/4)$

Completing Square Method

Any quadratic equation can be converted to the form $(x + a)^2 - b^2 = 0$ by adding and subtracting some terms. This method of finding the root of quadratic equation is called the method of completing the square.

Steps used in finding the roots by applying the square method are as follows:

(1)	$ax^2 + bx + c = 0$	$2x^2 + 9x - 20 = 0$ $a = 2, b = 9$ and $c = -20$
(2)	Divide by 'a' on both sides $x^2 + bx/a + c/a = 0$	Divide by '2' on both sides $x^2 + 9x/2 - 10 = 0$
(3)	add $-c$ on both sides $x^2 + bx/a + c/a = 0$ $ -c/a = -c/a$ —————— $x^2 + bx/a = -c/a$	add + 10 on both sides $x^2 + 9x/2 - 10 = 0$ $ + 10 = -20$ —————— $x^2 + 9x/2 = 10$
(4)	add $b^2/4a^2$ on both sides $x^2 + bx/a + b^2/4a^2$ $= -c/a + b^2/4a^2$	add $9^2/4 \times 2^2 = 81/16$ $x^2 + 9x/2 + 81/16$ $= 10 + 81/16$

[43]

(5)	$(x + b/2a)^2$ $= -c/a + b^2/4a^2$	$(x + 9/4)^2$ $= (160 + 81)/16$
(6)	$(x + b/2a)^2$ $= (-4ac + b^2)/4a^2$	$(x + 9/4)^2 = 241/16$
(7)	$(x + b/2a)^2$ $= (b^2 - 4ac)/4a^2$	$(x + 9/4)^2 = 241/16$
(8)	Taking square root on both sides $(x + b/2a)$ $= \pm (\sqrt{b^2 - 4ac})/2a$	Taking square root on both sides $(x + 9/4) = \pm \sqrt{241}/4$
(9)	Add $-b/2a$ on both sides $x = -b/2a$ $\pm (\sqrt{b^2 - 4ac})/2a$	Add $-9/4$ on both sides $x = -9/4 \pm \sqrt{241}/4$
(10)	$x = (-b \pm \sqrt{b^2 - 4ac})/2a$	$x = (-9 \pm \sqrt{241})/4$

The roots of the equations are
$(-9 + \sqrt{241})/4$ and $(-9 - \sqrt{241})/4$

Example 2 :
Find the roots of the equation $9 \times 2 - 15x + 6 = 0$ using completing square method.
Solution :
$$9 \times 2 - 15x + 6 = 0$$
$$9 \times 2 - 15x = -6$$
Here, leading coefficient $= a = 9$, $b = -15$ and $c = 6$
On dividing the whole equation by 9, we get
$$x^2 - 15x/9 = -6/9$$
$$x^2 - 5x/3 = -2/3$$
Now add $(-b/2a)^2 = -[-5/(2 \times 3)]^2$
$= (5/6)^2$ both sides
$$x^2 - 5x/3 + (5/6)^2 = -2/3 + (5/6)^2$$
$$(x - 5/6)^2 = -2/3 + 25/36$$
$$(x - 5/6)^2 = (-24 + 25)/36$$
$$(x - 5/6)^2 = 1/36$$
$$x - 5/6 = \pm 1/6$$
$$4\sqrt{x} = 5/6 \pm 1/6$$
$$x = 5/6 + 1/6$$
or $\quad x = 5/6 - 1/6$
$$x = 6/6 = 1$$
or $\quad x = 4/6 = 2/3$
So, the roots of the equation are 1 and 2/3

Multiple Choice Questions

1. The root of a quadratic euqation are 5 and –2. Then the equation is
   (a) $x^2 - 3x + 10 = 0$ (b) $x^2 - 3x - 10 = 0$
   (c) $x^2 + 3x - 10 = 0$ (d) $x^2 + 3x + 10 = 0$

2. If the sum of the roots of a quadratic equation is 6 and their product is 6, the equation is
   (a) $x^2 - 6x + 6 = 0$ (b) $x^2 + 6x - 6 = 0$
   (c) $x^2 - 6x - 6 = 0$ (d) $x^2 + 6x + 6 = 0$

3. If one root of the equation $3x^2 - 10x + 3 = 0$ is 1/3, then the other root is
   (a) $-\dfrac{1}{3}$ (b) $\dfrac{1}{3}$
   (c) -3 (d) 3

4. The quadratic equation whose one root it $(3 + 2\sqrt{3})$ is
   (a) $x^2 + 6x - 3 = 0$ (b) $x^2 - 6x - 3 = 0$
   (c) $x^2 + 6x + 3 = 0$ (d) $x^2 - 6x + 3 = 0$

5. If the sum of the roots of the equation $kx^2 + 2x + 3k = 0$ s equal to their products, then the value of the k is
   (a) $\dfrac{1}{3}$ (b) $-\dfrac{1}{3}$
   (c) $\dfrac{2}{3}$ (d) $-\dfrac{2}{3}$

6. The one root of $5x^2 + 13x + k = 0$ be the reciprocal of the other root, then the value of k is
   (a) 0 (b) 1
   (c) 2 (d) 5

7. The roots of the equation $ax^2 + bx + c = 0$ will be reciprocal of each oher if
   (a) $a = b$ (b) $b = c$
   (c) $c = a$ (d) None of the these

8. If roots of the equation $ax^2 + bx + c = 0$ are equal, then $c = ?$
   (a) $-\dfrac{b}{2a}$ (b) $\dfrac{b}{2a}$
   (c) $-\dfrac{b^2}{4a}$ (d) $\dfrac{b^2}{4a}$

9. If the equation $ax^2 + 6kx + 4 = 0$ has equal roots, then $k = ?$
   (a) 2 or 0 (b) -2 or 0
   (c) 2 or -2 (d) 0 only

10. If the equation $x^2 + 2(k + 2)x + 9k = 0$ has equal roots, then $k = ?$
    (a) 1 or 4 (b) -1 or 4
    (c) 1 or -4 (d) -1 or -4

11. If the equation $4x^2 - 3kx + 10 = 0$ has equal roots, then $k = ?$
    (a) $\pm\dfrac{2}{3}$ (b) $\pm\dfrac{1}{3}$
    (c) $\pm\dfrac{3}{4}$ (d) $\pm\dfrac{4}{3}$

Quadratic Equations

12. The roots of $ax^2 + bx + c = 0$, $a \neq 0$ are real and unequal, if $(b^2 - 4ac)$
    (a) > 0 (b) $= 0$
    (c) < 0 (d) None the these

13. In the equation $ax^2 + bx + c$, it the given that D = $(b^2 - 4ac) > 0$. Then the roots of the equation are
    (a) real and equal (b) real and unequal
    (c) imginary (d) None of these

14. If the equation $x^2 + 5kx + 16 = 0$ has no real roots then
    (a) $k > \dfrac{8}{5}$ (b) $k < -\dfrac{8}{5}$
    (c) $-\dfrac{8}{5} < k < \dfrac{8}{5}$ (d) None of these

15. If the equation $x^2 - kx + 1 = 0$ has no real roots then
    (a) $k < -2$ (b) $k > 2$
    (c) $-2 < k < 2$ (d) None of these

16. The roots of the equation $2x^2 - 6x + 7 = 0$ are
    (a) real, unequal and rational
    (b) real, unequal and irrational
    (c) real and equal
    (d) imaginary

17. The roots of the equation $2x^2 - 6x + 3 = 0$ are
    (a) real, unequal and rational
    (b) real, unequal and irrational
    (c) real and equal
    (d) imaginary

18. For the equation $ax^2 + bx + c = 0$, which of the following statements is incorrect ?
    (a) If $(b^2 - 4ac) < 0$, the roots are imginary
    (b) If $(b^2 - 4ac) = 0$, the roots are real and equal
    (c) If $(b^2 - 4ac) > 0$ and $(b^2 - 4ac)$ is a perfect square, then the roots are rational and unequal
    (d) $(b^2 - ac) < 0$, the roots are irrational

19. If the roots of $5x^2 - kx + 1 = 0$ are real and distinct, then
    (a) $-2\sqrt{5} < k < 2\sqrt{5}$
    (b) $k > 2\sqrt{5}$ only
    (c) $k < -2\sqrt{5}$ only
    (d) either $k > 2\sqrt{5}$ or $k < -2\sqrt{5}$

20. The roots of the equation $3x^2 + 7x + 8 = 0$ are
    (a) both real and equal
    (b) both real and unequal
    (c) both imginary
    (d) None of these

Answer Key

1. (b)	2. (a)	3. (d)	4. (b)	5. (d)	6. (d)	7. (c)	8. (d)	9. (c)	10. (a)
11. (d)	12. (a)	13. (b)	14. (c)	15. (c)	16. (d)	17. (b)	18. (d)	19. (d)	20. (c)

Explanatory Notes

1. (b)
$$(\alpha + \beta) = 5 + (-2) = 3 \; \alpha\beta$$
$$= 5 \times (-2) = -10$$
So, the equation is $x^2 - (\alpha + \beta)x + \alpha\beta = 0$
i.e. $x^2 - 3x - 10 = 0$

2. (a)
$$(\alpha + \beta) = 6 \text{ and } \alpha\beta = 6$$
∴ the equation is $x^2 - 6x + 6 = 0$

3. (d)
Let the other root be α. Then, Product of roots
$$= \frac{3}{3} = 1 \Rightarrow \frac{1 \times \alpha}{3} = 1 \Rightarrow \alpha = 3$$
So, the root is 3.

4. (b)
$$\alpha = (3 + 2\sqrt{3}) \text{ then } \beta$$
$$= (3 - 2\sqrt{3})$$
∴ $\alpha + \beta = 6$ and $\alpha\beta$
$$= (3 + 2\sqrt{3})(3 - 2\sqrt{3})$$
$$= (9 - 12) = -3$$
∴ the equation is $x^2 - 6x - 3 = 0$

5. (d)
$$\alpha + \beta = \frac{-2}{k}$$
and $\alpha\beta = \frac{3k}{k} = 3$
∴ $\frac{-2}{k} = 3$
$\Rightarrow k = \frac{-2}{3}$

6. (d)
Let the roots be α and $\frac{1}{\alpha}$. Then, their product
$$= 1$$
Also product of roots $= \frac{k}{5}$
∴ $\frac{k}{5} = 1$
$\Rightarrow k = 5$

7. (c)
Let the roots be α and $\frac{1}{\alpha}$. Then, their product
$$= 1$$
Given equation is $ax^2 + bx + c = 0$ product of its roots $= \frac{c}{a}$.
$\Rightarrow \frac{c}{a} = 1, \Rightarrow c = a$

8. (d)
The roots of $ax^2 + bx + c = 0$ are equal
$\Rightarrow b^2 - 4ac = 0$
∴ $b^2 - 4ac \Rightarrow c = \frac{b^2}{4a}$

9. (c)
The roots of $9x^2 + 6kx + 4 = 0$ are equal
$$36k^2 - 144 = 0$$
$$36k^2 = 144$$
$$k^2 = \frac{144}{36} = 4$$
$$k = \pm 2$$

10. (a)
The roots of $x^2 + 2(k+2) + 9k = 0$ are equal
$\Rightarrow 4(k+2)^2 = 36k$
$\Rightarrow (k+2)^2 = 9k$
$\Rightarrow k^2 + 4k + 4 = 9k$
$\Rightarrow k^2 + 5k + 4 = 0$
$\Rightarrow (k-4)(k-1) = 0$
$\Rightarrow k = 4$ or $k = 1$

11. (d)
The roots of $4x^2 - 3kx + 1)$ are equal
$\Rightarrow 9k - 16k = 0$
$$k^2 = \frac{16}{9}$$
$\Rightarrow k = \pm \frac{4}{3}$

12. (a)
The roots are real and unequal if $(b^2 - 4ac) > 0$

13. (b)
If D > 0, then the roots are real and unequal.

14. (c)
For no real roots, we must have :
$$(b^2 - 4ac) < 0$$

[46]

$\therefore \quad (25k^2 - 4 \times 16) < 0$

$\Rightarrow \quad 25k^2 < 64$

$\Rightarrow \quad k^2 < \dfrac{64}{25}$

$\Rightarrow \quad -\dfrac{8}{5} < k < \dfrac{8}{5}$

15. (c)

For no real roots we must have :

$(b^2 - 4ac) < 0$

$\therefore \quad k^2 - 4 < 0$

$\Rightarrow \quad k^2 < 4$

$\Rightarrow \quad -2 < k < 2$

16. (d)

$D = (-6)^2 - 4 \times 2 \times 7$
$= (36 - 56) = -20 < 0$

$\therefore$ the roots are imaginary

17. (b)

$D = (-6)^2 - 4 \times 2 \times 3$
$= (36 - 24) = 12 > 0$

and not a perfect square

$\therefore$ the roots are real, unequal and irrational.

18. (b)

If $(b^2 - ac) < 0$, then the roots may be rational or irrational.

19. (d)

The roots of $5x^2 - kx + 1 = 0$ are real and distinct.

$\therefore \quad (k^2 - 4 \times 5 \times 1) > 0$

$\Rightarrow \quad k^2 > 20$

$\Rightarrow \quad k^2 = \sqrt{20}$

or $\quad k < -\sqrt{20}$

$\Rightarrow \quad k > 2\sqrt{5}$

or $\quad k < -2\sqrt{5}$

20. (c)

$D = (b^2 - 4ac)$
$= (49 - 4 \times 3 \times 8)$
$= (49 - 96)$
$= -47 > 0$

Hence, both of the roots are imaginary. ◻

National Talent Search Examination (NTSE)-X

Previous Year Questions

1. Which constant should be added and subtracted to solve the quadratic equation $4x^2 - \sqrt{3x} - 5 = 0$ by the method of completing the square ?
   [NTSE 2001 – Haryna first stage paper]
   (a) $\dfrac{9}{10}$ (b) $\dfrac{3}{16}$
   (c) $\dfrac{3}{4}$ (d) $\dfrac{\sqrt{3}}{4}$

2. The roots of the equation $2x - \dfrac{3}{x} = 1$ are
   [NTSE 2012 – Delhi first stage paper]
   (a) $\dfrac{1}{2}, -1$ (b) $\dfrac{3}{2}, 1$
   (c) $\dfrac{3}{2}, -1$ (d) $\dfrac{-1}{2}, \dfrac{3}{2}$

3. For what real values of k, the equation $9x^2 + 8kx + 16 = 0$ has real and equal roots ?
   [NTSE 2004 – Kerala second stage paper]
   (a) $k = 2$ or -2 (b) $k = 3$ or -3
   (c) $k = \dfrac{4}{3}$ or $-\dfrac{4}{3}$ (d) None of these

4. For what values of k, the equation $kx^2 - 6x - 2 = 0$ has real roots ?
   [NTSE 2000 – MP second stage paper]
   (a) $k \leq -\dfrac{9}{2}$ (b) $k \geq -\dfrac{9}{2}$
   (c) $k \leq -2$ (d) None of these

5. If α and β are the roots of the equation $3x^2 + 8x + 2 = 0$, then $\left(\dfrac{1}{\alpha} + \dfrac{1}{\beta}\right) = ?$
   [NTSE 2003 – Jammu first stage paper]
   (a) $-\dfrac{3}{8}$ (b) $\dfrac{2}{3}$
   (c) -4 (d) 4

6. If $x = 3$ is a solution of the equation $3x^2 + (k-1)x + 9 = 0$ then $k = ?$
   [NTSE 2004 – Tripura first stage paper]
   (a) 11 (b) -11
   (c) 13 (d) -13

7. The sum of the roots of the equation $x^2 - 6x + 2 = 0$ is
   [NTSE 2003 – Gujrat second stage paper]
   (a) 2 (b) -2
   (c) 6 (d) -6

8. If the product of the roots of the equation $x^2 - 3x + k = 10$ is -2, then the value of k is
   [NTSE 2002 – Assam first stage paper]
   (a) -2 (b) -8
   (c) 8 (d) 12

9. The roots of the equation $2x^2 + 9x + 6 = 0$ is 2, then $a = ?$
   [NTSE 2012 – Manipur second stage paper]
   (a) 7 (b) -7
   (c) $\dfrac{7}{2}$ (d) $-\dfrac{7}{2}$

10. The ratio of the sum and product of the roots of the equation $7x^2 - 12x + 18 = 0$ is
    [NTSE 2004 – West Bengal first stage paper]
    (a) $7 : 2$ (b) $7 : 18$
    (c) $2 : 3$ (d) $3 : 2$

Quadratic Equations

Answer Key

| 1. (b) | 2. (c) | 3. (b) | 4. (b) | 5. (c) | 6. (b) | 7. (c) | 8. (c) | 9. (b) | 10. (c) |

Explanatory Notes

1. (b) $4x^2 - \sqrt{3}x - 5 = 0$

   $\Rightarrow \left(2x - \frac{\sqrt{3}}{4}\right)^2 - \frac{3}{16} - 5 = 0$

   $\therefore$ required number $= \frac{3}{16}$

2. (c)
   Given equation is
   $2x^2 - x - 3 = 0$
   $2x^2 - 3x + 2x - 3 = 0$
   $x(2x - 3) + (2x - 3) = 0$
   $(2x - 3)(x + 1) = 0$
   $\Rightarrow x = \frac{3}{2}$ or -1

3. (b)
   For real and equal roots, we have
   $(8k)^2 - 4 \times 9 \times 16 = 0$
   $64k^2 = 4 \times 9 \times 16$
   $k^2 = 4 \times 9 \times 16$
   $k^2 = 9$
   $k = \pm 3$

4. (b)
   For real roots we have :
   $(-6)^2 - 4k \times (-2) \geq 0$
   $\Rightarrow 36 + 8k \geq 0$
   $\Rightarrow 8k \geq -36$
   $\Rightarrow k \geq -\frac{9}{2}$

5. (c)
   We have :
   $(\alpha + \beta) = -\frac{8}{3}$ and $\alpha\beta = \frac{2}{3}$

   $\therefore \left(\frac{1}{\alpha} + \frac{1}{\beta}\right) = \frac{\beta + \alpha}{\alpha b} = \frac{\alpha + \beta}{\alpha b}$

   $= -\frac{8}{3} \times \frac{3}{2} = -4$

6. (b)
   Since $x = 3$ is a solution of
   $3x^2 + (k-1)x + 9 = 0$, we have :
   $27 + 3(k-1) + 9 = 0$
   $\Rightarrow 3(k-1) = -36$
   $\Rightarrow k - 1 = -12$
   $k = -11$

7. (c)
   Sum of roots $\alpha + \beta = \frac{-b}{a} = \frac{6}{1} = 6$

8. (c)
   Given equation is $x^2 - 3x + (k - 10) = 0$

   Product of roots $\alpha\beta = \frac{c}{a} = \frac{k-10}{1} = k - 10$

   $\therefore k - 10 = -2$
   $\Rightarrow k = -2 + 10$
   $\Rightarrow k = 8$

9. (b)
   Since 2 is a root of $2x^2 + ax + = 6$
   We have : $8 + 2a + 6 = 0 \Rightarrow 2a = -14, a = -7$

10. (c)
    Given equation is $7x^2 - 12x + 18 = 0$

    $\therefore \alpha + \beta = \frac{12}{7}$ and $ab = \frac{18}{7}$

    $\therefore$ Requird ratio $= \frac{12}{7} : \frac{18}{7} = 12 : 18 = 2 : 3$

UNIT 5
Arithmetic Progression

1. **Sequence:** Some numbers arranged in a definite order, according to a definite rule, are said to form a sequence.
2. **Progression:** A sequence which follows a definite pattern is called progression
3. **Arithmetic Progression** is a sequence of numbers, such that the difference of any 2 consecutive numbers is a constant.

   For example: 1, 3, 5, 7 ... this is a progression which has a difference of 2. Each number in the sequence is known as '**term**'. In this example, we can notice that the term after the first term is obtained by adding a fixed number to the previous terms.

   So, we can say that "an arithmetic progression (AP) is a list of numbers in which each term is obtained by adding a fixed number to the preceding term, except the first term". The fixed number which is being added is known as the **common difference**. The numbers can be positive, negative or zero in arithmetic progressions.

4. **Nth Term of Arithmetic Progression**

   Consider the first term as a_1, second term as a_2 and so on, till the last term is a_n. Last term is a_n and the difference between the term is d. The last term is a_n, because we do not know how many terms are in between the first and the last term. This can be represented by $a_1, a_2, a_3 ... a_n$. So, $a_3 - a_2 = a_2 - a_1 = d$.

5. **The last term a_n is also called as nth term or general term. It is also denoted by 'l'.**

   $$a_n = a + (n - 1) d$$

   Where 'a' is the first term, 'd' is the common difference and 'n' is the number of terms.

6. **Kinds of Arithmetic Progressions**

   There are 2 kinds of arithmetic progressions, namely:

   (i) **Finite Arithmetic Progression:** In this A.P, we find that the first term and the last term are available. Example: 1, 2, 4... 10, which means that the first term is 1 and the last term is 10.

   (ii) **Infinite Arithmetic Progression:** In this A.P, you can find that the first few terms are given, but we do not know where it will end. Example: 1, 3, 5, 7... here, the first few terms are available, but the last term is not.

7. **Arithmetic Progression Formulas**

   Let us see the important formulas in arithmetic progressions which are useful in solving problems.

   Let $a, a_2, a_3 .... a_n$ be terms in an arithmetic progression.

   (a) Common difference
   $$d = a_n - a_{n-1} = ... = a_3 - a_2 = a_2 - a_1$$

   (b) n^{th} term $a_n = a + (n-1)d$ where n is number of terms.

   (c) The nth term of an A.P. is the difference of the sum to first n terms and the sum to first (n–1) terms of it.
   i.e. $a_n = S_n - S_{n-1}$

   (d) Sum of first n terms in arithmetic progression is:
   $$S_n = \frac{n}{2}[2a + (n-1)d]$$
   or $$S_n = \frac{n}{2}[a + l]$$

   where 'l' is last term and $l = a_n$

Solved Examples

1. Which term of the arithmetic progression: 3, 8, 13, 18... is 78?
   Solution:
   Given 3, 8, 13, 18.......
   Here first term $\quad a = a_1 = 3$
   Common difference $\quad d = a_2 - a = 8 - 3 = 5$
   We know that $\quad a_n = a + (n-1) d$
   $\quad\quad 78 = 3 + (n-1)5$
   $\quad\quad 78 - 3 = (n-1)5$
   $\quad\quad 75 = (n-1)5$
   $\quad\quad 15 = n-1$
   $\quad\quad n = 16$
   Therefore 16th term is 78

2. Determine the AP whose third term is 16 and the 7th term exceeds the 5th term by 12.
   Solution: Let a and d be the first term and common difference of the AP.
   Given third term $\quad a_3 = 16$
   7th term exceeds 5th term by 12.
   $\quad\quad a_7 - a_5 = 12$
   $\{a + (7-1) d\} - \{a + (5-1) d\} = 12$
   $\quad (a + 6d) - (a + 4d) = 12$
   $\quad a + 6d - a - 4d = 12$
   $\quad\quad 2d = 12$
   $\quad\quad d = 6$

Therefore second term $a_2 = a_3 - d = 16 - 6 = 10$
First term $a = a_2 - d = 10 - 6 = 4$
Therefore AP is 4, 10, 16..............

3. Subba Rao started work in 1995 at an annual salary of Rs 5000 and received an increment of Rs 200 each year. After how many years did his income reach Rs. 7000?
   Solution:
   Initial salary a = Rs. 5000
   Increment every year d = Rs. 200
   Final salary a_n = Rs. 7000
   Number of years n = ?
   $$a_n = a + (n-1)d$$
   $$7000 = 5000 + (n-1)200$$
   $$7000 - 5000 = (n-1)200$$
   $$2000 = (n-1)200$$
   $$10 = n - 1$$
   $$11 = n$$
   $$n = 11$$
   Therefore at 11th year, his income will reach Rs 7000.

4. Which term of the AP, 3, 10, 17 will be 84 more than its 13th term?
   Solution:
   Let the nth term be 84 more than the 13th term.
   Now according to question,
   $a = 3, d = 10 - 3 = 7$
   So, 13th term = $a + 12d$
   $= 3 + 12 \times 7 = 87$
   Then n^{th} term = $84 + 87 = 171$
   $171 = a + (n-1)d$
   $171 = 3 + (n-1) \times 7$
   $171 - 3/7 + 1 = n$
   $168/7 + 1 = n$
   $24 + 1 = 25 = n$
   Therefore 25th term of the AP will be 84 more than 13th term.

5. A sum of Rs 700 is to be used to give seven cash prizes to students of a school for their overall academic performance. If each prize is Rs 20 less than its preceding prize, find the value of each prize.
   Solution:
   Let AP be x, $(x-20)$, $(x-40)$, $(x-60)$, $(x-80)$, $(x-100)$, $(x-120)$
   $S_n = 700, n = 7$ then,
   $700 = 7/2 (x + x-120)$
   $700 = 7/2(2x-120)$
   $700 = 7x - 420$
   $x = 160$
   Then the AP : 160, 140, 120, 100, 80, 60, 40

Multiple Choice Questions

1. The first term of AP is 6 and its common difference is −3. What is the 16th term of the AP ?
   (a) 51   (b) 39
   (c) −39   (d) −42

2. The first two terms of an AP are −5 and 6. Its 21st term is
   (a) 115   (b) −115
   (c) −215   (d) 215

3. Which term of the AP 21, 18, 15 ..... is −81 ?
   (a) 25th   (b) 18th
   (c) 35th   (d) 46th

4. Which term of the AP {72, 63, 54 ..... is 0 ?
   (a) 8th   (b) 9th
   (c) 10th   (d) 11th

5. Which term of the AP 25, 20, 15 ... is the first negative term ?
   (a) 9th   (b) 8th
   (c) 7th   (d) 10th

6. If then n^{th} term of an AP is $(7 - 4n)$, then its common difference is
   (a) 4   (b) −4
   (c) 3   (d) −3

7. What is the common difference of an AP in which $T_{18} - T_{14} = 32$?
   (a) 8   (b) −8
   (c) 4   (d) −4

8. If an AP, the 7th term is 4 and the common difference is −4, what is its first term ?
   (a) 16   (b) 20
   (c) 24   (d) 28

9. If, $(x + 2), 2x, (2x + 3)$ are three consecutive terms of an AP, then $x = ?$
   (a) 3   (b) 4
   (c) 5   (d) 6

10. If $(2P+1), 13, (5P-1)$ are three consecutive terms of the an AP, then $P = ?$
    (a) 4   (b) 5
    (c) 6   (d) 3

11. If $(k+1), 3k (4k+2)$ are three consecutive terms of an AP, then $k = ?$
    (a) 0   (b) 1
    (c) 2   (d) 3

12. If $\frac{4}{5}, a, 2$ are three consecutive terms of AP, then $a = ?$
    (a) 5   (b) $\frac{5}{4}$
    (c) $\frac{9}{5}$ (d) $\frac{7}{5}$

13. What is the next term of the AP $\sqrt{2}, \sqrt{8}, \sqrt{18}$ ... ?
    (a) $\sqrt{24}$ (b) $\sqrt{28}$
    (c) $\sqrt{30}$ (d) $\sqrt{32}$

14. What is the next term of the AP $\sqrt{8}, \sqrt{18}, \sqrt{32}$ ...?
    (a) $\sqrt{40}$ (b) $\sqrt{48}$
    (c) $\sqrt{50}$ (d) $\sqrt{54}$

15. The first term of an AP is P and its common difference is q. What is its 10th term ?
    (a) P + 10q (b) q + 10P
    (c) P + 9q   (d) q + 9P

16. The numbers −11, −7, −3, 1, 5 ... are
    (a) in AP with $d = -18$
    (b) in AP with $d = -4$
    (c) in AP with $d = 4$
    (d) not in AP

17. The 30th term of the AP, 10, 7, 4 ... ?
    (a) − 87 (b) 87
    (c) 77   (d) − 77

18. The 11th term of the AP −3, $-\dfrac{1}{2}$, 2 ... is
    (a) 22   (b) 28
    (c) − 38 (d) $48\dfrac{1}{2}$

19. If the nth term of on AP is (3n + 5), then its common difference is
    (a) 5 (b) 4
    (c) 3 (d) 2

20. The 4th term of an AP is 14 and its 12th term is 70. What is its first term ?
    (a) 7   (b) 10
    (c) − 7 (d) − 10

Arithmetic Progression

Answer Key

1. (c)	2. (d)	3. (c)	4. (b)	5. (c)	6. (b)	7. (a)	8. (d)	9. (c)	10. (a)
11. (d)	12. (d)	13. (d)	14. (c)	15. (c)	16. (c)	17. (d)	18. (a)	19. (c)	20. (c)

Explanatory Notes

1. (c)
   Here $a = 6$ and $d = -3$
   $\therefore \quad T_{16} = a + 15d = 6 + 15 \times (-3)$
   $= 6 - 45 = -39$

2. (d)
   Here $a = -5$ and $a + d = 6$
   so, $d = 6 - (-5) = 11$
   $\therefore \quad T_{21} = a + 20d = -5 + 20 \times 11$
   $= -5 + 220$
   $= 215$

3. (c)
   Here $a = 21$ and $d = (18 - 21) = -3$
   Let $T_n = -81$. Then $a + (n-1)d = -81$
   $\therefore \quad 21 + (n-1)(-3) = -81$
   $\Rightarrow \quad 3n = (24 + 81) = 105$
   $n = 35$

4. (b)
   Here $a = 72$ and $d = 63 - 72 = -9$
   Let $T_n = 0$. Then $a + (n-1)d = 0$
   $\therefore \quad 72 + (n-1)(-9) = 0$
   $9n = 81$
   $n = 9$
   $\therefore$ 9th term is 0

5. (c)
   Let the nth term be the first negative term, then
   $Tn < 0. \Rightarrow a + (n-1)d < 0$
   $\Rightarrow 25 + (n-1)(-5) < 0$
   $\Rightarrow 30 < 5n$
   $\Rightarrow 5n > 30$
   $\Rightarrow n > 6$
   $\therefore 7^{th}$ term is the first negative term.

6. (b)
   Let $Tn = (7 - 4n)$. Then
   $T_1 = (7 - 4 \times 1) = 3$
   and $T_{12} = (7 - 4 \times 2) = -1$
   $d = (T_2 - T_1) = (-1 - 3) = -4$

7. (a)
   $T_{18} - T_{14} = 32 \Rightarrow (a + 17d) - (a + 13d) = 32$
   $\Rightarrow 4d = 32$
   $\Rightarrow d = 8$

8. (d)
   $d = -4$, and $a + 6d = 4$
   $\therefore \quad a + 6 \times (-4) = 4$
   $\Rightarrow \quad a - 24 = 4$
   $\therefore \quad a = 28$

9. (c)
   Since $(x + 2), 2x, (2x + 3)$ are in AP, we have :
   $2x - (x + 2) = (2x + 3) - 2x$
   $x - 2 = 3$
   $x = 5$

10. (a)
    Since $(2P + 1), 13, (5P - 3)$ are in AP, we have :
    $13 - (2P + 1) = (5P - 3) - 13$
    $\Rightarrow (12 - 2P) = (5P - 16)$
    $7P = 28$
    $\Rightarrow P = 4$

11. (d)
    Since $(k + 1), 3k, (4k + 2)$ are in AP, we have :
    $3k - (k + 1) = (4k + 2) - 3k$
    $\Rightarrow 2k - 1 = k + 2$
    $\Rightarrow k = 3$

12. (d)
    Since $\frac{4}{5}, a, 2$ are in AP, we have :
    $a - \frac{4}{5} = 2 - a$
    $2a = \left(2 + \frac{4}{5}\right) = \frac{14}{5}$
    $\Rightarrow a = \frac{7}{5}$

13. (d)
    $T_1 = \sqrt{2}, T_2 = \sqrt{8} = \sqrt{4 \times 2} = 2\sqrt{2}$
    and $T_3 = \sqrt{18} = \sqrt{9 \times 2} = 3\sqrt{2}$
    $\Rightarrow T_1 = \sqrt{2}, T_2 = 2\sqrt{2}, T_3 = 3\sqrt{2}$
    $T_4 = 4\sqrt{2} = \sqrt{4 \times 4 \times 2} = \sqrt{32}$

14. (c)
    $T_1 = \sqrt{8} = \sqrt{4 \times 2} = 2\sqrt{2}, T_2 = \sqrt{18} = \sqrt{9 \times 2} = 3\sqrt{2}$
    $T_3 = \sqrt{32} = \sqrt{16 \times 2} = 4\sqrt{2}$
    $T_1 = 2\sqrt{2}, T_2 = 3\sqrt{2}, T_3 = 4\sqrt{2}$
    $T_4 = 5\sqrt{2} = \sqrt{5 \times 5 \times 2} = \sqrt{50}$

15. (c)
    Here $a = P$ and $d = q$
    $\therefore \quad$ 10th term $= a + 9d = (P + 9q)$

[53]

16. (c)
    We have
    $$(-7+11) = (-3+7) = (1+3)$$
    $$= (5-1) = 4$$
    So, the given numbers are in AP with $d = 4$

17. (d)
    This is an AP in which
    $a = 10$
    and $d = (7-10) = -3$
    $\therefore \quad T_{30} = a + 29d$
    $= 10 + 29 \times (-3)$
    $= 10 - 87$
    $= -77$

18. (c)
    Here $a = -3$ and $d = \left(\dfrac{-1}{2} + 3\right) = \dfrac{5}{2}$

    $\therefore \quad T_{11} = a + 10d$
    $= -3 + 10 \times \dfrac{5}{2}$
    $= -3 + 25$
    $= 22$

19. (c)
    Let $T_n = (3n + 5)$
    Then, $T_1 = (3 \times 1 + 5) = 8$
    and $T_2 = (3 \times 2 + 5) = 11$
    $\therefore \quad d = (T_2 - T_1)$
    $= (11 - 8) = 3$

20. (c)
    $a + 3d = 14$
    and $a + 11d = 70$
    on solving we get $d = 7$
    and $a = -7$
    $\therefore$ first term $= -7$

Arithmetic Progression

Previous Year Questions

1. The 8th term of an AP is 17 and its 14th term is 29. The common difference of the AP is
   [NTSE 2003 – Karnataka first stage paper]
   (a) 3   (b) 2
   (c) 5   (d) –2

2. The 17th term of an AP exceeds its 10th term by 21. The common difference of the AP is.
   [NTSE 2000 – Rajasthan second stage paper]
   (a) 3   (b) 2
   (c) – 3   (d) – 2

3. If the 3rd and 9th terms of an AP are 4 and – 8 repectively, which term of the AP is 0 ?
   [NTSE 2012 – Delhi first stage paper]
   (a) 5th   (b) 7th
   (c) 11th   (d) 13th

4. If 7 times the 7th term of an AP is equal to 11 times the 11th term, then its 18th term will be
   [NTSE 2005 – MP second stage paper]
   (a) 7   (b) 11
   (c) 18   (d) 0

5. Which term of the AP 21, 42, 63, 84.... is 210 ?
   [NTSE 2006 – Punjab second stage paper]
   (a) 9th   (b) 10th
   (c) 11th   (d) 12th

6. If 4, x_1, x_2, x_3, 28 are in AP, then x_3 = ?
   [NTSE 2001 – Assam first stage paper]
   (a) 19
   (b) 23
   (c) 22
   (d) Cannot be determined

7. The 20th term from the end of the AP, 3, 8, 13 .... 253 is
   [NTSE 2006 – Andhra Pradesh first stage paper]
   (a) 163   (b) 158
   (c) 153   (d) 148

8. The 4th term from the end of the AP – 11, – 8, – 5 ... 49 is
   [NTSE 2004 – Jammu second stage paper]
   (a) 58   (b) 43
   (c) 40   (d) 37

9. The second term of an AP is 13 and its 5th term is 25. What is the 17th term ?
   [NTSE 2003 – Bihar Second stage paper]
   (a) 73   (b) 77
   (c) 69   (d) 81

10. The sum of first 16 terms of the AP 10, 6, 2.... is
    [NTSE 2012 – Haryana second stage paper]
    (a) 320   (b) – 320
    (c) – 352   (d) – 400

National Talent Search Examination (NTSE)-X

Answer Key

| 1. (b) | 2. (a) | 3. (a) | 4. (d) | 5. (b) | 6. (c) | 7. (b) | 8. (c) | 9. (a) | 10. (b) |

Explanatory Notes

1. (b)
$$a + 7d = 1 \text{ and } a + 13d = 29$$
On solving are, we get
$$6d = 12 \Rightarrow d = 2$$

2. (a)
$$T_{17} - T_{10} = 21$$
$$\Rightarrow (a + 16d) - (a + 9d) = 21$$
$$\Rightarrow 7d = 21 \Rightarrow d = 3$$

3. (a)
$$T_3 = 4 \text{ and } T_9 = -8$$
$$\therefore a + 2d = 4 \text{ and } a + 8d = -8$$
On solving we get, $d = -2$ and $a = 8$
Let $T_n = 0$
Then, $a + (n-1)d = 0$
$\therefore 8 + (n-1) \times (-2) = 0$
$\Rightarrow 2n = 10, n = 5$
Hene $T_5 = 0$

4. (d)
Let a be the first term and d be the common difference. Then
$$7(a + 6d) = 11(a + 10d)$$
$$\Rightarrow 11a - 7a = 42d - 110d$$
$$\Rightarrow 4a = -68d \Rightarrow a = -17d$$
$$T_{18} = a + 17d$$
$$= (-17d) + 17d = 0$$

5. (b)
Here $a = 21$ and $d = (42 - 21) = 21$
Let $T_n = 210$. Then $a + (n-1)d = 210$
$\therefore 21 + (n-1) \times 1 = 210$
$1 + (n-1) = 10$,
$n = 10$
$\therefore T_{10} = 210$

6. (c)
Here $a = 4$ and $T_5 = 28$, $a + 4d = 28$
$\Rightarrow 4 + 4d = 28 \Rightarrow 4d = 24$
$d = 6$
$\therefore x_3 = T_4 = a + 3d = 4 + 3 \times 6$
$= 4 + 18 = 22$

7. (b)
Here $l = 253$, $d = (8-3) = 5$ and $n = 20$
n^{th} term from the end $= \{l - (n-1)d\}$
$\therefore$ 20th term from the end
$= (253 - 19 \times 5)$
$= (253 - 95) = 158$

8. (c)
Here $l = 49$, $d = (-8 + 11) = 3$
and $n = 4$
nth term from the end $= \{l - (n-1)d\}$
$\therefore$ 4th term from the end $= (49 - 3 \times 3) = 40$
$= (253 - 95) = 158$

9. (a)
$$T_2 = 13 \text{ and } T_5 = 25$$
$\therefore a + d = 13$ and $a + 4d = 25$
On solving, we get $d = 4$ and $a = 9$
$\therefore T_{17} = a + 16d$
$= 9 + 16 \times 4 = 73$

10. (b)
Here $a = 10$, $d = (6 - 10) = -4$ and $n = 16$
$$\therefore S_n = \frac{n}{2}[2a + (n-1)d]$$
$$\Rightarrow S_{16} = \frac{16}{2}[2 \times 10 + 15 \times (-4)]$$
$$= 8[20 - 60]$$
$$= 8(-40)$$
$$= -320$$

UNIT 6
Trigonometry

- **Trigonometric Ratios (SOHCAHTOA)**

The word **Trigonometry** is derived from three Greek words 'Trio' meaning thrice (3), 'gonia' meaning measure. Thus, Trigonometry is the study of a three-sided figure i.e. a triangle.

The three most used ratios to solve a right angled triangle are:
- Sine (sin)
- Cosine (cos)
- Tangent (tan)

The most important task of trigonometry is to find the remaining sides and angles of a triangle when some of its sides and angles are given. This problem is solved by using some ratios of the sides of a triangle with respect to its acute angles. These ratios of acute angles are called Trigonometric ratios of angles.

Let in ΔABC, the side opposite to 'A' is 'a', side opposite to 'B' is 'b' and side opposite to 'C' is 'c'.

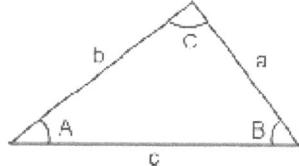

- **In a right angled triangle,**
  I. Adjacent side (A) is adjacent to the angle 'θ'
  II. Opposite side (O) is opposite the angle 'θ',
  III. The longest side is the Hypotenuse (H).

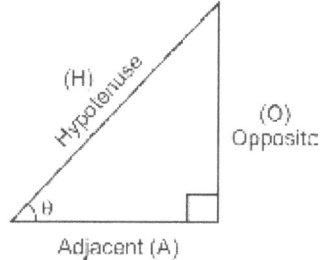

We define the following six trigonometric ratios.
SOH-CAH-TOA" is a helpful mnemonic for remembering the definitions of trigonometric functions on sine, cosine, and tangent i.e.

I. **Sine Function:**
   Sinθ = Opposite/ Hypotenuse = O/H (SOH)

II. **Cosine Function :**
   Cosθ = Adjacent / Hypotenuse =A/H (CAH)

III. **Tangent Function :**
   tanθ = Opposite / Adjacent = O/A (TOA)

IV. **Cosecant Function :**
   cosecθ = Hypotenuse / Opposite = H/O

V. **Secant Function:**
   Secθ = Hypotenuse /Adjacent = H/A

VI. **Cotangent Function :**
   Cotθ = Adjacent / Opposite = A/ H

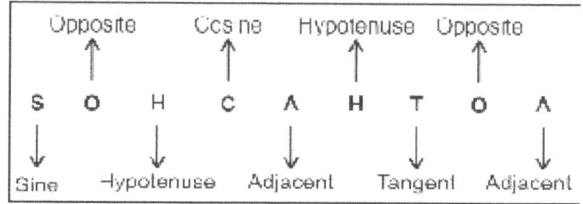

- **Trigonometric Ratios and Their Relation**

The Trigono metric-ratios sin θ, cos θ, and tan θ of an angle θ are very closely connected by relation. If any one of them is known, the other two can easily be calculated.

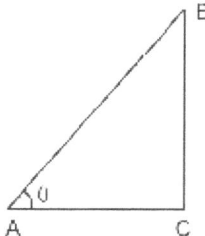

Here, Sin θ = BC / AB; Cos θ = AC / AB and tan θ = BC / AC

tan θ = (BC ÷ AB) / (AC ÷ AB) [Divide both numerator and denominator by AB]

tan θ = Sin θ / Cos θ [since BC / AB = Sin θ and AC / AB = Cos θ]

It is clear from the definitions of the Trigonometric-ratios that for any acute angle θ, we have,
- Cosec θ = 1 / sin θ or sin θ = 1 / Cosec θ
- Sec θ = 1 / cos θ or cos θ = 1 / sec θ
- Cot θ = 1 / tan θ or tan θ = 1 / cot θ
- Cot θ = cos θ / sin θ
- tan θ cot θ = 1

Trigonometry for Specific Angles

The ratios of the sides in a right triangle with respect to some acute angles are called trigonometry for specific-angles. The angles $0°$, $30°$, $45°$, $60°$ and $90°$ are useful angles in trigonometry, and their numerical values are easy to remember. These ratios are trigonometry for specific angles.

θ	0°	30°	45°	60°	90°
sinθ	0	$\frac{1}{2}$	$\frac{1}{\sqrt{2}}$	$\frac{\sqrt{3}}{2}$	1
cosθ	1	$\frac{\sqrt{3}}{2}$	$\frac{1}{\sqrt{2}}$	$\frac{1}{2}$	0
tanθ	0	$\frac{1}{\sqrt{3}}$	1	$\sqrt{3}$	Not difined
cotθ	Not defined	$\sqrt{3}$	1	$\frac{1}{\sqrt{3}}$	0
secθ	1	$\frac{2}{\sqrt{3}}$	$\sqrt{2}$	2	Not defined
cosecθ	Not defined	2	$\sqrt{2}$	$\frac{2}{\sqrt{3}}$	1

Complementary Angles in Trigonometry

Two angles are said to be complementary, if their sum is $90°$. It follows from the above definition that θ and $(90° - θ)$ are complementary angles in trigonometry for an acute angle θ.

In $\triangle ABC$, $\angle B = 90°$
$\therefore \angle 4 + \angle A + \angle C = 90°$
$\angle C = 90° - \angle A$

$\sin(90° - A) = \cos A$	$\tan(90° - A) = \cot A$
$\cos(90° - A) = \sin A$	$\cot(90° - A) = \tan A$
$\sec(90° - A) = \csc A$	$\csc(90° - A) = \sec A$

This means
$$\sin 70° = \cos 20°$$

The co-function of the sine is the cosine and 20° is the complement of 70°.

Trigonometric Equations

An equation involving trigonometric ratios of an angle θ is said to be a trigonometric equations, if it is satisfied for all values of θ for which the given trigonometric ratios are defined.

Some trigonometric equations (identities) are as follows:

I. $\sin^2 θ + \cos^2 θ = 1$
II. $\sin^2 θ = 1 - \cos^2 θ$
III. $\cos^2 θ = 1 - \sin^2 θ$
IV. $1 + \tan^2 θ = \sec^2 θ$
V. $\tan^2 θ = \sec^2 θ - 1$
VI. $\sec^2 θ - \tan^2 θ = 1$
VII. $1 + \cot^2 θ = \csc^2 θ$
VIII. $\cot^2 θ = \csc^2 θ - 1$
IX. $\csc^2 θ - \cot^2 θ = 1$

These trigonometric equations are true for any angle θ for which the trigonometric ratios are meaningful.

Solved Examples

1. In $\triangle ABC$, right angled at A, if AB = 12, AC = 5 and BC = 13, find all the six Trigonometric-ratios of angle B.

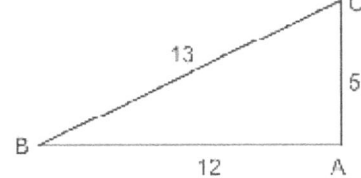

Solution:
Using definition of trigonometric ratios, we have
Sin B = AC / BC = 5 / 13
Cos B = AB / BC = 12 / 13
Tan B = AC / AB = 5 / 12
Cosec B = BC / AC = 13 / 5
Sec B = BC / AB = 13 / 12
Cot B = AB / AC = 12 / 5

2. If cosec A = 2, find the value of tan A.

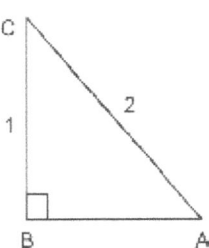

Solution:
Since Cosec A = AC/BC
  2 / 1 = AC / BC
So, Let AC = 2k, BC = 1k
By Pythagorean Theorem,
  $AC^2 = AB^2 + BC^2$
$\Rightarrow (2k)^2 = AB^2 + (1k)^2$
$\Rightarrow 4k^2 = AB^2 + k^2$
  $AB^2 = 4k^2 - k^2 \Rightarrow AB = \sqrt{3}\,k$

Trigonometry

So, tan A = BC / AB = 1k /√(3) k
tan A = 1/√(3)

3. ΔABC is right angled at B and ∠A = ∠C. Is cos A equal to cos C?
   Solution:
   We know ∠A = ∠C
   AB = BC
   [Sides opposite to equal angles are equal]
   Cos A = AB / AC
   = BC / AC [substitute AB = BC]
   = Cos C
   Cos A = Cos C

4. Evaluate: (sin² 45⁰ + cos² 45⁰) / tan² 60⁰
   Solution:
   (sin² 45⁰ + cos² 45⁰) / tan² 60⁰
   = 1 / tan² 60⁰   [since sin²θ + cos²θ = 1]
   = 1/ (√3)²
   = 1 / 3

5. 2 sin² 30⁰ tan 60⁰ − 3 cos² 60⁰ sec²30⁰
   Solution :
   2 sin²30⁰ tan 60⁰ − 3 cos²60⁰ sec²30⁰
   = 2 (1/ 2)² × √3 − 3 (1/2)² × (2 / √3)²
   = 2 × 1 /4 × √3 − 3 × 1/4 × 4 / 3
   = √3 / 2 − 1
   = (√3 − 2) / 2

6. Solve tan 5A = 1 for 0⁰ < A < 90⁰
   Solution:
   tan 5A =1   5A = 45⁰
   A = 45⁰/5   A = 9⁰

7. Find the acute angles A and B, if sin(A + 2B) = √3 / 2 and cos (A + 4B) = 0, A > B.
   Solution :
   sin(A + 2B) = √3 / 2
   sin(A + 2B) = sin 60⁰
   A + 2B = 60   ..... (1)
   cos (A + 4B) = 0
   cos (A + 4B) = cos 90⁰
   A + 4B = 90   ..... (2)
   Subtract equation (1) from (2) we get
   2B = 30⁰
   B = 15⁰
   From equation (1), we have
   A + 2(15⁰) = 60⁰
   A + 30⁰ = 60⁰
   A = 60⁰ − 30⁰
   A = 30⁰

8. Evaluate : cos 37⁰ / sin 53⁰
   Solution:
   cos 37⁰/sin 53⁰ = cos(90 − 53)/sin 53 = sin 53⁰/sin 53⁰
   = 1

9. Show that : (cos 70⁰)/(sin 20⁰) + (cos 59⁰)/sin 31⁰ − 8 sin² 30⁰ = 0
   Solution : Consider
   (cos 70⁰) / (sin 20⁰) + (cos 59⁰) / sin 31⁰ − 8 sin² 30⁰
   = [cos (90⁰ − 20⁰)] / [sin 20⁰] + [cos(90⁰ − 31⁰)]/sin 31⁰ − 8 × (1/2)²
   = sin 20⁰ / sin 20⁰ + sin 31⁰ / sin 31⁰ − 8 × 1/ 4
   = 1 + 1 − 2 = 0
   ∴ (cos 70⁰)/(sin 20⁰) + (cos 59⁰)/sin 31⁰− 8 sin² 30⁰ = 0

10. 1/(1 + sin θ) + 1/(1 − sin θ) = 2 sec²θ
    Solution :
    Consider 1/(1 + sin θ) + 1/(1 − sin θ)
    LCM = (1 + sin θ)(1 − sin θ)
    = [1 (1 − sin θ) + 1 (1 + sin θ)]/(1 + sin θ)(1 − sin θ)
    = (1 − sin θ + 1 + sin θ)/(1 + sin θ) (1 − sin θ)
    = 2 / (1 − sin²θ)
    [use identity (a + b) (a − b) = a² − b²]
    = 2/cos²θ
    = 2 sec²θ
    ∴ 1 / (1 + sin θ) + 1/(1 − sin θ) = 2 sec²θ

11. Prove that : cos θ / (1− sin θ) = (1 + sin θ) / cos θ
    Solution:
    Consider cos θ / (1− sin θ)
    Multiply top (numerator) and bottom (denomi-nator) by (1 + sin θ)
    = cos θ (1 + sin θ) / (1− sin θ) (1 + sin θ)
    = cos θ (1 + sin θ) / (1− sin²θ)
    [using this identity (a + b) (a − b) = a²− b²]
    = cos θ (1 + sin θ) / cos²θ)
    = (1 + sin θ) / cos θ
    ∴ cos θ / (1− sin θ) = (1 + sin θ) / cos θ

12. Cos² θ + 1 / (1 + cot² θ) = 1
    Solution : Consider Cos² θ + 1/ (1 + cot² θ)
    = Cos² θ + 1/ cosec² θ   [since 1 + cot²θ = cosec²θ]
    = cos²θ + sin²θ   [since 1/cosec² θ = sin²θ]
    = 1   [since sin²θ + cos²θ = 1]
    ∴ Cos² θ + 1 / (1 + cot² θ) = 1

Multiple Choice Questions

1. If $3x$ = cosec θ and $\frac{3}{x}$ = cot θ then $3\left(x^2 - \frac{1}{x^2}\right) = ?$

   (a) $\frac{1}{27}$ (b) $\frac{1}{81}$

   (c) $\frac{1}{3}$ (d) $\frac{1}{9}$

2. If $2x$ = sec A and $\frac{2}{x}$ = tan A, then $2\left(x^2 - \frac{1}{x^2}\right) = ?$

   (a) $\frac{1}{2}$ (b) $\frac{1}{4}$

   (c) $\frac{1}{8}$ (d) $\frac{1}{16}$

3. If $(\tan \theta + \cot \theta) = 5$, then $(\tan^2 \theta + \cot^2 \theta) = ?$
   (a) 27
   (b) 25
   (c) 24
   (d) 23

4. If $(\cos \theta + \sec \theta) = \frac{5}{2}$, then $(\cos^2 \theta + \sec^2 \theta) = ?$
   (a) $\frac{21}{4}$
   (b) $\frac{17}{4}$
   (c) $\frac{29}{4}$
   (d) $\frac{33}{4}$

5. If $\tan \theta = \frac{1}{\sqrt{7}}$, then $\frac{(\cosec^2 \theta - \sec^2 \theta)}{(\cosec^2 \theta + \sec^2 \theta)} = ?$
   (a) $-\frac{2}{3}$
   (b) $-\frac{3}{4}$
   (c) $\frac{2}{3}$
   (d) $\frac{3}{4}$

6. If $\cot \theta = \frac{15}{8}$, then $\frac{(2 + 2\sin \theta)(1 - \sin \theta)}{(1 + \cos \theta)(2 - 2\cos \theta)} = ?$
   (a) $\frac{64}{225}$
   (b) $\frac{225}{64}$
   (c) $\frac{64}{289}$
   (d) $\frac{289}{64}$

7. If the given ΔABC, it is given that $\angle B = 90°$ AB = 24 cm and BC = 7 cm. Then cos A = ?

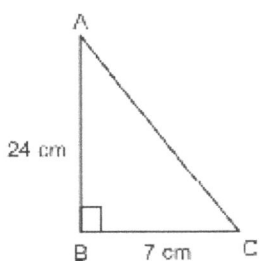

   (a) $\frac{7}{24}$
   (b) $\frac{7}{25}$
   (c) $\frac{24}{25}$
   (d) None of these

8. If $\sin \alpha = \frac{1}{2}$ and $\cos \beta = \frac{1}{2}$, then $(\alpha + \beta) = ?$
   (a) 0°
   (b) 30°
   (c) 60°
   (d) 90°

9. If $(\sin \theta - \cos \theta) = 0$, then $(\sin^4 \theta - \cos^4 \theta) = ?$
   (a) 1
   (b) $\frac{1}{2}$
   (c) $\frac{1}{4}$
   (d) $\frac{3}{4}$

10. If ΔABC is right angled at C, then cos (A + B) = ?
    (a) 0
    (b) $\frac{1}{2}$
    (c) 1
    (d) $\frac{\sqrt{3}}{2}$

11. A pole 6 m high casts a shadow $2\sqrt{3}$ m long on the ground. The sun's attitude is
    (a) 30°
    (b) 45°
    (c) 60°
    (d) 90°

12. $(\tan 30° \cosec 60° + \tan 60° \sec 30°) = ?$
    (a) $2\frac{1}{3}$
    (b) $2\frac{2}{3}$
    (c) $3\frac{1}{3}$
    (d) $1\frac{2}{3}$

13. If $(\cos 30° + \sin 30° + \sin 45°)(\sin 90° + \cos 60° - \cos 95°) = ?$
    (a) $\frac{5}{6}$
    (b) $\frac{5}{8}$
    (c) $\frac{3}{5}$
    (d) $\frac{7}{4}$

14. $(\sin^2 30° + 4 \cot^2 45° - \sec^2 60°) = ?$
    (a) 0
    (b) $\frac{1}{4}$
    (c) 4
    (d) 1

15. If $\sec 5A = \cosec (A - 30°)$, where 5A is an acute angle, then $\angle A = ?$
    (a) 35°
    (b) 25°
    (c) 20°
    (d) 27°

16. If A and B are acute angles such that sin A = cos B, then (A + B) = ?
    (a) 45°
    (b) 60°
    (c) 90°
    (d) 180°

17. $\sin 70° \sin 20° + \cos 20° \cosec 70° = ?$
    (a) 0
    (b) 1
    (c) −1
    (d) 2

18. $\cot (90 - \theta) = ?$
    (a) $\cot \theta$
    (b) $-\cot \theta$
    (c) $\tan \theta$
    (d) $-\tan \theta$

19. If $\cos 9\alpha = \sin \alpha$ and $9\alpha < 90°$, then $\tan 5\alpha = ?$
    (a) $\frac{1}{\sqrt{3}}$
    (b) $\sqrt{3}$
    (c) 1
    (d) 0

20. If $\cos (\alpha + \beta) = 0$ then $\sin (\alpha - \beta) = ?$
    (a) $\cos \beta$
    (b) $\cos 2\beta$
    (c) $\sin \alpha$
    (d) $\sin 2\alpha$

Trigonometry

Answer Key

1. (c)	2. (a)	3. (d)	4. (b)	5. (d)	6. (b)	7. (c)	8. (d)	9. (b)	10. (a)	11. (c)
12. (b)	13. (d)	14. (b)	15. (c)	16. (c)	17. (d)	18. (c)	19. (c)	20. (b)		

Explanatory Notes

1. (c)
   We know that $\csc^2\theta - \cot^2\theta = 1$

   $\therefore \quad (3x)^2 - \left(\dfrac{3}{x}\right)^2 = 1$

   $\Rightarrow \quad 9x^2 - \dfrac{9}{x^2} = 1$

   $\Rightarrow \quad 9\left(x^2 - \dfrac{1}{x^2}\right) = 1$

   $\Rightarrow \quad \left(x^2 - \dfrac{1}{x^2}\right) = \dfrac{1}{9}$

   $\Rightarrow \quad 3\left(x^2 - \dfrac{1}{x^2}\right) = \left(3 \times \dfrac{1}{9}\right) = \dfrac{1}{3}$

2. (a)
   We know that
   $\sec^2 A - \tan^2 A = 1$

   $\therefore \quad (2x)^2 - \left(\dfrac{2}{x}\right)^2 = 1$

   $4x^2 - \dfrac{4}{x^2} = 1$

   $\Rightarrow \quad 4\left(x^2 - \dfrac{1}{x^2}\right) = 1$

   $\Rightarrow \quad \left(x^2 - \dfrac{1}{x^2}\right) = \dfrac{1}{4}$

   $\Rightarrow \quad 2\left(x^2 - \dfrac{1}{x^2}\right) = \left(2 \times \dfrac{1}{4}\right) = \dfrac{1}{2}$

3. (d)
   $(\tan\theta + \cot\theta)^2 = 5^2$
   $\Rightarrow \tan^2\theta + \cot^2\theta + 2\tan\theta\cot\theta = 25$
   $\Rightarrow \tan^2\theta + \cot^2\theta + 2 = 25$
   $\Rightarrow \tan^2\theta + \cot^2\theta = 23$

4. (b)
   $(\cos\theta + \sec\theta)^2 = \left(\dfrac{5}{2}\right)^2$

   $\Rightarrow \cos^2\theta + \sec^2\theta + 2\cos\theta\sec\theta = \dfrac{25}{4}$

   $\Rightarrow \cos^2\theta + \sec^2\theta + 2 = \dfrac{25}{4}$

   $\Rightarrow \cos^2\theta + \sec^2\theta = \left(\dfrac{25}{4} - 2\right) = \dfrac{17}{4}$

5. (d)
   $\tan\theta = \dfrac{1}{\sqrt{7}} \quad \Rightarrow \quad \cot\theta = \sqrt{7}$

   $\Rightarrow \sec^2\theta = (1 + \tan^2\theta)$

   $= \left(1 + \dfrac{1}{7}\right) = \dfrac{8}{7}$

   and $\csc^2\theta = (1 + \cot^2\theta)$
   $= (1 + 7) = 8$

   $\therefore \dfrac{\csc^2\theta - \sec^2\theta}{\csc^2\theta + \sec^2\theta} = \dfrac{\left(8 - \dfrac{8}{7}\right)}{\left(8 + \dfrac{8}{7}\right)} = \dfrac{48}{64} = \dfrac{3}{4}$

6. (b)
   $\dfrac{(2 + 2\sin\theta)(1 - \sin\theta)}{(1 + \cos\theta)(2 - 2\cos\theta)} = \dfrac{2(1 + \sin\theta)(1 - \sin\theta)}{2(1 + \cos\theta)(1 - \cos\theta)}$

   $= \dfrac{1 - \sin^2\theta}{1 - \cos^2\theta} = \dfrac{\cos^2\theta}{\sin^2\theta}$

   $= \cot^2\theta$

   $= (\cot\theta)^2 = \left(\dfrac{15}{8} \times \dfrac{15}{8}\right)$

   $= \dfrac{225}{64}$

7. (c)
   $AC^2 = AB^2 + BC^2 = (24)^2 + 7^2$
   $= (576 + 49) = 625$

   $AC = \sqrt{625} = 25$ cm

   $\therefore \cos A = \dfrac{AB}{AC} = \dfrac{24}{25}$

8. (d)
   $\sin\alpha = \dfrac{1}{2} = \sin 30° \Rightarrow \alpha = 30°$

   $\cos\beta = \dfrac{1}{2} = \cos 60°$

   $\Rightarrow \quad \beta = 60°$
   $\therefore \quad \alpha + \beta = (30° + 60°) = 90°$

[61]

9. (b)
$$\sin\theta - \cos\theta = 0$$
$$\Rightarrow \sin\theta = \cos\theta \Rightarrow \tan\theta = 1$$
$$\theta = 45°$$
$$\therefore (\sin^4\theta + \cos^4\theta) = (\sin 45°)^4 + (\cos 45°)^4$$
$$= \left(\frac{1}{\sqrt{2}}\right)^4 + \left(\frac{1}{\sqrt{2}}\right)^4 = \frac{1}{4} + \frac{1}{4} = \frac{2}{4} = \frac{1}{2}$$

10. (a)
Clearly $A + B = 90°$
$\Rightarrow \cos(A + B) = \cos 90° = 0$
$$[\because \angle C = 90°]$$

11. (c)
Let AB be the pole and AC be its shadow.
Then AB = 6m
and AC = $2\sqrt{3}$ m

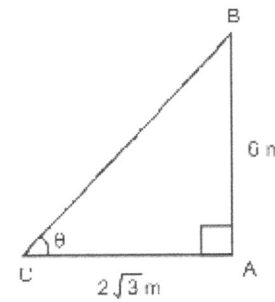

Let $\angle ACB = \theta°$
Then, $\tan\theta = \dfrac{AB}{AC} = \dfrac{6}{2\sqrt{3}}$
$= \sqrt{3}\quad \theta = 60°$

12. (b)
$(\tan 30° \operatorname{cosec} 60° + \tan 60° \sec 30°)$
$$= \left(\frac{1}{\sqrt{3}} \times \frac{2}{\sqrt{3}}\right) + \left(\sqrt{3} \times \frac{2}{\sqrt{3}}\right) = \left(\frac{2}{3} + 2\right) = 2\frac{2}{3}$$

13. (d)
$(\cos 0° + \sin 30° + \sin 45°)$
$(\sin 90° + \cos 60° - \cos 45°)$
$$= \left(1 + \frac{1}{2} + \frac{1}{\sqrt{2}}\right)\left(1 + \frac{1}{2} - \frac{1}{\sqrt{2}}\right)$$
$$= \left(\frac{3}{2} + \frac{1}{\sqrt{2}}\right)\left(\frac{3}{2} - \frac{1}{\sqrt{2}}\right) = \frac{9}{4} - \frac{1}{2} = \frac{7}{4}$$

14. (b)
$(\sin^2 30° + 4\cot^2 45° - \sec^2 60°)$
$$= \left(\frac{1}{2}\right)^2 + 4\times(1)^2 - 2^2 = \left(\frac{1}{4} + 4 - 4\right) = \frac{1}{4}$$

15. (c)
$$\sec 5A = \operatorname{cosec}(A - 30°)$$
$$= \operatorname{cosec}(90° - 5A)$$
$$= \operatorname{cosec}(A - 30°)$$
$\Rightarrow 90° - 5A = A - 30°$
$\Rightarrow 6A° = 120°$
$\Rightarrow A = 20°$

16. (c)
$\sin A = \cos B = \sin(90° - B)$
$\Rightarrow A = 90° - B$
$\Rightarrow A + B = 90°$

17. (d)
$\sec 70° \sin 20° + \cos 20° \operatorname{cosec} 70°$
$= \sec 70° \sin(90° - 70°) + \cos 20° \operatorname{cosec}(90° - 20°)$
$= \sec 70° \cos 70° + \cos 20° \sec 20°$
$= 1 + 1 = 2$

18. (b)
$$\cot(90° - \theta) = \tan\theta$$

19. (c)
$\cos 9\alpha = \sin\alpha = \cos(90° - \alpha)$
$\Rightarrow 9\alpha = 90° - \alpha$
$\Rightarrow 10\alpha = 90°;\ \alpha = 9°$
$\therefore 5\alpha = 45°$
and hence $\tan 5\alpha = \tan 45° = 1$

20. (b)
$\cos(\alpha + \beta) = 0 \Rightarrow \alpha + \beta = 90°$
$\Rightarrow \alpha = (90° - \beta)$
$\therefore (\alpha - \beta) = (90° - 2\beta)$
$\Rightarrow \sin(\alpha - \beta) = \sin(90° - 2\beta)$
$= \cos 2\beta$

Trigonometry

Previous Year Questions

1. cos (40° + θ) − sin (50° − θ) = ?
   [NTSE 2004 – Punjab first stage paper]
   (a) 1 (b) 0
   (c) sin 2θ (d) None of these

2. sin (45° + θ) − cos (45° − θ) = ?
   [NTSE 2000 – Jammu second stage paper]
   (a) 2 cos θ (b) 2 sin θ
   (c) 0 (d) 1

3. cosec (75° + θ) − sec (15° − θ) = ?
   [NTSE 2001 – Haryana first stage paper]
   (a) 2 sec θ (b) 2 cosec θ
   (c) 0 (d) 1

4. If sin (θ + 34°) = cos θ and θ is acute, then θ = ?
   [NTSE 2003 – Himachal Pradesh first stage paper]
   (a) 56° (b) 66°
   (c) 28° (d) 42°

5. Sin θ cos (90° − θ) + cos θ sin (90° − θ) = ?
   [NTSE 2000 – Bihar second stage paper]
   (a) 0 (b) 1
   (c) 2 (d) $\frac{3}{2}$

6. If tan (A + B) = $\sqrt{3}$ and tan (A − B) = $\frac{1}{\sqrt{3}}$, where A ≥ B and (A + B) is acute, then A = ?
   [NTSE 2012 – Chandigarh first stage paper]
   (a) 15° (b) 30°
   (c) 45° (d) 60°

7. In ΔABC, ∠B = 90° AB = 3 cm and AC = 6 cm. Then ∠A = ?
   [NTSE 2005 – Assam first stage paper]

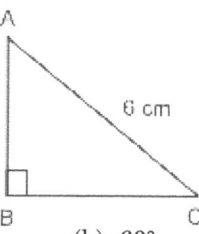

   (a) 30° (b) 60°
   (c) 45° (d) None of these

8. In ΔABC, ∠B = 90°, ∠A = 30° and AB = 9 cm. Then BC = ?
   [NTSE 2004 – Goa first stage paper]

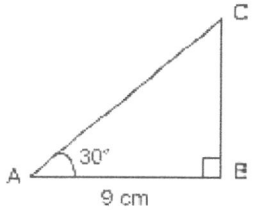

   (a) 3 cm (b) $2\sqrt{3}$ cm
   (c) $3\sqrt{3}$ cm (d) 6 cm

9. The value of (cos 60° cos 30° − sin 60° sin 30°) is
   [NTSE 2012 – Delhi first stage paper]
   (a) 0 (b) $\frac{\sqrt{3}}{2}$
   (c) $\frac{1}{2}$ (d) 1

10. (sin 60° cos 30° − sin 60° sin 30°) = ?
    [NTSE 2001 – Tamilnadu second stage paper]
    (a) 0 (b) 1
    (c) $\frac{1}{2}$ (d) $\frac{\sqrt{3}}{2}$

Answer Key

| 1. (b) | 2. (c) | 3. (c) | 4. (c) | 5. (b) | 6. (c) | 7. (b) | 8. (c) | 9. (a) | 10. (c) |

Explanatory Notes

1. (b)
$\cos(40° + \theta) - \sin(50° - \theta)$
$= \cos(40° + \theta) - \sin\{90° - (40° + \theta)\}$
$= \cos(40° + \theta) - \cos(40° + \theta)$
$= 0$

2. (c)
$\sin(45° + \theta) - \cos(45° - \theta)$
$= \sin(45° + \theta) - \cos\{90° - (45° + \theta)\}$
$= \operatorname{cosec}(45° + \theta) - \sin(45° + \theta)$
$= 0$

3. (c)
$\operatorname{cosec}(75° + \theta) - \sec(15° - \theta)$
$= \operatorname{cosec}(75° + \theta) - \sec\{90° - (75° + \theta)\}$
$= \operatorname{cosec}(75° + \theta) - \operatorname{cosec}(75° + \theta)$
$= 0$

4. (c)
$\sin(\theta + 34°) = \cos\theta$
$\Rightarrow \sin(\theta + 34° +) = \sin(90° - \theta)$
$\therefore \theta + 34° = 90° - \theta$
$\Rightarrow 2\theta = (90° - 34°) = 56°$
$\theta = 28°$

5. (b)
$\sin\theta \cos(90 - \theta) + \cos\theta \sin(90° - \theta)$
$= \sin^2\theta + \cos^2\theta = 1$

6. (c)
$\tan(A + B) = \sqrt{3} = \tan 60°$
$\Rightarrow A + B = 60°$ ...(i)
$\tan(A - B) = \dfrac{1}{\sqrt{3}} = \tan 30°$
$\Rightarrow A - B = 30°$ ...(ii)
on adding (i) and (ii), we get
$2A = 90°$
$\Rightarrow A = 45°$

7. (b)
$\sin C = \dfrac{AB}{AC} = \dfrac{3}{6} = \dfrac{1}{2}$
$= \sin 30°$
$\Rightarrow \angle C = 30°$
$\therefore \angle A = (90° - \angle C)$
$= (90° - 30°)$
$= 60°$

8. (c)
We have :
$\dfrac{BC}{AB} = \tan 30° = \dfrac{1}{\sqrt{3}}$
$= \dfrac{BC}{9} = \dfrac{1}{\sqrt{3}}$
$\therefore BC = \left(9 \times \dfrac{1}{\sqrt{3}}\right)$ cm
$= 3\sqrt{3}$ cm

9. (a)
$(\cos 60° \cos 30° - \sin 60° \sin 30°)$
$= \left(\dfrac{1}{2} \times \dfrac{\sqrt{3}}{2}\right) - \left(\dfrac{\sqrt{3}}{2} \times \dfrac{1}{2}\right)$
$= \left(\dfrac{\sqrt{3}}{4} - \dfrac{\sqrt{3}}{4}\right) = 0$

10. (c)
$(\sin 60° \cos 30° - \cos 60° \sin 30°)$
$= \left(\dfrac{\sqrt{3}}{2} \times \dfrac{\sqrt{3}}{2}\right) - \left(\dfrac{1}{2} \times \dfrac{1}{2}\right)$
$= \left(\dfrac{3}{4} - \dfrac{1}{4}\right) = \dfrac{2}{4} = \dfrac{1}{2}$

UNIT 7
Height and Distance

Introduction
Sometimes, we are required to find the height of a tower, a tree, a building and the distance of a ship from light house, width of a river etc. We cannot measure them accurately though we can find them using the knowledge of trigonometric ratio.

Line of sight
When we see an object standing on the ground. The line of sight is the line from our eye to the object, we see.

Angle of Elevation

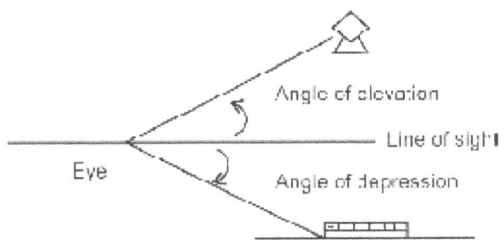

When the object is above the horizontal level of our eye, we have to turn our head upwards to see an object. In this process, our eyes move through an angle which is called 'angle of elevation'.

Angle of Depression
When the object is on the ground and the observer is on a building, the object is below the level of the eye of the observer. The observer has to turn his head downward to see the object. In doing so, his eyes move through an angle which is called 'angle of depression'.

Important Formulae

Trigonometric Identities
1. $\cos^2\theta + \sin^2\theta = 1$
2. $\tan^2\theta + 1 = \sec^2\theta$

Sine Sum and Difference Formulas
1. $\sin(\theta_1 + \theta_2) = \sin\theta_1\cos\theta_2 + \cos\theta_1\sin\theta_2$
2. $\sin(\theta_1 - \theta_2) = \sin\theta_1\cos\theta_2 - \cos\theta_1\sin\theta_2$

Sine Double Angle Formula
$\sin 2\theta = 2\sin\theta\cos\theta$

Cosine Sum and Difference Formulas
1. $\cos(\theta_1 + \theta_2) = \cos\theta_1\cos\theta_2 - \sin\theta_1\sin\theta_2$
2. $\cos(\theta_1 - \theta_2) = \cos\theta_1\cos\theta_2 + \sin\theta_1\sin\theta_2$

Cosine Double Angle Formula
$$\cos 2\theta = \cos^2\theta - \sin^2\theta$$
$$= 2\cos^2\theta - 1$$
$$= 1 - 2\sin^2\theta$$

From this Cosine Double Angle Formula, we obtain Half Angle Formulas.

Half Angle Formulas

1. $\cos^2\theta = \dfrac{1+\cos?}{2}$ or equivalently

   $\cos\theta = \mp\sqrt{\dfrac{1+\cos?}{2}}$

2. $\sin^2\theta = \dfrac{1-\cos?}{2}$ or equivalently

   $\sin\theta = \mp\sqrt{\dfrac{1-\cos?}{2}}$

Table-1 : Trigonometric Functions for Special Angles

θ	0	$\dfrac{\pi}{6}$	$\dfrac{\pi}{4}$	$\dfrac{\pi}{3}$	$\dfrac{\pi}{2}$
	0	30°	45°	60°	90°
sin (θ)	0	$\dfrac{1}{2}$	$\dfrac{\sqrt{2}}{2}$	$\dfrac{\sqrt{3}}{2}$	1
cos (θ)	1	$\dfrac{\sqrt{3}}{2}$	$\dfrac{\sqrt{2}}{2}$	$\dfrac{1}{2}$	0
tan (θ)	0	$\dfrac{\sqrt{3}}{3}$	1	$\sqrt{3}$	U
cos (θ)	U	2	$\sqrt{2}$	$\dfrac{2}{\sqrt{3}}$	1
sec (θ)	1	$\dfrac{2}{\sqrt{3}}$	$\sqrt{2}$	2	U
cot (θ)	U	$\sqrt{3}$	1	$\dfrac{\sqrt{3}}{3}$	0

Solved Examples

1. Qutab Minar casts of shadow 150 m long at the same time when Vikas Minar casts a shadow 120 m long on the ground. If the height of Vikas Minar is 80 m, find the height of Qutab Minar.
   a. 100 m   b. 180 m
   c. 150 m   d. 120 m
   Solution: Option (a) is correct.
   Explanation:
   Let the height of Qutab Minar be x m, then
   $x : 150 = 80 : 120$
   On solving, we get $x = 100$ m

2. The angle of elevation of the sun, when the length of the shadow of a tree is 3 times the height of the tree, is:
   a. 30°   b. 60°
   c. 45°   d. 90°
   Solution: Option (a) is correct.
   Explanation:
   Let AB be the tree and AC be its shadow.
   $\angle ACB = \theta$
   Then, $\dfrac{AC}{AB} = \sqrt{3}$
   $\Rightarrow \cot \theta = \sqrt{3}$
   $\therefore \theta = 30°$

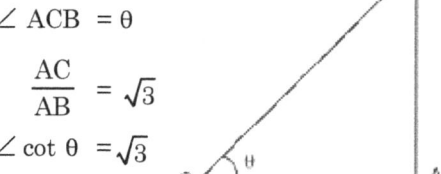

3. From a point P on a level ground, the angle of elevation of the top tower is 30°. If the tower is 100 m high, the distance of point P from the foot of the tower is:
   a. 149 m   b. 156 m
   c. 173 m   d. 200 m
   Solution: Option (c) is correct.
   Explanation:
   Let AB be the tower.

   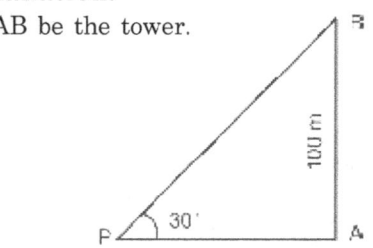

   Then, $\angle APB = 30°$ and AB = 100 m
   $\dfrac{AB}{AP} = \tan 30° = \dfrac{1}{\sqrt{3}}$
   $\Rightarrow AP = (AB \times \sqrt{3})$ m
   $= 100\sqrt{3}$ m
   $= (100 \times 1.73)$ m
   $= 173$ m

Practice Exercise

1. An observer 1.6 m tall is 203 m away from a tower. The angle of elevation from his eye to the top of the tower is 30°. The height of the tower is:
   a. 21.6 m   b. 23.2 m
   c. 24.72 m   d. None of these

2. The angle of elevation of a ladder leaning against a wall is 60° and the foot of the ladder is 4.6 m away from the wall. The length of the ladder is:
   a. 5.6 m   b. 4.6 m
   c. 7.8 m   d. 9.2 m

3. A man standing at a point P is watching the top of a tower, which makes an angle of elevation of 30° with the man's eye. The man walks some distance towards the tower to watch its top and the angle of elevation becomes 60°. What is the distance between the base of the tower and the point P?
   a. 43 units   b. 8 units
   c. 12 units   d. Data inadequate

4. Two hips are sailing in the sea on the two sides of a lighthouse. The angles of elevation of the top of the lighthouse observed from the ships are 30° and 45° respectively. If the lighthouse is 100 m high, the distance between the two ships is:
   a. 173 m   b. 200 m
   c. 273 m   d. 300 m

5. A man is standing on the deck of a ship, which is 8 m above the water level. He observes the angle of elevation of the top of a hill as 60⁰ and the angle of depression of the base of the hill as 30⁰. Calculate the distance of the hill from the ship and the height of the hill.
   a. $4\sqrt{3}$ m, 24 m   b. $8\sqrt{3}$ m, 24 m
   c. $8\sqrt{3}$ m, 32 m   d. $4\sqrt{3}$ m, 36 m

Height and Distance

6. A portion of a 30 m long tree is broken by a tornado and the top strikes the ground making the angle of 30° with the ground level. The height of the point where the tree is broken equals

   a. 10m
   b. $\dfrac{30}{\sqrt{3}}$ m
   c. $34\sqrt{3}$ m
   d. 60 m

7. A tree 6 m tall casts 4 m long shadow. At the same time, a flag pole casts 50 m long shadow. How long is the flag pole?

   a. 75 m
   b. 100 m
   c. 150 m
   d. 50 m

8. The reduced form of $\cos^6 x + \sin^6 x + 3 \cos^2 x \sin^2 x$ is equal to

   a. 2
   b. 0
   c. $\sin^3 x + \cos^3 x^2$
   d. 1

9. 300 m from the foot of a cliff on the level ground, the angle of elevation of the top of a cliff is 30°. Find the height of the cliff.

   a. 150.50 m
   b. 173.20 m
   c. 144.20 m
   d. 314.20 m

10. We have an angle of $2\dfrac{1}{2}°$. How big will it look through a glass that magnifies the things three times?

    a. $2\dfrac{1}{2}° \times 4$
    b. $2\dfrac{1}{2}° \times 3$
    c. $2\dfrac{1}{2}° \times 2$
    d. None of these

Answer Key

| 1. (a) | 2. (d) | 3. (d) | 4. (c) | 5. (c) | 6. (a) | 7. (a) | 8. (d) | 9. (b) | 10. (d) |

Explanatory Notes

1. (a)
   Let AB be the observer and CD be the tower.

   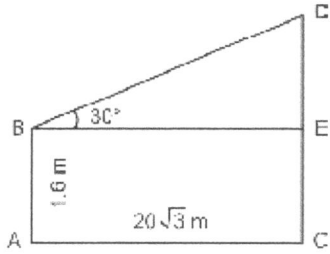

   Draw BE ⊥ CD
   Then,   CE = AB = 1.6 m
                  BE = AC = $20\sqrt{3}$ m

   $$\frac{DE}{BE} = \tan 30° = \frac{1}{\sqrt{3}}$$

   ⇒   DE $= \frac{20\sqrt{3}}{\sqrt{3}} = 20$ m

   ∴   CD = CE + DE = (1.6 + 20) m = 21.6 m

2. (d)
   Let AB be the wall and BC be the ladder.

   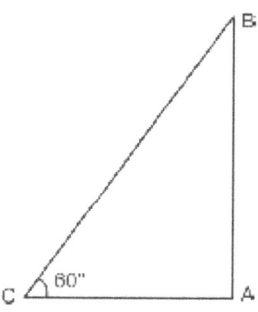

   Then, ∠ACB = 60° and AC = 4.6 m

   $$\frac{AC}{BC} = \cos 60° = \frac{1}{2}$$

   ⇒   BC = 2 × AC
                    = (2 × 4.6) m
                    = 9.2 m

3. (d)
   One of AB, AD and CD must have been given.

   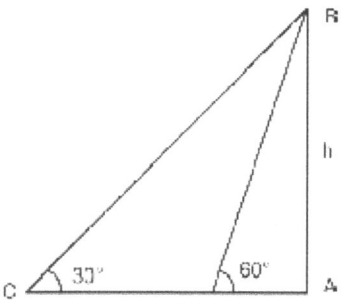

   So, the data is inadequate.

4. (c)
   Let AB be the lighthouse and C and D be the positions of the ships.

   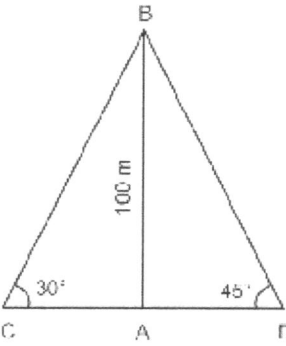

   Then, AB = 100 m, ∠ACB = 30° and ∠ADB = 45°

   $$\frac{AB}{AC} = \tan 30° = \frac{1}{\sqrt{3}}$$

   ⇒   AC = AB × $\sqrt{3}$ = $100\sqrt{3}$ m

   $$\frac{AB}{AD} = \tan 45° = 1$$

                  AD = AB = 100 m
                  CD = (AC + AD)
                     = ($100\sqrt{3}$ + 100) m
                     = 100 ($\sqrt{3}$ + 1)
                     = (100 × 2.73) m
                     = 273 m

Height and Distance

5. (c)

Let B be the man, D the base of the hill, x be the distance of hill from the ship and h + 8 be the height of the hill.

$\angle ADB = 45°, \angle DBC = 30°$

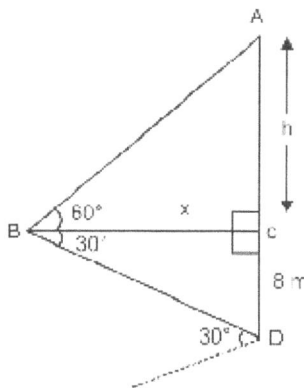

In $\triangle ABC$

$$\tan 60° = \frac{AC}{BC}$$

$$\sqrt{3} = \frac{h}{x} \Rightarrow h = x\sqrt{3} \quad \ldots (1)$$

In $\triangle BCD$

$$\tan 30° = \frac{CD}{BC}$$

$$\frac{1}{\sqrt{3}} = \frac{8}{x} \Rightarrow x = 8\sqrt{3}$$

From (1) $h = x\sqrt{3} = (8\sqrt{3})\sqrt{3} = 24$

Height of the hill = h + 8 = 24 + 8 = 32 m

Distance of the hill from the ship = $8\sqrt{3}$ m

6. (a)

$$\sin 30° = \frac{30-x}{x}$$

or $$\frac{1}{2} = \frac{30-x}{x}$$

$\Rightarrow \quad x = 20$

$\therefore \quad AB = (30 - 20)$
$\quad = 10$ m

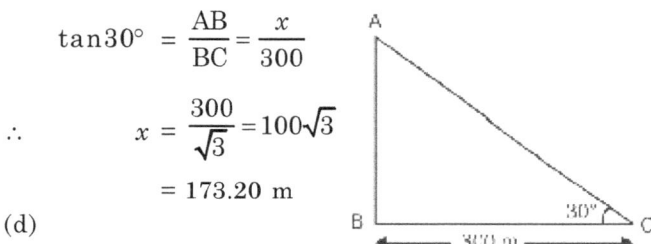

7. (a)

Clearly, 6:4 = h:50

$$h = \frac{50 \times 6}{4} = 75\,m$$

8. (d)

$\cos^6 x + \sin^6 x + 3\cos^2 x \, \sin^2 x$
$= (\cos^2 x)^3 + (\sin^2 x)^3 + 3\sin^2 x \cos^2 x \, (\sin^2 x + \cos^2 x)$
$= (\sin^2 x + \cos^2 x)^3 = 1$

9. (b)

$$\tan 30° = \frac{AB}{BC} = \frac{x}{300}$$

$\therefore \quad x = \frac{300}{\sqrt{3}} = 100\sqrt{3}$

$\quad = 173.20$ m

10. (d)

The angle will not change.

UNIT 8
Co-ordinate Geometry

1. Two perpendicular number lines intersecting at point zero are called coordinate axes. The horizontal number line is the x-axis (denoted by X'OX) and the vertical number line is the y-axis (denoted by Y'OY).

2. The point of intersection of x axis and y axis is called origin denoted by 'O'.

3. Cartesian plane is a plane obtained by putting the coordinate axes perpendicular to each other in the plane. It is also called coordinate plane or xy plane.

4. The x-coordinate of a point is its perpendicular distance from y axis.

5. The y-coordinate of a point is its perpendicular distance from x axis.

6. The point where the x axis and the y axis intersect is represented by coordinate points (0, 0) and is called the origin. It is denoted by 'O' on a Cartesian plane.

7. The abscissa of a point is the x-coordinate of the point.

8. The ordinate of a point is the y-coordinate of the point.

9. If the abscissa of a point is x and the ordinate of the point is y, then (x, y) are called the coordinates of the point.

10. The axes divide the Cartesian plane into four parts called the quadrants (one fourth part), numbered I, II, III and IV anticlockwise from OX.

11. The origin O has zero distance from both the axes.

12. The coordinate of a point on the x axis are of the form (x, 0) and that of the point on y axis are (0, y)

13. The signs of coordinates depicts the quadrant in which it lies. The coordinates of a point are of the form (+, +) in the first quadrant, (–, +) in the second quadrant, (–, –) in the third quadrant and (+, –) in the fourth quadrant.

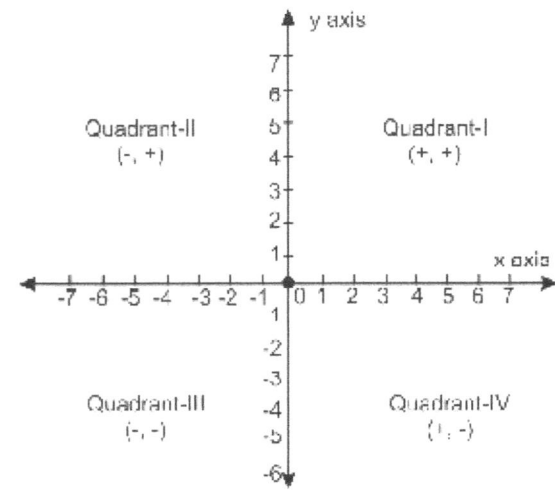

14. To plot a point P (3, 4) in the Cartesian plane, start from origin count 3 units on the positive x axis, then move 4 units towards positive y axis and mark the point P as shown in the figure below :

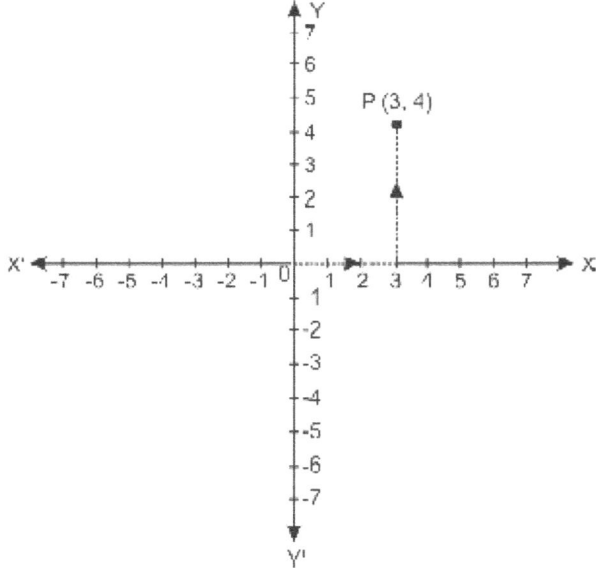

15. If $x \neq y$, then $(x, y) \neq (y, x)$ and if $(x, y) = (y, x)$, then $x = y$.

Co-ordinate Geometry

16. Three points A, B and C are collinear if the distances AB, BC, CA are such that the sum of two distances is equal to the third.
17. Three points A, B and C are the vertices of an equilateral triangle if the distances
    AB = BC = CA.
18. The points A, B and C are the vertices of an isosceles triangle if the distances AB = BC or BC = CA or CA = AB.
19. Three points A, B and C are the vertices of a right triangle if $AB^2 + BC^2 = CA^2$.
20. For the given four points A, B, C and D
    (i)   AB = BC = CD = DA; AC = BD
          $\Rightarrow$ ABCD is a square.
    (ii) AB = BC = CD = DA; AC ≠ BD
          $\Rightarrow$ ABCD is a rhombus.
    (iii) AB = CD, BC = DA; AC = BD
          $\Rightarrow$ ABCD is a rectangle.
    (iv) AB = CD, BC = DA; AC ≠ BD
          $\Rightarrow$ ABCD is a parallelogram.
21. Diagonals of a square, rhombus, rectangle and parallelogram always bisect each other.
22. Diagonals of rhombus and square bisect each other at right angle.
23. Four given points are collinear, if the area of quadrilateral is zero.
24. Centroid is the point of intersection of the three medians of a triangle.
25. Centroid divides the median in the ratio of 2:1.
26. The incentre is the point of intersection of internal bisector of the angles. It is also the centre of the circle touching all the sides of a triangle.
27. Circumcentre is the point of intersection of the perpendicular bisectors of the sides of the triangle.
28. Orthocentre is the point of intersection of perpendicular drawn from the vertices on opposite sides (called altitudes) of a triangle and can be obtained by solving the equations of any two altitudes.
29. If the triangle is equilateral, the centroid, incentre, orthocentre, circumcentre coincides.
30. If the triangle is right angled triangle, then orthocentre is the point where right angle is formed.
31. If the triangle is right angled triangle, then circumcentre is the midpoint of hypotenuse.
32. Orthocentre, centroid and circumcentre are always collinear and centroid divides the line joining Orthocentre and Circumcentre in the ratio of 2:1.
33. In an isosceles triangle, centroid, orthocentre, incentre, circumcentre lies on the same line.
34. Angle bisector divides the opposite sides in the ratio of remaining sides.
35. Three given points are collinear, if the area of triangle is zero.
36. The distance between $P(x_1, y_1)$ and $Q(x_2, y_2)$ is
    $$\sqrt{(x_2 - x_1)^2 + (y_2 - y_1)^2}$$
37. The Point P which divides the line segment joining the points $A(x_1, y_1)$ and $B(x_2, y_2)$ internally in the ratio $l:m$ is
    $$\left(\frac{lx_2 + mx_1}{l+m}, \frac{ly_2 + my_1}{l+m} \right).$$
38. The Point P which divides the line segment joining the points and is externally in the ratio $l:m$ is.
    $$\left(\frac{lx_2 - mx_1}{l-m}, \frac{ly_2 - my_1}{l-m} \right)$$
39. Midpoint of the line segment of joining the points (x_1, y_1) and (x_2, y_2) is
    $$\left(\frac{x_1 + x_2}{2}, \frac{y_1 + y_2}{2} \right).$$
40. The area of the triangle formed by the points (x_1, y_1), (x_2, y_2) and (x_3, y_3) is $\frac{1}{2} \sum x_1 (y_2 - y_3)$
    $= \frac{1}{2} \{ x_1(y_2 - y_3) + x_2(y_3 - y_1) + x_3(y_1 - y_2) \}$

Solved Examples

1: Write the coordinate of the point P when it divides the line AB internally in the ratio of 2:3 where $A(x_1, y_1) = (5, 3)$ and $B(x_2, y_2) = (7, 9)$.

Solution:
Given: $(x_1, y_1) = (5, 3)$
$(x_2, y_2) = (7, 9)$
$m : n = 2 : 3$

Step 1: Section formula for internal division:
$$\left(\frac{mx_2 + nx_1}{m+n}, \frac{my_2 + ny_1}{m+n} \right)$$

Step 2:
$$\frac{mx_2 + nx_1}{m+n} = \frac{2 \times 7 + 3 \times 5}{2+3}$$
$$\frac{14 + 15}{5} = \frac{29}{5} = 5.8$$

Step 3:
$$\frac{my_2 + ny_1}{m+n} = \frac{2 \times 9 + 3 \times 3}{2+3} = \frac{18 + 9}{5}$$
$$= \frac{27}{5} = 5.4$$

Answer: P(x, y) = (5.8, 5.4)

2: Write the coordinate of the point P when it divides the line AB externally in the ratio of 3:1 where $A(x_1, y_1) = (9, 4)$ and $B(x_2, y_2) = (5, 1)$.

Solution:
Given: $(x_1, y_1) = (9, 4)$
$(x_2, y_2) = (5, 1)$
$m : n = 3 : 1$

Step 1: Section formula for external division:
$$\left(\frac{mx_2 - nx_1}{m - n}, \frac{my_2 - ny_1}{m - n}\right)$$

Step 2:
$$\frac{mx_2 - nx_1}{m - n} = \frac{3 \times 5 - 1 \times 9}{3 - 1}$$
$$\frac{15 - 9}{2} = \frac{6}{2} = 3$$

Step 3:
$$\frac{my_2 - ny_1}{m - n} = \frac{3 \times 1 - 1 \times 4}{3 - 1}$$
$$= \frac{3 - 4}{2} = -\frac{1}{2}$$

Answer: $P(x, y) = (3, -\frac{1}{2})$

3: Find the distance between the following pair of points: A (1, 2) and B (4, 5).

Solution: Using the distance formula, we have
$$AB = \sqrt{(x_2 - x_1)^2 + (y_2 - y_1)^2}$$
$$= \sqrt{(4 - 1)^2 + (5 - 2)^2}$$
$$= \sqrt{3^2 + 3^2} = \sqrt{18} = 3\sqrt{2}$$

4: Find the midpoint value for the points (−2, 4) and (6, −10).

Solution:
Given points are (−2, 4) and (6, −10)
$(x_1, y_1) = (-2, 4)$
$(x_2, y_2) = (6, -10)$

Midpoint Formula $= \left(\dfrac{x_1 + x_2}{2}, \dfrac{y_1 + y_2}{2}\right)$

$= \left(\dfrac{-2 + 6}{2}, \dfrac{4 + (-10)}{2}\right)$

$= (2, -3)$

So the midpoint is (2, −3).

5: Find the value of 'p' so that (−4, 4.5) is the midpoint of (p, 4) and (−3, 6).

Solution:
By using midpoint formula, $\left(\dfrac{x_1 + x_2}{2}, \dfrac{y_1 + y_2}{2}\right)$, we have

$\dfrac{p - 3}{2}, \dfrac{4 + 6}{2} = (-4, 4.5)$

$\Rightarrow \dfrac{p - 3}{2} = -4$

$p - 3 = -8$
$p = -5$

The value of 'p' is −5.

Multiple Choice Questions

1. The distance of the point (4, 3) from the origin is:
   (a) 1 unit   (b) 3 units
   (c) 5 units   (d) 7 units

2. The distance between the points A (2, −3) and B (2, 2) is
   (a) 4 units   (b) 5 units
   (c) 3 units   (d) 2 units

3. What point on x-axis is equidistant from the points A (7,6) and B (−3, 4) ?
   (a) (0, 4)   (b) (−4, 0)
   (c) (3, 0)   (d) (0, 3)

4. The distance between the points A (0, 5) and B (−5, 0) is
   (a) 5 units   (b) $2\sqrt{5}$ units
   (c) $\sqrt{10}$ units   (d) $5\sqrt{2}$ units

5. A point P divides the join of A (5, −2) and B (9,6) in the ratio 3 :1. The co-ordinate of P are
   (a) (4, 7)   (b) (8, 4)
   (c) (12, 8)   (d) $\left(\dfrac{11}{2}, 5\right)$

6. In what ratio does the point P (1, 2) divide the join of A(−2, 1) and B (7, 4) ?
   (a) 1 : 2   (b) 2 : 1
   (c) 3 : 2   (d) 2 : 3

7. The point which divides the line segment joining the points A(7, −6) and B(3,4) in the ratio 1 : 2 lies in
   (a) I quadrant   (b) II quadrant
   (c) III quadrant (d) IV quadrant

8. In what ratio does the x-axis divide the join of A(2, −3) and B (5, 6) ?
   (a) 2 : 3   (b) 3 : 5
   (c) 1 : 2   (d) 2 : 1

Co-ordinate Geometry

9. In what ratio does the y-axis divide the join of the P(–4, 2) and Q (8, 3) ?
   (a) 3 : 1 (b) 1 : 3
   (c) 2 : 1 (d) 1 : 2

10. The midpoint of the line segment joining the points A(–2, 8) and B(–6, –4) is :
    (a) (4, 2) (b) (–4, 2)
    (c) (2, 6) (d) (–4, –6)

11. If P (–1, 1) is the midpoint of the line segment joining A(–3, b) and B (1, b + 4), then b = ?
    (a) 1 (b) –1
    (c) 2 (d) 0

12. If $P\left(\dfrac{9}{3}, 4\right)$ is the midpoint of the line segment joining A (–6, 5) and B(–2, 3), then a = ?
    (a) –4 (b) –12
    (c) 12 (d) –6

13. If the distance between the points A(2, –2) and B(–1, x) is 5, then
    (a) $x = -3$ or $x = 4$ (b) $x = 3$ or $x = -4$
    (c) $x = -6$ or $x = 2$ (b) $x = 6$ or $x = -2$

14. The line $2x + y = 4 = 0$ divides the line segment joining A(2, –2) and B(3, 7) in the ratio :
    (a) 2 : 5 (b) 2 : 9
    (c) 2 : 7 (d) 2 : 3

15. If A(4, 2), B(6, 5) and C(1,4) be the vertices of ΔABC and CD is a median, then the co-ordinates of D are :
    (a) $\left(\dfrac{5}{2}, 3\right)$ (b) $\left(5, \dfrac{7}{2}\right)$
    (c) $\left(\dfrac{7}{2}, \dfrac{9}{2}\right)$ (d) None of these

16. If A(–1, 0), B(5, –2) and C(8, 2) are the vertices of a DABC, then its centroid is
    (a) (12, 0) (b) (6, 0)
    (c) (0, 6) (d) (4, 0)

17. Two vertices of ΔABC are A(–1, 4) and B(5, 2) and its centroid is G(0, –3). Then the co-ordinates of C are:
    (a) (4, 3) (b) (4, 15)
    (c) (–4, –15) (d) (–15, –4)

18. If the distance between the points A(4, P) and B(1, 0) is 5, then
    (a) P = 4 only (b) P = – 4 only
    (c) P = ± 4 (d) P = 0

19. The three vertices of a parallelogram ABCD are A(–2, 3), B(6,7) and C(8,3). The fourth vertex D is
    (a) (1, 0) (b) (0, 1)
    (c) (–1, 0) (d) (0, –1)

20. The points A(–4, 0), B(4, 0) and C(0, 3) are the vertices of a triangle, which is
    (a) isosceles (b) equilateral
    (c) scalene (d) right angled

National Talent Search Examination (NTSE)-X

Answer Key

| 1. (c) | 2. (b) | 3. (c) | 4. (d) | 5. (b) | 6. (a) | 7. (d) | 8. (c) | 9. (d) | 10. (b) |
| 11. (b) | 12. (b) | 13. (c) | 14. (b) | 15. (c) | 16. (d) | 17. (c) | 18. (c) | 19. (d) | 20. (a) |

Explanatory Notes

1. (c)
$$OA^2 = (4-0)^2 + (-3-0)^2$$
$$= 4^2 + (-3)^2 = 16 + 9 = 25$$
$$\Rightarrow OA = \sqrt{25} = 5 \text{ units}$$

2. (b)
$$AB^2 = (2-2)^2 + (2+3)^2$$
$$= (0^2 + 5^2)$$
$$= (0 + 25) = 25$$
$$\Rightarrow OA = \sqrt{25} = 5 \text{ units}$$

3. (c)
Let the required point be $P(x, 0)$. Then
$$AP^2 = BP^2$$
$$\Rightarrow (7-x)^2 + (6-0)^2 = (-3-x)^2 + (4-0)^2$$
$$= x^2 - 14x + 85$$
$$= x^2 + 6x + 25$$
$$\Rightarrow 20x = 60$$
$$\Rightarrow x = 3$$
Hence, the required point is $P(3,0)$

4. (d)
$$AB^2 = (-5-0)^2 + (0-5)^2$$
$$= (-5)^2 + (-5)^2$$
$$= 25 + 25 = 50$$
$$\Rightarrow AB = \sqrt{50} = 5\sqrt{2} \text{ units}$$

5. (c)
The coordinates of P are
$$P\left(\frac{3 \times 9 + 1 \times 5}{3 \times 1}, \frac{3 \times 6 + 1 \times (-2)}{3 + 1}\right)$$
i.e. $P\left(\frac{32}{4}, \frac{16}{4}\right)$ or $(8, 4)$

6. (a)
Let the required ratio be $k : 1$. Then
$$P\left(\frac{7k-2}{k+1}, \frac{4k+1}{k+1}\right) \Rightarrow \frac{7k-2}{k+1} = 1$$
$$7k - 2 = k + 1 \Rightarrow 6k = 3 \Rightarrow k = \frac{1}{2}$$
$\therefore$ required ratio : $\frac{1}{2} : 1 = 1 : 2$

7. (c)
Let $P(x, y)$ be the point which divides AB in the ratio $1 : 2$. Then,
$$x = \frac{1 \times 3 + 2 \times 7}{1 + 2} = \frac{3 + 14}{3} = \frac{17}{3}$$
and $$y = \frac{1 \times 4 + 2 \times (-6)}{1 + 2} = \frac{4 - 12}{3} = \frac{-8}{3}$$
$\therefore$ required point is $P\left(\frac{17}{3}, \frac{-8}{3}\right)$
which lies in the IV quadrant.

8. (c)
Let x-axis divide AB in the ratio $k : 1$. Then,
$$P\left(\frac{5k+2}{k+1}, \frac{6k-3}{k+1}\right) \Rightarrow \frac{6k-3}{k+1} = 0$$
$$6k - 3 = 0 \Rightarrow 6k = 3 \Rightarrow k = \frac{1}{2}$$
$\therefore$ required ratio $= \frac{1}{2} : 1 = 1 : 2$

9. (d)
Let y-axis divide PQ in the ratio $k : 1$. Then,
$$R\left(\frac{8k-4}{k+1}, \frac{3k+2}{k+1}\right) \Rightarrow \frac{8k-2}{k+1} = 0$$
$$\Rightarrow 8k - 4 = 0$$
$$\Rightarrow 8k = 4 \Rightarrow k = \frac{4}{8} = \frac{1}{2}$$
$\therefore$ required ratio $= \frac{1}{2} : 1 = 1 : 2$

10. (b)
Co-ordinates of the midpoint of AB are
$$M\left(\frac{-2-6}{2}, \frac{8-4}{2}\right) \text{ i.e. } M(-4, 2)$$

11. (b)
Midpoint of AB is $P\left(\frac{-3+1}{2}, \frac{b+b+4}{2}\right)$
i.e. $P\left(\frac{-2}{2}, \frac{2b+4}{2}\right)$ i.e. $P(-1, b+2)$
$\therefore b + 2 = 1 \Rightarrow b = -1$

Co-ordinate Geometry

12. (b)

    We have : $\dfrac{-6 + (-2)}{2} = \dfrac{9}{3}$

    $\dfrac{9}{3} = \dfrac{-8}{2}$

    $= -4$,

    $\Rightarrow \quad a = -12$

13. (c)

    $AB^2 = 5^2 = 25$

    $\Rightarrow \quad (-1 - 2)^2 + (x + 2)^2 = 25$

    $\Rightarrow \quad (-3)^2 + (x + 2)^2 = 25$

    $\Rightarrow \quad x^2 + 4x + 13 = 25$

    $\Rightarrow \quad x^2 + 4x - 12 = 0$

    $\Rightarrow \quad (x + 6)(x - 2) = 0$

    $\Rightarrow \quad x = -6$

    or $\quad x = 2$

14. (b)

    Let the required ratio be $k : 1$

    Then the point of division is $\left(\dfrac{3k + 2}{k + 1}, \dfrac{7k - 2}{k + 1}\right)$

    This point lies on $2x + y - 4 = 0$

    $\therefore \dfrac{2(3k + 2)}{k + 1} + \dfrac{7k - 2}{k + 1} = 4$

    $\Rightarrow \quad 6k + 4 + 7k - 2 = 4k + 4$

    $\Rightarrow \quad 9k = 2 \Rightarrow k = \dfrac{2}{9}$

    $\therefore$ required ratio $= \dfrac{2}{9} : 1 = 2 : 9$

15. (c)

    Coordinates of D = Cordinates of midpoint of BC

    $= \left(\dfrac{6 + 1}{2}, \dfrac{5 + 4}{2}\right)$ i.e. $\left(\dfrac{7}{2}, \dfrac{9}{2}\right)$

16. (d)

    Coordinates of centroid are

    $\left(\dfrac{-1 + 5 + 8}{3}, \dfrac{0 - 2 + 2}{3}\right)$ i.e. $(4, 0)$

17. (c)

    Let (x, y) be the required point. Then

    $\dfrac{-1 + 5 + x}{3} = 0$ and $\dfrac{4 + 2 + y}{3} = -3$

    $\Rightarrow \quad 4 + x = 0$ and $6 + y - 9$

    $\Rightarrow \quad x = -4$

    and $\quad y = -15$

    $\therefore$ coordinates of C are $(-4, -15)$

18. (c)

    $AB^2 = 25$

    $\Rightarrow \quad (4 - 1)^2 + (P - 0)^2 = 25$

    $\Rightarrow \quad 3^2 + P^2 = 25$

    $\Rightarrow \quad P^2 = 16$

    $P = \pm 4$

19. (d)

    Let the fourth vertex be D(a, b). Then,

    Midpoint of AC = midpoint of BD

    $\Rightarrow \left(\dfrac{-2 + 8}{2}, \dfrac{3 + 3}{2}\right) = \left(\dfrac{6 + a}{2}, \dfrac{7 + b}{2}\right)$

    $\Rightarrow \quad \dfrac{6 + a}{2} = \dfrac{6}{2} = 3$

    and $\quad \dfrac{7 + b}{2} = 3$

    $\Rightarrow \quad 6 + a = 6$ and $7 + b = 6$

    $\Rightarrow \quad a = 0$ and $b - 1$

    Hence the required point is D(0, -1)

20. (a)

    $AB^2 = (4 + 4)^2 + (0 - 0)^2$

    $= (8^2 + 0^2) = (64 + 0) = 64$

    $AB = \sqrt{64} = 8$ units

    $BC^2 = (0 - 4)^2 + (3 - 0)^2$

    $= (-4)^2 + (3)^2 = (16 + 9)$

    $= 25$

    $BC = \sqrt{25} = 5$ units

    $AC^2 = (0 + 4)^2 + (3 - 0)^2$

    $= (4^2 + 3^2) = (16 + 9)$

    $\Rightarrow \quad AC = \sqrt{25} = 5$ units

    $\therefore \triangle ABC$ is isosceles.

National Talent Search Examination (NTSE)-X

Previous Year Questions

1. If the points A(2, 3), B(5, k) and C(6, 7) are collinear, then **[NTSE 2001 – MP first stage paper]**
   (a) $k = 4$ (b) $k = 6$
   (c) $k = -\dfrac{3}{2}$ (d) $k = \dfrac{11}{4}$

2. If the points A(1, 2), O(0, 0) and C(a, b) are collinear, then **[NTSE 2003 – Delhi second stage paper]**
   (a) $a = b$ (b) $a = 2b$
   (c) $2a = b$ (d) $a + b = 0$

3. The area of $\triangle ABC$ with vertices A (a, $b + c$), B (b, $c + a$) and C(c, $a + bs$) is **[NTSE 2012 – Jammu first stage paper]**
   (a) $(a + b + c)^2$ (b) $a + b + c$
   (c) abc (d) 0

4. The point which lies on the perpendicular bisector of the line segment joining the points A(– 2, –5) and B(2, 5) is **[NTSE 2006 – Assam first stage paper]**
   (a) (0, 0) (b) (0, 2)
   (c) (2, 0) (d) (–2, 0)

5. The area of $\triangle ABC$ with vertices A(3,0), B(7, 0) and C(8, 4) is **[NTSE 2003 – Haryana first stage paper]**
   (a) 14 sq. units (b) 28 sq. units
   (c) 8 sq. units (d) 6 sq. units

6. AOBC is a rectangle whose three vertices are A(0,3) O(0,0) and B(5, 0). Length of each of its diagonal is **[NTSE 2005 – Andhra Pradesh second stage paper]**
   (a) 5 units (b) 3 units
   (c) $\sqrt{34}$ units (d) 4 units

7. Find the value of a, so that the point (3, a) lies on the line represented by $2x - 3y = 5$. **[NTSE 2004 – Gujrat second stage paper]**
   (a) $\dfrac{1}{3}$ (b) $\dfrac{2}{3}$
   (c) $\dfrac{4}{3}$ (d) $\dfrac{5}{3}$

8. Find the ceontroid of $\triangle ABC$ whose vertices are A(2, 2) B(– 4, – 4) and C (5, – 8) **[NTSE 2000 – UP second stage paper]**
   (a) $\left(1, -\dfrac{10}{3}\right)$ (b) $\left(-1, \dfrac{10}{3}\right)$
   (c) $\left(-1, -\dfrac{10}{3}\right)$ (d) $\left(1, \dfrac{10}{3}\right)$

9. The line segment joining the points A(4,–5) and B (4, 5) is divided by the point P such that $\dfrac{AP}{AB} = \dfrac{2}{5}$. Find the coordinates of P. **[NTSE 2004 – Tamilnadu first stage paper]**
   (a) (4, 1) (b) (4, – 1)
   (c) (– 4, 1) (d) (– 4, – 1)

10. A is a point on y-axis at a distance of 4 units from x-axis lying below x-axis. The coordinates of A are **[NTSE 2012 – Bihar stage paper]**
    (a) (4, 0) (b) (0, 4)
    (c) (– 4, 0) (d) (0, – 4)

Co-ordinate Geometry

Answer Key

| 1. (b) | 2. (c) | 3. (d) | 4. (a) | 5. (c) | 6. (c) | 7. (a) | 8. (a) | 9. (b) | 10. (d) |

Explanatory Notes

1. (b)
   Here $(x_1 = 2, y_1 = 3)$ $(x_2 = 5, y_2 = k)$
   $(x_3 = 6, y_3 = 7)$
   Since the given points are collinear, we must have :
   $x_1(y_2 - y_3) + x_2(y_3 - y_1) + x_3(y_1 - y_2) = 0$
   $2(k - 7) + 5(7 - 3) + 6(3 - k) = 0$
   $\Rightarrow 2k - 14 + 20 + 18 - 6k = 0$
   $4k = 24 \Rightarrow k = 6$

2. (c)
   Here $(x_1 = 1, y_1 = 2)$ $(x_2 = 0, y_2 = 0)$ and
   $(x_3 = a, y_3 = b)$
   Since the given points are collinear, we have :
   $x_1(y_2 - y_3) + x_2(y_3 - y_1) + x_3(y_1 - y_2) = 0$
   $1.(0 - b) + 0.(b - 2) + a.(2 - 0) = 0$
   $\Rightarrow -b + 0 + 2a = 0$
   $\Rightarrow 2a = b$

3. (d)
   Here $(x_1 = a, y_1 = b + c)$ $(x_2 = b, y_2 = c - a)$ and
   $(x_3 = c, y_3 = a + b)$
   $\therefore \Delta = \frac{1}{2}\{x_1(y_2 - y_3) + x_2(y_3 - y_1) + x_3(y_1 - y_2)\}$
   $= \frac{1}{2}(a(c + a - a - b) + b(a + b - b - c) + c(b + c - c - a)]$
   $= \frac{1}{2}\{a(c - b) + b(a - c) + c(b - a) = \frac{1}{2} \times 0 = 0$

4. (d)
   Midpoint of AB is $\left(\frac{-2 + 2}{2}, \frac{-5 + 5}{2}\right) = (0, 0)$
   $\therefore$ required point is (0, 0)

5. (c)
   Here $(x_1 = 3, y_1 = 0)$ $(x_2 = 7, y_2 = 0)$ and
   $(x_3 = 8, y_3 = 4)$
   $\therefore$ area of $\Delta ABC = \frac{1}{2}\{x_1(y_2 - y_3) + x_2(y_3 - y_1)$
   $+ x_3(y_1 - y_2)\}$
   $= \frac{1}{2}\{3(0 - 4) + 7(4 - 0) + 8(0 - 0)\}$
   $= \frac{1}{2}\{-12 + 28 + 0\}$
   $= \frac{1}{2} \times 16 = 8$ sq. uints

6. (c)
   Diagonal $AB = \sqrt{(0-5)^2 + (3-0)^2}$
   $= \sqrt{(-5)^2 + (3)^2}$
   $= \sqrt{25 + 9} = \sqrt{34}$ units

7. (a)
   Since (3, a) lines on the line $2x - 3y = 5$, we have
   $2 \times 3 - 3a = 5$
   $3a = 1 \Rightarrow a = \frac{1}{3}$

8. (a)
   Let $(x_1 = 2, y_1 = 3)$ $(x_2 = 4, y_2 = k)$ and
   $(x_3 = 6, y_3 = -3)$
   $\therefore \Delta = 0$
   $\Rightarrow x_1(y_2 - y_3) + x_2(y_3 - y_1) + x_3(y_1 - y_2) = 0$
   $\Rightarrow 2(k + 3) + 4(-3 - 3) + 6(3 - k) = 0$
   $-4k = 0 \Rightarrow k = 0$

9. (b)
   The end points of AB are A(4, -5) and B(4, 5)
   $\therefore x_1 = 4, y_1 = -5$
   $x_2 = 4, y_2 = 5$
   Given that
   (AP = 2, AB = 5)
   $\Rightarrow$ PB = (AB - AP) = (5 - 2) = 3
   $\therefore$ AP : PB = 2 : 3)
   so M = 2 and n = 3
   Let the required point be P(x, y)
   By the section formula we have,
   $x = \frac{(mx_2 + nx_1)}{m + n}, y = \frac{mx_2 + ny_1}{m + n}$
   $x = \frac{2 \times 4 + 3 \times 4}{(2 + 3)}, y = \frac{(2 \times 5 + 3 \times (-5))}{(2 + 3)}$
   $x = 4, y = -1$

10. (d)
    Clearly, the point y-axis, below x-axis, at a distance of 4 units from x–axis is A(0, -4).

UNIT 9
Triangles & Quadrilaterals

- **Quadrilateral** is a polygon having 4 sides. ABCD is a quadrilateral and AC and BD are its diagonals.

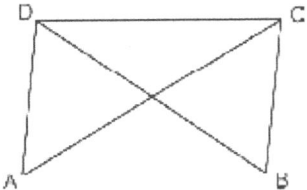

- **Types of Quadrilaterals**
  There are different types of quadrilaterals based on their properties. The names of quadrilaterals are as follows:
  - Parallelogram
  - Rectangle
  - Rhombus
  - Square
  - Trapezium

  These are some special quadrilaterals.

- **Parallelogram**
  A parallelogram has its opposite pairs of sides parallel. Its other properties are:
  (i) The opposite sides are equal.
  (ii) The opposite angles are equal.
  (iii) The diagonals bisect each other.

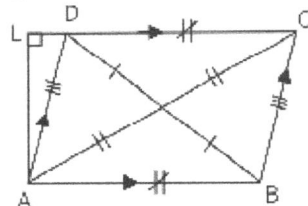

  In the figure above, the perpendicular AL to DC has been drawn. AL is called the height of ABCD.

- **Rectangle**
  Rectangle is a parallelogram having all angles equal. Its other properties are:
  (i) The diagonals are equal.
  (ii) Each angle is a right angle.

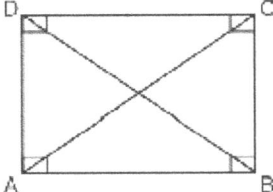

- **Rhombus**
  Rhombus is a parallelogram having all sides equal. Its other properties are:
  (i) The diagonals bisect each other at right angles.
  (ii) The diagonals bisect the angles at each vertex.

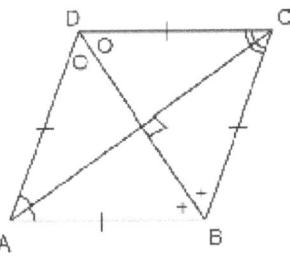

- **Square**
  Square is a parallelogram having all its sides equal and all its angles equal. Its other properties are:
  (i) The diagonals bisect each other at right angles and are equal.
  (ii) The diagonals bisect the angles at each vertex and each half is equal to 45°.

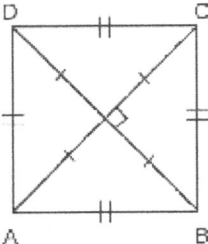

- **Trapezium**
  Trapezium is a quadrilateral having one pair of opposite sides parallel. A trapezium with non-parallel sides equal is called an isosceles trapezium.

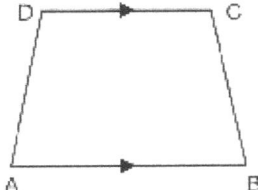

TRIANGLES

■ **Key Concepts**

1. If two triangles ABC and PQR are congruent under the corresponding A ↔ P, B ↔ Q and C ↔ R, then symbolically, it is expressed as ΔABC ≅ ΔPQR.

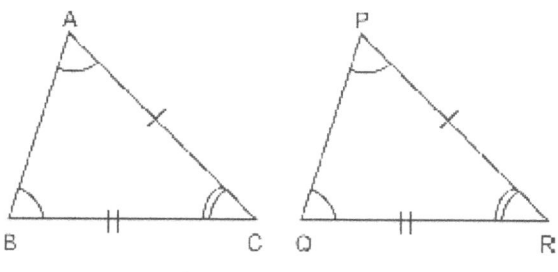

Congruence of Triangles

2. **Properties of Congruence of Triangles**
   - **Reflexive Property:** Every triangle is congruent to itself.
   - **Symmetric Property:** If ΔABC ≅ DEF, then ΔDEF ≅ ΔABC
   - **Transitive Property :** If ΔABC ≅ ΔDEF, ΔDEF ≅ ΔJKL, then ΔABC ≅ ΔJKL.

   The above properties prove the congruence of triangles.

3. **Determination of Congruence of Triangles**

   Angle Angle Angle (AAA): When three angles of two triangles are equal, both triangles are similar triangles. That is, the corresponding angles have equal measurement.

   Side Side Side (SSS): When three corresponding sides of two triangles are equal, the triangles are similar triangles.

   Side Angle Side (SAS): When two sides in one triangle are in the same ratio to the corresponding sides of the other triangle and the included angles are equal, both triangles are similar.

   Angle-Angle-Side (AAS): When two pairs of angles of two triangles are equal in measurement and pair of corresponding sides is equal in length, the triangles are called as congruent triangles.

   Right-angle-Hypotenuse-Side (RHS): When two right-angled triangles have their hypotenuses equal in length and the shorter sides of two right triangles are equal in length, the triangles are called as congruent triangles.

4. Two circles of the same radii are congruent.
5. Two squares of the same sides are congruent.
6. Each angle of an equilateral triangle is of 60°.
7. In congruent triangles corresponding parts are equal and we write this as 'CPCT' for corresponding parts of congruent triangles.
8. SAS congruence rule holds but ASS or SSA rule does not.
9. Angles opposite to equal sides of an isosceles triangle are equal.
10. The sides opposite to equal angles of a triangle are equal.
11. RHS stands for Right Angle–Hypotenuse–Side.
12. If two sides of a triangle are unequal, then the greater angle is opposite to the greater side.
13. If two angles of a triangle are unequal, the greater side is opposite to the greater angle.
14. The sum of any two sides of a triangle is greater than the third side.
15. The difference between any two sides of a triangle is less than the third side.
16. If the sum of two adjacent angles is 180°, then the non-common arms of the angles form a line.
17. **Similar Triangles**

    Similar Triangles are two triangles that have congruent corresponding angles and the ratios of corresponding sides are in pro-portion. This proportion is also called as similarity ratio. The similar triangles are also called as equiangular triangle. This is because in equilateral triangles, both the triangles have equal angles. The similar triangles have common shape but different sizes.

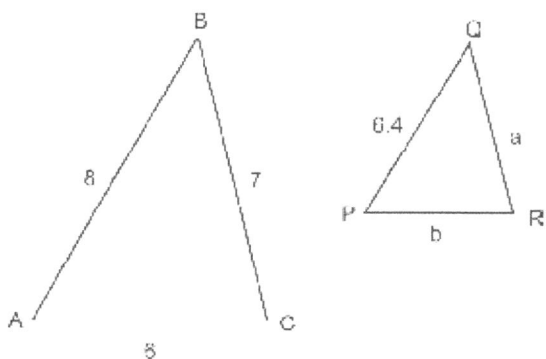

In the above figures, the two triangles are of same shape but different sizes. And so, the above two triangles are called similar triangles.

18. **Properties of Similar Triangles**
    - **Corresponding** Angles of both the triangles are equal.
      < P = < A, < Q = < B, < R = < C
    - The corresponding sides of the triangles have same ratio.
      AB/PQ = BC/QR = AC/PR = X, where X is called the similarity ratio.

19. **Rules of Similar Triangles**

    There are three rules to test the similarity of triangles.
    (i) Angle Angle Angle (AAA)
    (ii) Side Side Side (SSS)
    (iii) Side Angle Side (SAS)

AAA Similarity: When three angles of the triangles are equal, the two triangles are similar triangles, i.e. the corresponding angles have equal measurement.

SSS Similarity: When three corresponding sides of the triangles are equal, the triangles are similar triangles.

SAS Similarity: When two sides in one triangle are in the same proportion to the corresponding sides of the other and the included angles are equal, both triangles are similar triangles.

20. Two geometrical figures are called congruent if they superpose exactly on each other that is they are of same shape and sizes.

21. Two figures are similar, if they are of the same shape but of different sizes.

22. **Basic Proportionality Theorem (Thales Theorem):** If a line is drawn parallel to one side of a triangle to intersect other two sides in distinct points, the other two sides are divided in the same ratio.

23. **Converse of Basic Proportionality Theorem:** If a line divides any two sides of a triangle in the same ratio, then the line is parallel to the third side.

24. A triangle in which two sides are equal is called an isosceles triangle.

25. **Pythagoras Theorem:** In a right triangle, the square of the hypotenuse is equal to the sum of the squares of the other two sides.

26. **Converse of Pythagoras Theorem:** If in a triangle, square of one side is equal to the sum of the squares of the other two sides, then the angle opposite the first side is a right angle.

Solved Examples

1. The similar triangles ABC and PQR are shown below. Find the value of a and b in the triangle PQR.

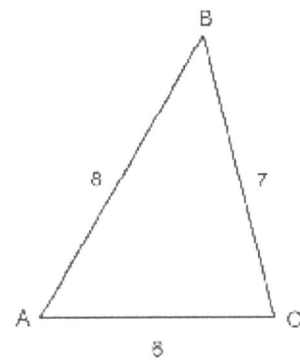

Solution: We know that the corresponding sides of the triangles have same ratio,

That is, AB/PQ = BC/QR = AC/PR
Consider, AB/PQ = BC/QR
$8/6.4 = 7/a$
Apply cross multiplication,
$8a = 7 \times 6.4$
$8a = 44.8$
$a = 5.6$
QR = a = 5.6
Consider BC/QR = AC/PR
$7/5.6 = 6/b$
Apply cross multiplication,
$7b = 33.6$
$b = 33.67$
$b = 4.8$
PR = b = 4.8

2. Prove that AP = BQ (see the given figure).

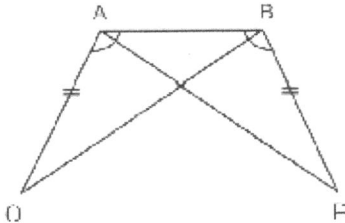

Solution: It is given that,
$\angle BAQ = \angle ABP$
$AQ = BP$
To Prove : $AP = BQ$
Proof:

Statement	Reason
In $\triangle ABP$ and $\triangle ABQ$	
1. BP = AQ	data
2. AB = AB	common
3. $\angle ABP = \angle BAQ$	data
4. $\triangle ABP \cong \triangle BAQ$	(S.A.S)
5. $AP \cong BQ$	Statement (4)

3. In the figure, AD bisects BE, $\angle B = \angle E$; prove that
   (i) $\angle A = \angle D$ (ii) AB = DE

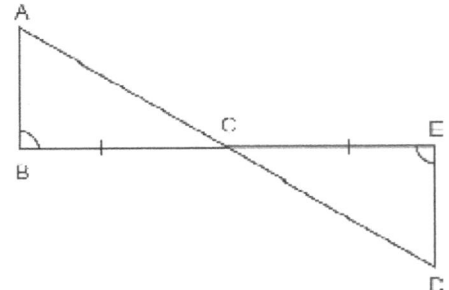

Solution: It is given that,
BC = CE and ∠B = ∠E
To Prove:
(i) ∠A = ∠D   (ii) AB = DE
Proof:

Statement	Reason
In △ABC and △CED	
1. ∠B = ∠E	Data
2. ∠ABC = ∠DEC	Vertically opposite angles
3. BC = CE	data
4. △ABC ≅ △DEC	(A.A.S)
5. ∴ ∠A = ∠D	Statement (4)
6. AB = CE	Statement (4)

4. Equilateral △ABD and △ACE are drawn on the sides of △ABC
   Prove that CD = BE

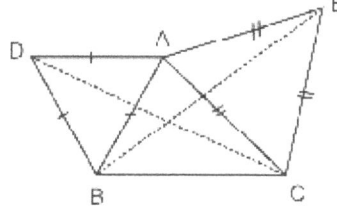

Solution:
It is given that,
ABC is a triangle. ABD and ACE are equilateral triangles.
To Prove: CD = BE
Construction: Join BE and CD.
Proof:

Statement	Reason
1. ∠BAD = ∠CAE	each ∠ = 60° [∠s of eq. △s]
2. ∠BAD + ∠BAC = ∠CAE + ∠BAC	adding ∠BAC to both sides
3. ∠CAD = ∠BAE	statement (2)
In △ACD and △ABE	
4. AD = AB	sides of an equilateral triangle
5. AC = AE	sides of an equilateral triangle
6. ∠CAD = ∠BAE	Statement (3)
7. △ACD ≅ △AEB	(S.A.S)
8. DC = BE	Statement (7)

5. A 13 m long ladder reaches a window of a building 12 m above the ground. Determine the distance of the foot of the ladder from the building.
   Solution:

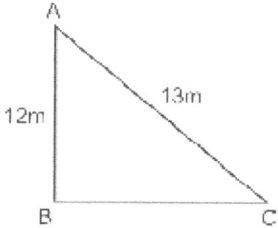

Distance of the foot of the ladder from the building
= BC
= $\sqrt{(13)^2 - (12)^2}$
= $\sqrt{169 - 144}$
= $\sqrt{25}$ = 5 m

6. Find the height of an equilateral triangle of side 12 cm. Find each of its altitude.
   Solution:

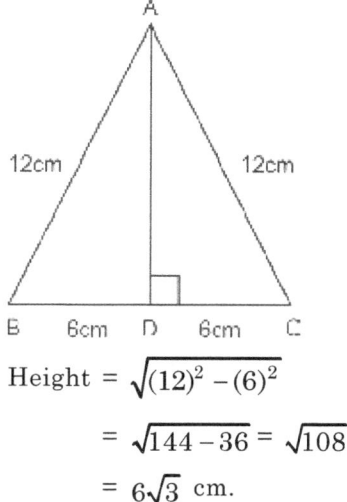

Height = $\sqrt{(12)^2 - (6)^2}$
= $\sqrt{144 - 36}$ = $\sqrt{108}$
= $6\sqrt{3}$ cm.

Multiple Choice Questions

1. In a $\triangle ABC$, it is given that AD is the internal bisetor of $\angle A$. If BD = 4 cm, DC = 5 cm and AB = 6 cm, then AC = ?

   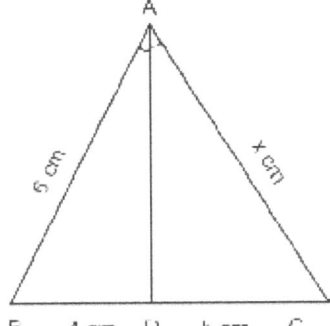

   (a) 4.5 cm (b) 8 cm
   (c) 9 cm (d) 7.5 cm

2. In a $\triangle ABC$, it is given that AD is the internal bisetor of A. If AB = 10 cm, AC = 14 cm and BC = 6 cm, then CD = ?

   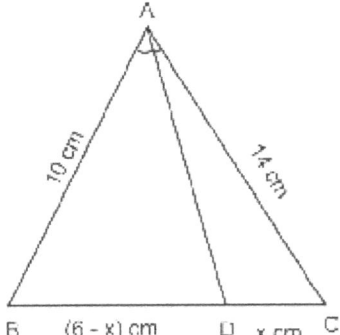

   (a) 4.8 cm (b) 3.5 cm
   (c) 7 cm (d) 10.5 cm

3. In a triangle, the perpendicular from the vertex to the base bisects the base. The triangle is
   (a) right-angled
   (b) isosceles
   (c) scalene
   (d) obtuse-angled

4. In an equilateral triangle ABC, if AD + BC then which of the following is true ?

   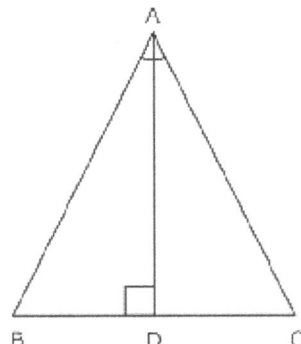

   (a) $2AB^2 = 3AD^2$ (b) $4AB^2 = 3AD^2$
   (c) $3AB^2 = 4AD^2$ (d) $3AB^2 = 2AD^2$

5. In a rhombus of side 10 cm, one of the diagonals is 12 cm long. The length of the second diagonal is
   (a) 20 cm (b) 18 cm
   (c) 16 cm (d) 22 cm

6. In lengths of the diagonals of a rhombus are 24 cm and 10 cm. The length of each side of the rhombus is
   (a) 12 cm (b) 13 cm
   (c) 14 cm (d) 17 cm

7. If the diagonals of a quadrilateral divide each other proportionally, then it is a
   (a) parallelogram (b) trapezium
   (c) rectangle (d) square

8. In the given figure, ABCD is a traperzium whose diagonals AC and BD intersect at O such that OA = (3x – 1) cm, OB = (2x + 1) cm, OC = (5x – 3) cm and OD = (6x – 5) cm. Then x = ?

   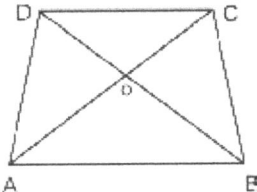

   (a) 2 (b) 3
   (c) 2.5 (d) 4

9. The line segments joining the mid points of the adjacent sides of a quadrilateral form
   (a) a parallelogram
   (b) a rectangle
   (c) a square
   (d) a rhombus

10. If the bisector of an angle of a triangle bisects the opposite side, then the triangle is
    (a) scalene (b) equilateral
    (c) isosceles (d) right angled

11. $\triangle ABC \sim \triangle DEF$ and the perimeters of $\triangle ABC$ an $\triangle DEF$ are 30 cm and 18 cm respectively. If BC = 9 cm, then EF ?
    (a) 6.3 cm (b) 5.4 cm
    (c) 7.2 cm (d) 4.5 cm

12. $\triangle ABC \sim \triangle DEF$ such that AB = 9.1 cm and De = 6.5 cm. If the perimeter of $\triangle DEF$ is 25 cm. What is the perimeter of $\triangle ABC$?
    (a) 35 cm (b) 28 cm
    (c) 42 cm (d) 40 cm

13. In $\triangle ABC$, it is given that AB = 9 cm, BC = 6 cm and CA = 7.5. Also, $\triangle DEF$ is given such that EF = 8 cm and $\triangle DEF \sim \triangle ABC$. Then, perimeter of $\triangle DEF$ is
    (a) 2.25 cm (b) 25 cm
    (c) 27 cm (d) 30 cm

Triangles & Quadrilaterals

14. It is given that ΔABC ~ ΔDEF. If ∠A = 30°, ∠C = 50°, AB = 5 cm, AC = 8 cm and DF = 7.5 cm, then which of the following is true ?
    (a) DE = 12 cm, ∠F = 50°
    (b) DE = 12 cm, ∠F = 100°
    (c) EF = 12 cm, ∠D = 100°
    (d) EF = 12 cm, ∠D = 30°

15. In ΔABC and ΔDEF, it is given that $\dfrac{AB}{DE} = \dfrac{BC}{FD}$, then
    (a) ∠B = ∠E   (b) ∠A = ∠D
    (c) ∠B = ∠D   (d) ∠A = ∠F

16. In ΔDEF and ΔPQR, it is given that ∠D = ∠Q and ∠R = ∠E, then which of the following is not true ?
    (a) $\dfrac{EF}{PR} = \dfrac{DF}{PQ}$
    (b) $\dfrac{DE}{PQ} = \dfrac{EF}{RP}$
    (c) $\dfrac{DE}{QR} = \dfrac{DF}{PQ}$
    (d) $\dfrac{EF}{RP} = \dfrac{DE}{QR}$

17. In ΔABC and ΔDEF, we have $\dfrac{AB}{DE} = \dfrac{BC}{EF} = \dfrac{AC}{DF} = \dfrac{5}{7}$, then ar (ΔABC) : ar (ΔEF) = ?
    (a) 5 : 7   (b) 24 : 49
    (c) 49 : 25   (d) 125 : 343

18. In ΔABC ~ ΔDEF such that ar (ΔABC) = 36 cm² and ar (ΔDEF) : 49 cm². Then the ratio of their corresponding sides is
    (a) 36 : 49   (b) 6 : 7
    (c) 7 : 6   (d) $\sqrt{6} : \sqrt{7}$

19. Two isosceles triangles have their corresponding angles equal and their areas are in the ratio 25 : 36. The ratio of their corresponding height is
    (a) 25 : 36   (b) 36 : 25
    (c) 5 : 6   (d) 6 : 5

20. The line segments joining the mid points of the sides of a triangle form four triangles, each of which is
    (a) congruent to the original triangle
    (b) similar to the original triangle
    (c) an isosceles triangle
    (d) an equilateral triangle.

Answer Key

1. (d)	2. (b)	3. (b)	4. (c)	5. (c)	6. (b)	7. (b)	8. (a)	9. (a)	10. (c)	11. (b)
12. (a)	13. (d)	14. (b)	15. (c)	16. (b)	17. (b)	18. (b)	19. (c)	20. (b)		

Explanatory Notes

1. (d)
   We know that BD : DC = AB : BC
   $\therefore 4 : 5 = 6 : x \Rightarrow \dfrac{4}{5} = \dfrac{6}{x} \Rightarrow 4x = 30 \Rightarrow x = 7.5$ cm

2. (b)
   Let CD be x cm. Then BD = $(6 - x)$ cm.
   Now BD : CD = AB : AC
   $\Rightarrow \dfrac{6-x}{x} = \dfrac{10}{14} = \dfrac{5}{7} \Rightarrow 42 - 7x = 5x$
   $\Rightarrow 12x = 4x \Rightarrow x = 3.5$
   $\therefore$ CD = 3.5 cm

3. (b)
   In an isosceles triangle, the perpendicular from the vetex bisects the base.

4. (c)
   $AB^2 = BD^2 + AD^2$

   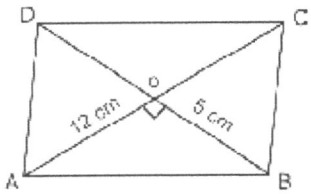

   $\Rightarrow \quad AB^2 = \left(\dfrac{1}{2} AB\right)^2 + AD^2$
   $\Rightarrow \quad AB^2 = \dfrac{1}{4} AB^2 + AD^2$
   $\Rightarrow \quad \dfrac{3}{4} AB^2 = AD^2$
   $\Rightarrow \quad 3AB^2 = 4AD^2$

5. (c)
   Let ABCD be a rhombus whose diagonals AC and BD interest at O.
   We know that the diagonals of a rhombus bisect each other at right angles.

   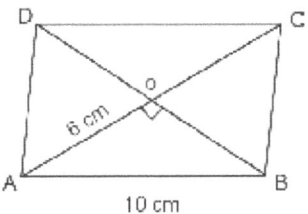

   Now, AB = 10 cm, OA = $\dfrac{1}{2}$ AC = 6 cm
   and $\angle AOB = 90°$
   $\therefore OB^2 = (AB^2 - OA^2) = \{(10)^2 - (6)^2\}$
   $\qquad = (100 - 36) = 64$ cm
   $\Rightarrow \quad OB = \sqrt{64} = 8$ cm
   $\Rightarrow \quad BD = (2 \times OB)$
   $\qquad = (2 \times 8)$ cm = 16 cm

6. (b)
   Let ABCD be a rhombus whose diagonals AC and BD interest at O, then
   OA = 12 cm, OB = 5 cm and $\angle AOB = 90°$

   $AB^2 = (OA^2 + OB^2) = (12)^2 + (5)^2 = 144 + 25 = 169$
   $\therefore AB = \sqrt{169} = 13$ cm
   $\therefore$ each side = 13 cm

7. (b)
   The diagonals of a tapezium divide each other proportionally.

8. (a)
   We know that the diagonals of trapezium divide each other proportionally.
   $\therefore \dfrac{OA}{OC} = \dfrac{OB}{OD} \Rightarrow \dfrac{3x-1}{5x-3} = \dfrac{2x+1}{6x-5}$
   $\therefore (3x - 1)(6x - 5) = (5x - 3)(2x + 1)$
   $\qquad 18x^2 - 21x + 5 = 10x^2 - x - 3$
   $\Rightarrow \quad 8x^2 - 20x + 8 = 0$
   $\Rightarrow \quad 2x^2 - 5x + 2 = 0$
   $\Rightarrow \quad 2x^2 - 4x - x + 2 = 0$
   $\Rightarrow \quad 2x(x - 2) - 2(x - 2) = 0$
   $\Rightarrow \quad (x - 2)(2x - 1) = 0$
   $\Rightarrow \quad x = 2$
   or $\quad x = \dfrac{1}{2}$
   But $x = \dfrac{1}{2}$ gives $(6x - 5) < 0$ and the distance cannot be negative.
   $\therefore \quad x = 2$

9. (a)
   The line segments joining the mid-points of the adjacent sides of a quadrilateral form a parallelogram

10. (c)
Let AD be the bisector of ∠A and △ABC such that BD = DC. Then
$$\frac{AB}{AC} = \frac{BD}{DC} = 1$$
⇒ AB = AC
So, the given triangle is isosceles.

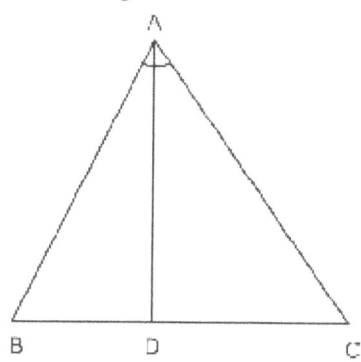

11. (b)
$$\frac{\text{Perimeter of }\triangle ABC}{\text{Perimeter of }\triangle DEF} = \frac{BC}{EF}$$
Let EF = x cm. Then
$$\frac{9}{x} = \frac{30}{18} \Rightarrow 30x = 18 \times 9$$
$$x = \frac{18 \times 9}{30} = \frac{27}{5} = 5.4 \text{ cm}$$

12. (a)
$$\frac{\text{Perimeter of }\triangle ABC}{\text{Perimeter of }\triangle DEF} = \frac{AB}{DE}$$
Let the perimeter of △ABC be p cm. Then,
$$\frac{9.1}{6.5} = \frac{p}{25} \Rightarrow \frac{7}{5} = \frac{p}{25}$$
∴ $p = \frac{25 \times 7}{5} = 35$ cm
∴ Perimeter of △ABC is 35 cm.

13. (d)
Perimeter of △ABC = (9 + 6 + 7.5) cm = 22.5 cm
Let the perimeter of △DEF be p cm. Then
$$\frac{\text{Perimeter of }\triangle DEF}{\text{Perimeter of }\triangle ABC} = \frac{EF}{BC} \Rightarrow \frac{p}{22.5} = \frac{8}{6}$$
∴ $p = \frac{22.5 \times 8}{6} = \frac{225 \times 8}{60} = 30$
Hence, the perimeter of △DEF is 30 cm

14. (b)
∠B = 180° − (30° + 50°) = 100°
since, △ABC ~ △DEF, we have :
∠D = ∠A = 30°, ∠F = ∠B = 100° and ∠E = ∠C = 50°
Let DE = x cm. Then,
$$\frac{AB}{DF} = \frac{AC}{DE} \Rightarrow \frac{5}{7.5} = \frac{8}{x}$$
∴ $5x = 8 \times 7.5$

⇒ $x = \frac{8 \times 7.5}{5} = 12$
Hence DE = 12 cm and ∠F = 100°

15. (c)
Clearly B ↔ D, A ↔ E and C ↔ F.
∴ ∠B = ∠D

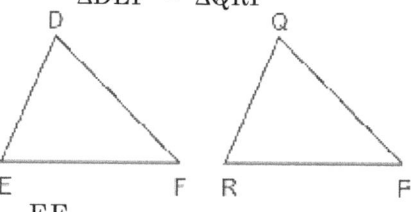

16. (b)
∠D = ∠Q, ∠E = ∠R
and ∠F = ∠P
∴ △DEF ~ △QRP
∴ $\frac{DE}{PQ} = \frac{EF}{RP}$ is not true.

17. (b)
$ar(\triangle ABC) : ar(\triangle DEF) = \left(\frac{AB}{DE}\right)^2 = \left(\frac{5}{7}\right)^2$
$= \frac{25}{49} = 25 : 49$

18. (b)
$$\frac{(AB)^2}{(DE)^2} = \frac{ar(ABC)}{ar(DEF)} = \frac{36}{49}$$
⇒ $\frac{AB}{DE} = \frac{6}{7} = 6 : 7$

19. (c)
Let h_1 and h_2 be the corresponding heights. Then,
$$\frac{h_1^2}{h_2^2} = \frac{25}{36}$$
⇒ $\left(\frac{h_1}{h_2}\right)^2 = \left(\frac{25}{36}\right) = \left(\frac{5}{6}\right)^2$
⇒ $\frac{h_1}{h_2} = \frac{5}{6}$
⇒ $h_1 : h_2 = 5 : 6$

20. (b)
The line sements joining the mid points of the sides of a triangle form four triangles each of which is similar to the original triangle.

Previous Year Questions

1. A vertical stick 1.8 m long casts a shadow 45 cm long on the ground. At the same time, what is the length of the shadow of a pole 6 m high ?
   [NTSE 2003 – Kerala second stage paper]
   (a) 2.4 m   (b) 1.35 m
   (c) 1.5 m   (d) 13.5 m

2. A vertical pole 6 m long casts a shadow of length 3.6 m on the ground. What is the height of a tower which casts a shadow of length 18 m at the same time ?
   [NTSE 2005 – Haryana first stage paper]
   (a) 10.8 m   (b) 28.8 m
   (c) 32.4 m   (d) 30 m

3. A ladder 25 m long just reaches the top of a building 24 m high from the ground. What is the distance of the foot of the ladder from the building?
   [NTSE 2000 – Manipur first stage paper]
   (a) 7 cm   (b) 14 cm
   (c) 21 cm   (d) 24.5 cm

4. In the given figure, O is point inside a ΔPQR such that $\angle POR = 90°$, then OP = 6 cm and OR = 8 cm. If PQ = 24 cm and $\angle QPR = 90°$, then QR = ?
   [NTSE 2012 – Delhi first stage paper]

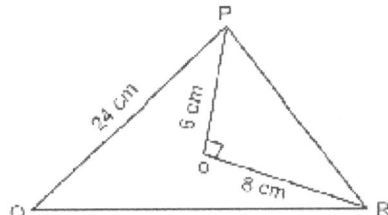

   (a) 28 cm   (b) 25 cm
   (c) 26 cm   (d) 32 cm

5. The hypotenuse of a right triangle is 25 cm. The other two sides are such that one is 5 cm longer than the other. The lengths of these sides are :
   [NTSE 2004 – Maharashtra second stage paper]
   (a) 10 cm, 15 cm   (b) 15 cm, 20 cm
   (c) 12 cm, 17 cm   (d) 13 cm, 18 cm

6. The height of an equilateral triangle having each side 12 cm is   *[NTSE 2001 – Bihar first stage paper]*
   (a) $6\sqrt{2}$ cm   (b) $6\sqrt{3}$ cm
   (c) $3\sqrt{6}$ cm   (d) $6\sqrt{6}$

7. In a ΔABC, it is given that AB = 6 cm, AC = 8 cm and AD is the bisector of $\angle A$. Then BD : DC = ?
   [NTSE 2012 – UP first stage paper]

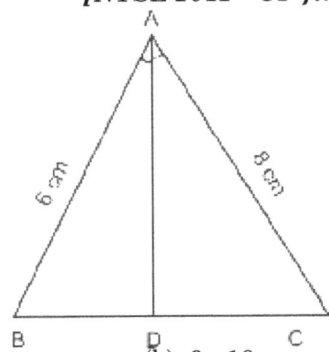

   (a) 3 : 4   (b) 9 : 16
   (c) 4 : 3   (d) $\sqrt{3} : 2$

8. In an isosceles ΔABC, if AC = BC and $AB^2 = 2AC^2$, then $\angle C = ?$ *[NTSE 2004 – Delhi second stage paper]*
   (a) 30°   (b) 45°
   (c) 60°   (d) 90°

9. In ΔABC, if AB = 16 cm, BC = 12 cm and AC = 20 cm, then ΔABC is
   [NTSE 2003 – MP first stage paper]
   (a) acute-angled   (b) right-angled
   (c) obtuse-angled   (d) None of these

10. In $\Delta ABC \sim \Delta DEF$, it is given that $\angle B = \angle E$, $\angle F = \angle C$ and AB = 3, then the two triangles are
    [NTSE 2005 – Andhra Pradesh first stage paper]
    (a) Congruent but not similar
    (b) Similar but not congruent
    (c) Neither congruent nor similar
    (d) Similar as well as congruent.

Triangles & Quadrilaterals

Answer Key

1. (c)	2. (d)	3. (a)	4. (c)	5. (b)	6. (b)	7. (a)	8. (d)	9. (b)	10. (b)

Explanatory Notes

1. (c)
   Let the required length of the shadow be x meters. Then, ratio of actual lengths = ratio of lengths of shadows.
   $$\therefore \quad \frac{1.8}{6} = \frac{0.45}{x}$$
   $$\Rightarrow \quad 1.8x = 6 \times 0.45 = 2.7$$
   $$\Rightarrow \quad x = \frac{2.7}{1.8} = \frac{3}{2} = 1.5 \text{ m}$$
   Hence, the length of the required shadow is 1.5 m

2. (d)
   Let the height of the tower be x meters.
   Then, ratio of actual heights
   $$= \text{ratio of lenghs of shadow}$$
   $$\therefore \quad \frac{6}{x} = \frac{3.6}{18}$$
   $$\Rightarrow \quad 3.6 \times x = 6 \times 18$$
   $$\Rightarrow \quad x = \frac{6 \times 18}{3.6} = 30 \text{ m}$$
   Hence, the height of the tower is 30 cm.

3. (a)
   Let AB be the ladder and BC be the wall.
   Then   AB = 25 m
   and   BC = 24 m

   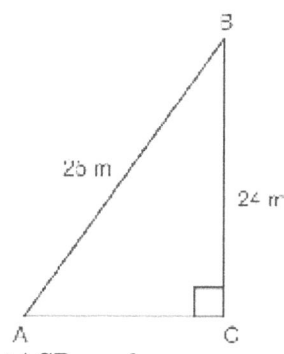

   From, right $\triangle ACB$, we have
   $$AC^2 = (AB)^2 - (BC)^2$$
   $$= (25)^2 - (24)^2 = 625 - 576$$
   $$AC^2 = 49$$
   $$AC = \sqrt{49} = 7 \text{ m}$$
   Hence, the distane of the foot of the ladder from the wall is 7 m.

4. (c)
   From right triangle $\triangle POR$, we have
   $$PR^2 = (OP^2 + OR^2) = (6^2 + 8^2)$$
   $$= (36 + 64) = 100$$
   $$\Rightarrow \quad PR = \sqrt{100} = 10 \text{ cm}$$
   From right triangle $\triangle QPR$, we have
   $$QR^2 = (PQ^2 + PR^2)$$
   $$= (24)^2 + (10)^2$$
   $$= 576 + 100 = 676$$
   $$\Rightarrow \quad QR = \sqrt{676} = 26 \text{ cm}$$

5. (c)
   Let the two sides be x cm and $(x + 5)$ cm. Then,
   $$x^2 + (x+5)^2 = (25)^2$$
   $$x^2 + (x^2 + 10x + 25) = 625$$
   $$2x^2 + 10x + 25 = 625$$
   $$\Rightarrow \quad x^2 + 5x - 300 = 0$$
   $$x^2 + 20x - 15x - 300 = 0$$
   $$x(x + 20) - 15(x + 20) = 0$$
   $$\Rightarrow \quad x(x + 20) - 15(x + 20) = 0$$
   $$(x - 15)(x + 20) = 0 \quad \Rightarrow x = 15$$
   $\therefore$ required sides are 15 cm and 20 m.

6. (b)
   Let $\triangle ABC$ be an equilateral triangle having each side 12 cm. Draw AD $\perp$ BC. Then, D is the mid point of BC.
   In right triangle $\triangle ADB$, we have
   $$AB = 12 \text{ cm and } BD = 6 \text{ cm}$$
   $$\therefore \quad AD^2 = (AB^2 - BD^2)$$
   $$= (12)^2 - (6)^2$$
   $$= (144 - 36) = 108$$
   $$\Rightarrow \quad AD = \sqrt{108} = \sqrt{36 \times 3}$$
   $$= 6\sqrt{3} \text{ cm}$$
   $\therefore$ its height = $6\sqrt{3}$ cm.

7. (a)
   We know that BD : DC = AB : AC = 6 : 8 = 3 : 4

8. (a)
   $$AB^2 = 2AC^2 = AC^2 + AC^2$$
   $$= BC^2 + AC^2 \quad [AC = BC]$$
   $\therefore$ by converse of pythagoras theorem,
   we have : $\angle C = 90°$

9. (b)
   $$AB^2 + BC^2 = (16)^2 + (12)^2 = 256 + 144$$
   $$= 400 = (20)^2 = AC^2$$
   $\therefore \triangle ABC$ is right-angled.

10. (b)
    $\angle B = \angle E, \angle C = \angle F$ and $\angle A = \angle D$
    $\therefore \quad \triangle ABC \sim \triangle DEF$
    But AB = 3DE $\Rightarrow$ AB $\neq$ DE
    $\triangle ABC$ and $\triangle DEF$ are not congruent
    So, the given triangles are similar but not congruent.

UNIT 10
Circles

- **Circle**

  Circle is a set of those points in a plane, which are at a constant distance from a fixed point in the plane.

  A circle is a plane figure bounded by one curved line, every point of which is equally distant from a certain point within, which is called its centre.

  Origin: Origin refers to the centre of a circle.

  Radius: The distance from the centre of a circle to any given point on the circle is known as the radius of a circle.

  Diameter: Any straight line drawn through the centre and ending at both ways by the circumference is called diameter. Diameter is just the double of radius.

  Circumference: The distance around a circle, which is the bounding line is called the circumference.

  Chord: A straight line joining any two points on the circumference of a circle is called a chord.

  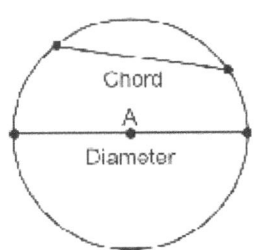 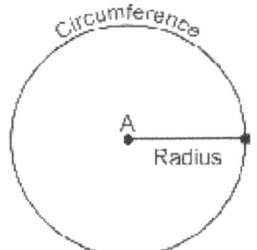

  Arc: Any portion of the circumference of a circle is referred as an arc.

  Sector: A sector is that part of a circle, which lies between an arc and two radii joining the extremities of the centre. The most important sector is a quadrant, which is one-fourth of the circle.

  Tangent of a circle: It is a line perpendicular to the radius that touches only one point on the circle.

  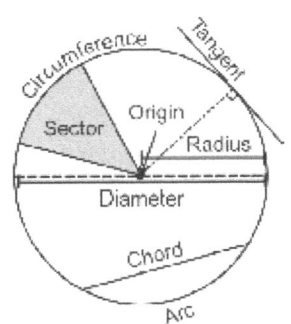

  Pi (π): An approximate value of π is 22/7 which is correct to two decimal places. A more accurate value of π is 3.14159 which is correct to five decimal places.

- **Key Points on Circles**
  1. A diameter of circle is its longest chord.
  2. A line can meet a circle at the most in two points.
  3. In a circle, perpendicular from the centre to a chord bisects the chord.
  4. In a circle, the line joining the midpoint of a chord to the centre is perpendicular to the chord.
  5. Equal chords of a circle are equivalent from the centre of the circle.
  6. In a circle, the chords which subtend equal angles at the centre are equal.
  7. The two points of intersections determine a chord of the circle.
  8. In a circle, equal chords subtend equal angles at the centre.
  9. Triangle is a polygon with 3 sides.
  10. Quadrilateral is a polygon with 4 sides.
  11. The chords corresponding to congruent arcs are equal.
  12. If two arcs of a circle (or of congruent circles) are congruent, then the corresponding chords are equal.
  13. If two chords of a circle (or of congruent circles) are equal, then their corresponding arcs (minor, major or semi-circular) are congruent.
  14. One and only one circle can be drawn through three non-collinear points.
  15. An infinite number of circles can be drawn through a given point P.
  16. An infinite number of circles can be drawn through the two given points.
  17. Perpendicular bisectors of two chords of a circle, intersect each other at the centre of the circle.
  18. The angle subtended by an arc at the centre is double the angle subtended by it at any point on the remaining part of the circle.
  19. Angles in the same segment of a circle are equal.
  20. An angle in a semi–circle is a right angle.
  21. The arc of a circle subtending a right angle at any point of the circle in its alternate segment is a semi-circle.
  22. If a line segment joining two points subtends equal angles at two other points lying on the same side of the line segment, the four points are con-cyclic, i.e., lie on the same circle.
  23. An angle in a semi–circle is a right angle.

Circles

24. The arc of a circle subtending a right angle at any point of the circle in its alternate segment is a semi-circle.
25. If the sum of any pair of opposite angles of a quadrilateral is 180°, then the quadrilateral is cyclic.
26. Any exterior angle of a cyclic quadrilateral is equal to the interior opposite angle.

■ **Circle Formulas**
Diameter of a Circle $(d) = 2 \times$ Radius
Radius of a Circle $(r) = \dfrac{\text{diameter}}{2}$
Circumference of a Circle $= 2\pi r$
Area of a Circle $= 2\pi r$

Solved Examples

1. The radius of the bicycle wheel of a boy, Ali is 29 cm. He cycles from his house to school and the wheel has made 350 complete turns. Find the distance of the school from his house, giving your answer in metres, correct to the nearest metre.
   (Take $\pi = \dfrac{22}{7}$)

   Solution:
   The radius of the bicycle wheel $r = 29$ cm
   The circumference of the wheel cm
   $2\pi r = 2 \times 3.142 \times 29$
   The wheel has made 350 complete turns for the journey.
   ∴ The distance of the school from Ali's home
   $= 2 \times 3.142 \times 29 \times 350$ cm
   $= \dfrac{(2 \times 3.142 \times 29 \times 350)}{100} m$
   $= 638$ m (to the nearest to metre)

2. A wheel has radius 35 cm. How many times will it turn on a car that travels 22 m?
   (Take $\pi = \dfrac{22}{7}$)

   Solution:
   The radius of the wheel, $r = 35$ cm
   ∴ Its circumference $= 2\pi \times 35$ cm
   $2\pi r = 2 \times \dfrac{22}{7} \times 35 = 220$ cm
   i.e. the distance moved in 1 complete turn $= 220$ cm
   The total distance moved $= 22$ m $= 2200$ cm
   ∴ The number of turns of the wheel
   $= 2200 \div 220 = 10$ turns

3. Calculate the circumference of a wheel which has a diameter $= 35$ cm.
   (Take $\pi = \dfrac{22}{7}$)

   Solution:
   The circumference C $= 33$ cm
   If its diameter $= d$ meters,
   ∴ $\pi \times d = 33$
   ⇒ $d = 33 \div \pi$
   $d = 33 \times \dfrac{7}{22} = \dfrac{21}{2} = 10\dfrac{1}{2}$

Multiple Choice Questions

1. What is the area of a circle whose circumference is 176 m?
   (a) 2164 m² (b) 2364 m²
   (c) 2464 m² (d) 2564 m²

2. What is the radius of a circle with area 7850 m²? [Take p =3.14]
   (a) 55 m (b) 65 m
   (c) 60 m (d) 50 m

3. A circular plot has area 706.5 m². How long wire is required to fence the plot? [Take p = 3.14]
   (a) 94.20 m (b) 94.02 m
   (c) 96.00 m (d) 98.20 m

4. A circular ground of radius 20 m has a pathway of width 9 m around it on its outside. Find the area of the circular pathway.
   (a) 1386 m² (b) 1468 m²
   (c) 1238 m² (d) 1086 m²

5. The ratio of the radii of two circles is 5:9. What is the ratio of their areas?
   (a) 49:125 (b) 36:81
   (c) 25:81 (d) 64:81

6. In a circle whose radius is 13 cm, a chord is at a distance of 12 cm from the centre. How long is the chord?
   (a) 15 cm (b) 25 cm
   (c) 10 cm (d) 20 cm

7. A chord AB of a circle with radius 17 cm is 8 cm from its centre O. Find the area of the triangle ABO.
   (a) 110 cm² (b) 125 cm²
   (c) 121 cm² (d) 120 cm²

8. Two parallel chords AB and CD of a circle of radius 5 cm lie on opposite sides of the centre. OM and ON are perpendiculars from O to AB and CD. If AB = 8 cm and CD = 6 cm, then find the distance between them

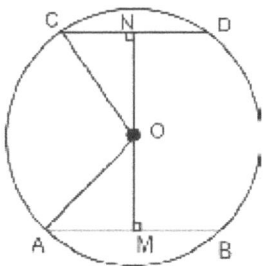

(a) 7 cm (b) 8 cm
(c) 9 cm (d) 5 cm

9. What is the semi-perimeter of a circle in which a chord of 10 cm length is at a distance of 12 cm from its centre?
(a) 50.80 cm (b) 40.82 cm
(c) 42.25 cm (d) 45.81 cm

10. Two equal parallel chords are on opposite sides of the centre of a circle with radius r. What is the sum of the lengths of the chords if they are 'r' cm apart?
(a) $2r\sqrt{3}$ cm (b) $r\sqrt{3}$ cm
(c) $2r\sqrt{2}$ cm (d) $5r\sqrt{3}$ cm

11. AA' is a diameter of a circle with centre O. B and B' are points on the circle. Find the sum
$\angle ABO + \angle AB'A' + \angle OBA' + \angle A'BA$
(a) 180° (b) 235°
(c) 330° (d) 270°

12. In the given figure, $\angle ABA' = 35^0$. Find the measures of angle ACA'.

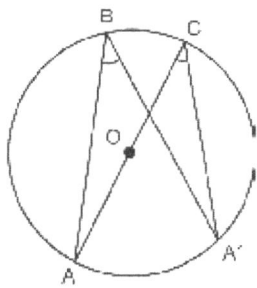

(a) 60° (b) 35°
(c) 70° (d) 135°

13. In the given circle centred at O, LM is a diameter. OP is perpendicular to LM. N is any point on the circle. Find the measure of $\angle LNP$ in the given figure.

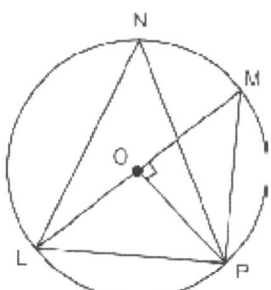

(a) 45° (b) 60°
(c) 75° (d) 30°

14. In the given figure, find the value of x.

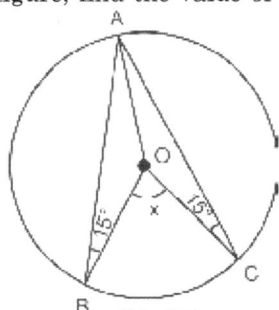

(a) 75° (b) 30°
(c) 60° (d) 45°

15. In the given figure, O is the centre of the circle. Find the measure of $\angle BCO$ and $\angle ABC$

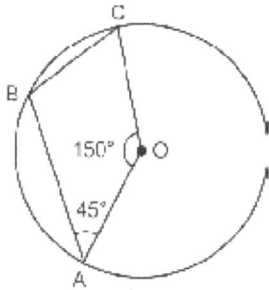

(a) $\angle ABC = 115^0$ and $\angle BCO = 60^0$
(b) $\angle ABC = 105^0$ and $\angle BCO = 30^0$
(c) $\angle ABC = 120^0$ and $\angle BCO = 90^0$
(d) $\angle ABC = 105^0$ and $\angle BCO = 60^0$

16. In the given circle with centre O, the degree measure of angle DOB is 210°. Find the measures of $\angle DAB$ and $\angle DCB$

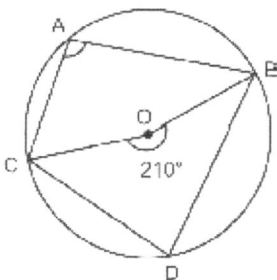

(a) $\angle DAB = 120^0$ and $\angle DCB = 75^0$
(b) $\angle DAB = 105^0$ and $\angle DCB = 60^0$
(c) $\angle DAB = 105^0$ and $\angle DCB = 75^0$
(d) $\angle DAB = 120^0$ and $\angle DCB = 60^0$

17. A diagonal of a cyclic quadrilateral passes through the centre O. Is the quadrilateral a rectangle?
(a) Yes (b) No
(c) Uncertain (d) Can't say

18. In the given figure, triangle ABC is an equilateral triangle and triangle ACD is an isosceles triangle with AD = CD Find the measures of angles BAC and ACD

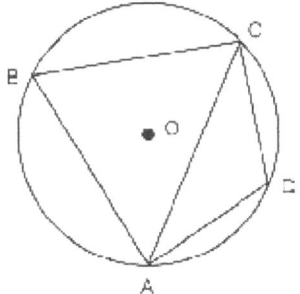

(a) $\angle BAC = 60^0, \angle ACD = 30^0$
(b) $\angle BAC = 90^0, \angle ACD = 30^0$
(c) $\angle BAC = 60^0, \angle ACD = 45^0$
(d) $\angle BAC = 60^0, \angle ACD = 15^0$

19. In the given figure, the circle is centered at O and KN is produced to P. If angle KOM = 150°, find the measures of angles KLM and MNP.

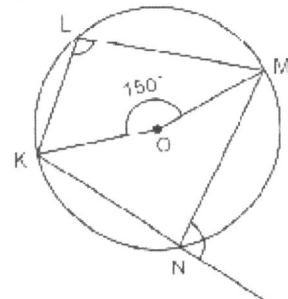

(a) 75° (b) 120°
(c) 135° (d) 105°

20. In the given figure, O is the centre and KL is the diameter.

$\angle KMN = 30^0$ and $\angle LNM = 20^0$

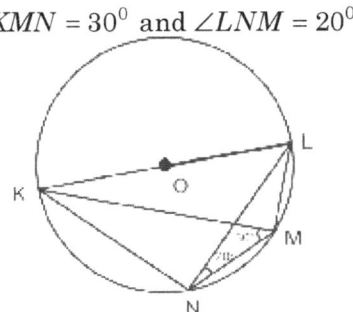

Find the measures of the angles of the quadrilateral KLMN.
(a) The four angles K, L, M and N measure 60°, 90°, 120° and 110° respectively
(b) The four angles K, L, M and N measure 60°, 70°, 120° and 110° respectively
(c) The four angles K, L, M and N measure 30°, 70°, 90° and 110° respectively
(d) The four angles K, L, M and N measure 60°, 70°, 120° and 90° respectively.

National Talent Search Examination (NTSE)-X

Answer Key

1. (c)	2. (d)	3. (a)	4. (a)	5. (c)	6. (c)	7. (d)	8. (a)	9. (b)	10. (a)
11. (d)	12. (b)	13. (a)	14. (c)	15. (d)	16. (c)	17. (b)	18. (a)	19. (d)	20. (b)

Explanatory Notes

1. (c)
   Let the radius of the circle be r meters.
   $$2\pi r = 176$$
   Circumference = 176 m
   $$r = 176 \times \frac{7}{22} \times \frac{1}{2}$$
   $$= 28 \text{ m}$$
   Area $= \pi r^2$
   $$= \frac{22}{7} \times 28^2 = 2464 \text{ m}^2$$

2. (d)
   Let the radius of the circle be r meters.
   $$\pi r^2 = 7850$$
   $$r^2 = \frac{7850}{3.14}$$
   $$= 2500 \text{ m}^2$$
   $$r = \sqrt{2500} = 50 \text{ m}$$
   Radius of the circle is 50 m

3. (a)
   Let the radius of the plot be r meters.
   $$\pi r^2 = 706.5$$
   $$r^2 = 706.5 \times \frac{1}{\pi}$$
   $$r^2 = \frac{706.5}{3.14} = 225$$
   $$r = \sqrt{225} = 15 \text{ m}$$
   Circumference $= 2\pi r$
   $$= 2 \times 3.14 \times 15$$
   $$= 94.20 \text{ m}$$
   Length of wire = 94.20 m

4. (a)
   Let r be the radius of the ground and r' be the width of the path.
   Area of circular ground $= \pi r^2$
   $$\pi(20)^2 = 400\pi$$
   Area of the ground including the pathway $= \pi r^2$
   $$= \pi(20+9)^2$$
   $$= 29^2 \pi = 841\pi$$
   Area of circular pathway $= 841\pi - 400\pi$
   $$= 441\pi$$
   $$= 1386 \text{ m}^2$$
   The area of the pathway is 1386 m²

5. (c)
   Let the radii be r' and r".
   $$r' : r" = 5 : 9$$
   Let the radii be 5x and 9x.
   Ratio of areas $= \dfrac{\pi r'^2}{\pi r"^2}$
   $$= 5^2 : 9^2 = 25 : 81$$
   Required ratio = 25 : 81

6. (c)
   Let AB be a chord of the circle with centre O and radius 13 cm. Let OM intersects AB at the mid-point of AB.

   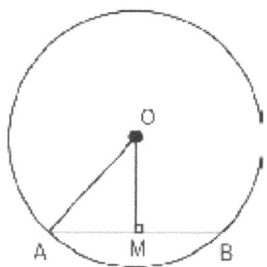

   Hence, AB = 2AM and $OM \perp AB$.
   In triangle OAM, OA = 13 cm, OM = 12 cm.
   Applying Pythagoras Theorem to the triangle, we get
   $$OA^2 = OM^2 + AM^2$$
   $$13^2 = 12^2 + AM^2$$
   $$169 = 144 + AM^2$$
   $$AM = \sqrt{169-144} = \sqrt{25} = 5 \text{ cm}$$
   $$AB = 2AM = 2 \times 5 = 10 \text{ cm}$$
   The length of the chord is 10 cm.

7. (d)
   Consider the following figure.

   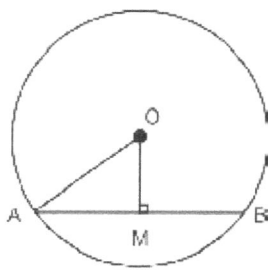

   A line perpendicular from O to AB meets it in M. The point M is the mid-point of the chord AB.

[92]

Applying Pythagoras theorem to triangle AMO, we get
$$AO^2 = AM^2 + MO^2$$
$$17^2 = AM^2 + 8^2$$
$$289 = AM^2 + 64$$
$$AM^2 = 289 - 64 = 225$$
$$AM = \sqrt{225} = 15 \text{cm}$$
$$AB = 2AM = 2 \times 15 = 30 \text{cm}$$

Area of triangle
$$OAB = \frac{1}{2} \times AB \times OM$$
$$= \frac{1}{2} \times 30 \times 8$$
$$= 15 \times 8$$
$$= 120 \text{cm}^2$$

Area of triangle OAB = 120 cm²

8. (a)
Perpendicular ON and OM bisect the chords AB and CD.
Hence, AM = MB = 8/2 = 4 cm and CN = ND = 6/2 = 3cm.
Also, OA = OC = 5 cm
Consider the right triangles AMO and CNO and apply Pythagoras theorem
$$OA^2 = AM^2 + OM^2$$
$$5^2 = 4^2 + OM^2$$
$$25 = 16 + OM^2$$
$$OM = \sqrt{25-16} = \sqrt{9} = 3 \text{ cm}$$
$$OC^2 = ON^2 + CN^2$$
$$5^2 = ON^2 + 3^2$$
$$25 = ON^2 + 9$$
$$ON = \sqrt{25-9} = \sqrt{16} = 4 \text{cm}$$

The distance between the two chords is equal to the sum of ON and OM
$$ON + OM = 4 + 3 = 7 \text{cm}$$
The distance between the two chords is 7cm.

9. (b)

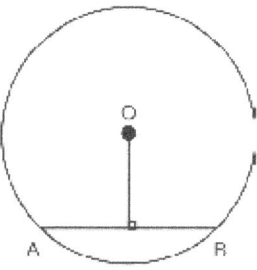

Let the circle be centred at O and AB be the given chord. Let OM be the perpendicular to the chord from O. OM = 12 cm OM divides AB.

Hence, AM = MB = 10/2 = 5 cm
In triangle AMO,
AM = 5 cm, OM = 12 cm
Applying Pythagoras theorem to triangle AMO, we get
$$OA^2 = AM^2 + OM^2$$
$$= 5^2 + 12^2$$
$$= 25 + 144 = 169$$
$$OM = \sqrt{169} = 13 \text{cm}$$

Radius of the circle = 13 cm
Semi-perimeter of the circle = πr
$$= 3.14 \times 13 \text{cm}$$
$$= 40.82 \text{cm}$$

10. (a)

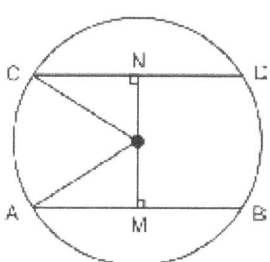

Let AB and CD be the two equal chords. They are equidistant from the centre since they are equal chords. ON and OM are perpendiculars from O to the two chords.
OM = ON
The distance between the two chords = r
ON + OM = r
ON = OM = r/2
In the triangles OCN and OAM, we apply Pythagoras theorem
$$OA^2 = AM^2 + OM^2$$
$$r^2 = AM^2 + \left(\frac{r}{2}\right)^2$$
$$r^2 - \frac{r^2}{4} = AM^2$$
$$AM^2 = \frac{3r^2}{4}$$
$$AM = \frac{r\sqrt{3}}{2} \text{ cm}$$
$$AB = 2AM = r\sqrt{3}$$
$$AB + CD = 2r\sqrt{3} \text{ cm}$$

The sum of the lengths of the two chords is
$$2r = 2r\sqrt{3} \text{ cm}$$

11. (d)
Consider the figure.

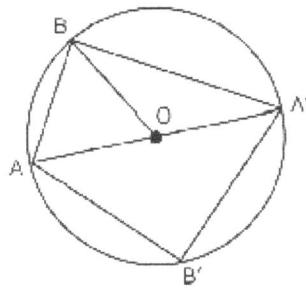

Since AA' is a diameter, we know that the angles in the two semi circles shall be 90°

$\angle ABO + \angle AB'A' + \angle OBA' + \angle A'BA$

$= (\angle ABO + \angle OBA') + \angle AB'A' + \angle A'BA$

$= 90^0 + 90^0 + 90^0$

$= 270^0$

12. (b)
In the given figure, $\angle ABA'$ and $\angle ACA'$ are angles subtended by the same arc and hence they are equal $\angle ACA' = 35^0$

13. (a)
In the given figure, $\angle LPM$ is a right angle since it lies in the semi-circle.
Consider ΔLPO and ΔMPO,
LO = MO (both are equal to the radius)

$\angle LOP = \angle MOP = 90^0$

OP = OP (common line)
Hence, the two triangles are congruent by SAS.
Thus, LP = MP
Hence triangle LPM is isosceles

$\angle PLM = \angle PML$

In triangle LPM,

$\angle LPM + \angle PML + \angle PLM = 180^0$

$90^0 + \angle PML + \angle PML = 180^0$ ($\angle PLM = \angle PML$)

$\angle PML = \dfrac{180^0 - 90^0}{2} = 45^0$

The two angles PML and PNL lie in the same segment and hence they are equal.

$\angle LNP = 45^0$

14. (c)
In the two triangles AOB and AOC,
AO = OB and AO = OC and hence the two triangles are isosceles.
Therefore, we have

$\angle OAB = \angle OBA$ and $\angle OCA = \angle OAC$

$\angle BAC = \angle BAO + \angle CAO = 15^0 + 15^0$

$= 30^0$

Now, we know that the central angle subtended by an arc is twice the angle subtended by the arc in the remaining circle.
Hence, $\angle BOC = 2 \times 30^0 = 60^0$

15. (d)
In the given figure, we consider the reflex angle AOC

$\angle AOC = 360^0 - 150^0 = 210^0$

The angles AOC and ABC are subtended by the same major arc and hence

$\angle ABC = \dfrac{1}{2} \times \angle AOC = \dfrac{1}{2} \times 210^0 = 105^0$

In quadrilateral ABCO,

$\angle A + \angle B + \angle C + \angle O = 360^0$

$45^0 + 105^0 + \angle C + 150^0 = 360^0$

$\angle C = 60^0$

Thus, $\angle ABC = 105^0$ and $\angle BCO = 60^0$

16. (c)
In the given figure, $\angle DAB$ is the angle subtended by the arc DOB in the circle, whereas $\angle DOB = 210^0$ is the central angle.

Hence, $\angle DAB = \dfrac{1}{2} \angle DOB = 105^0$

Now, since the quadrilateral ABCD is a cyclic quadrilateral, we have

$\angle DAB + \angle DCB = 180^0$

$\angle DCB = 180^0 - 105^0 = 75^0$

Hence, $\angle DAB = 105^0$ and $\angle DCB = 75^0$

17. (b)
Consider the cyclic quadrilateral ABCD.

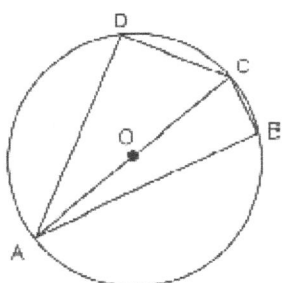

The diagonal AC of the quadrilateral passes through the centre. Hence, opposite angles D and B are right angles. However, angles A and C are not right angles. Hence, the quadrilateral is not a rectangle.

18. (a)
Since triangle ABC is equilateral, each angle is 60°.

Hence, $\angle ABC = \angle BCA = \angle BAC = 60^0$

In the cyclic quadrilateral ADCB, the opposite angles are supplementary.

Hence, $\angle ABC + \angle ADC = 180^0$

$\angle ADC = 180^0 - \angle ABC$

$= 180^0 - 60^0 = 120^0$

Since triangle ADC is isosceles and AD = CD, $\angle CAD = \angle DCA$

In triangle ADC,

$\angle ADC + \angle DCA + \angle CAD = 180^0$

$120^0 + \angle DCA + \angle DCA = 180^0$

$\angle DCA = \dfrac{(180^0 - 120^0)}{2} = 30^0$

Hence, $\angle BAC = 60^0, \angle ACD = 30^0$

19. (d)

In the given figure, $\angle KOM$ is the central angle subtended by the arc KM.

Hence, $\angle KNM = \dfrac{1}{2} \times \angle KOM = \dfrac{1}{2} \times 150^0$

$\angle KNM = 75^0$, $\angle KNP$ is a straight angle and hence,

$\angle MNP = 180^0 - \angle KNM = 180^0 - 75^0$,

$\angle MNP = 105^0$

$\angle KLM = \angle MNP = 105^0$ (Exterior angle of a cyclic quadrilateral)

20. (b)

In the given figure, $\angle KNL = \angle KML = 90^0$ since they are angles in the semi-circle.

Hence, $\angle KNM = \angle KNL + \angle LNM = 90^0 + 20^0$,

$\angle KNM = 110^0$

Similarly, $\angle LMN = \angle LMK + \angle KMN = 90^0 + 30^0$,

$\angle LMN = 120^0$

Opposite angles of a quadrilateral are supple-mentary.

Hence, $\angle NKL = 180^0 - \angle LMN = 180^0 - 120^0$,

$\angle NKL = 60^0$

Similarly, $\angle KLM = 180^0 - \angle MNK = 180^0 - 110^0$,

$\angle MLK = 70^0$

Hence, the four angles K, L, M and N measure 60°, 70°, 120° and 110° respectively.

Previous Year Questions

1. The circumference of a circle is equal to the sum of the circumference of two circles having diameters 36 cm and 20 cm. The radius of the new circle is
   [NTSE 2004 – MP first stage paper]
   (a) 16 cm (b) 28 cm
   (c) 42 cm (d) 56 cm

2. The area of a square is the same as the area of circle. Their perimeters are in the ratio.
   [NTSE 2000 – Kerala second stage paper]
   (a) 1 : 1 (b) 2 : π
   (c) π : 2 (d) $\sqrt{\pi} : 2$

3. The areas of two circles are in the ratio 4 : 9. The ratio of their circumference is
   [NTSE 2012 – UP first stage paper]
   (a) 2 : 3 (b) 3 : 2
   (c) 4 : 9 (d) 9 : 4

4. The area of a circle is equal to the sum of the areas of two circles of radii 24 cm and 7 cm. The diameter of the the new circle is
   [NTSE 2001 – Goa first stage paper]
   (a) 25 cm (b) 31 cm
   (c) 50 cm (d) 62 cm

5. If the sum of the areas of two circles with radii R_1 and R_2 is equal to the area of a circle of Radius R, then
   [NTSE 2006 – Chandigarh first stage paper]
   (a) $R_1 + R_2 = R$ (b) $R_1 + R_2 < R$
   (c) $R_1^2 + R_2^2 < R^2$ (d) $R_1^2 + R_2^2 = R^2$

6. If the sum of the circumferences of two circles with radii R_1 and R_2 is equal to the area of a circle of Radius R, then
   [NTSE 2004 – Jammu second stage paper]
   (a) $R_1 + R_2 = R$ (b) $R_1 + R_2 < R$
   (c) $R_1 + R_2 > R$ (d) None of these

7. The diameter of a wheel is 40 cm. How many revolutions will it make in covering 176 m ?
   [NTSE 2012 – Delhi first stage paper]
   (a) 140 (b) 150
   (c) 160 (d) 166

8. The radius of a wheel is 0.25 m. How many revolutions will it make in covering 11 km ?
   [NTSE 2001 – Haryana first stage paper]
   (a) 2800 (b) Rs. 4000
   (c) 5500 (d) Rs. 7000

9. The length of an arc of the sector of a circle of radius R making a central angle of $x°$ is
   [NTSE 2004 – WB second stage paper]
   (a) $\dfrac{2\pi R x}{180}$ (b) $\dfrac{2\pi R x}{360}$
   (c) $\dfrac{\pi R^2 x}{180}$ (d) $\dfrac{\pi R^2 x}{360}$

10. A chord of a circle of radius 28 cm subtends an angle of 45° at the centre of the circle. The area of the minor segment is : $\left(\sqrt{2} = 1.414\right)$
    [NTSE 2002 – Andhra Pradesh first stage paper]
    (a) 30.256 cm² (b) 30.356 cm²
    (c) 30.456 cm² (d) 30.856 cm²

Circles

Answer Key

| 1. (b) | 2. (d) | 3. (a) | 4. (a) | 5. (d) | 6. (a) | 7. (a) | 8. (d) | 9. (b) | 10. (d) |

Explanatory Notes

1. (b)
   Circumference of a new circle
   $= (2\pi \times 18 + 2\pi \times 10)$
   $= (2\pi + 28)$ cm
   $2\pi R = 2\pi \times 28$
   $\Rightarrow R = 28$ cm

2. (d)
   $a^2 = \pi R^2 \Rightarrow \dfrac{R^2}{a^2} = \dfrac{1}{\pi}$
   $\Rightarrow \dfrac{R}{a} = \dfrac{1}{\sqrt{\pi}}$
   Ratio of their perimeters
   $= \dfrac{2\pi R}{4a} = \dfrac{\pi}{2} \times \left(\dfrac{R}{a}\right)$
   $= \dfrac{\pi}{2} \times \dfrac{1}{\sqrt{\pi}} = \dfrac{\sqrt{\pi}}{2}$
   $= \sqrt{\pi} : 2$

3. (a)
   $\dfrac{\pi R_1^2}{\pi R_2^2} = \dfrac{4}{9}; \dfrac{R_1^2}{R_2^2} = \dfrac{4}{9}$
   $\Rightarrow \left(\dfrac{R_1}{R_2}\right)^2 = \left(\dfrac{2}{3}\right)^2$
   $\Rightarrow \dfrac{R_1}{R_2} = \dfrac{2}{3}$
   Ratio of their circumferences
   $= \dfrac{2\pi R_1}{2\pi R_2} = \dfrac{R_1}{R_2} = \dfrac{2}{3}$
   $= 2 : 3$

4. (a)
   Area of a new circle $= \{\pi \times (24)^2 + \pi \times (7)^2\}$ cm^2
   $= \{\pi \times (576 + 49)\}$ cm^2
   $= (625\pi)$ cm^2
   $\therefore \pi R^2 = 625\pi \Rightarrow R^2 = (25)^2$
   $\Rightarrow R = 25$
   $\therefore$ Radius of the new circle = 25 cm

5. (d)
   $\pi R_1^2 + \pi R_2^2 = \pi R^2 \Rightarrow R_1^2 + R_2^2 + R^2$

6. (a)
   $2\pi R_1 + 2\pi R_2 = 2\pi R \Rightarrow R_1 + R_2 = R$

7. (b)
   Distance covered in 1 revolution
   $= \pi d$
   $= \left(\dfrac{22 \times 40}{7}\right)$ cm $= \dfrac{880}{7}$ cm
   $\therefore$ Number of revolutions
   $= \left(176 \times 100 \times \dfrac{7}{880}\right) = 140$

8. (a)
   Circumference of the wheel = $2\pi R$
   $= \left(2 \times \dfrac{22}{7} \times \dfrac{25}{100}\right) m = \dfrac{11}{7} m$
   $\therefore$ Number of revolutions
   $= \left(11000 \times \dfrac{7}{11}\right) = 7000$

9. (b)
   Clearly the length of the arc $= \dfrac{2\pi R x}{360}$

10. (d)
    Here $r = 28$ cm $\theta = 45°$
    $\therefore$ area of the minor segment
    $= \left\{\dfrac{\pi r^2 \theta}{360} - \dfrac{1 r^2 \sin\theta}{2}\right\}$ cm^2
    $= \left\{\dfrac{22}{7} \times 28 \times 28 \times \dfrac{45}{360} - \dfrac{1}{2} \times 28 \times 28 \times \sin 45°\right\}$ cm^2
    $= (308 - 277.144)$ cm^2
    $= 30.856$ cm^2

UNIT 11
Mensuration

- **Results on Triangles**
  - Sum of the angles of a triangle is 180°.
  - The sum of any two sides of a triangle is greater than the third side.
  - **Pythagoras Theorem:**
    In a right-angled triangle,
    (Hypotenuse)² = (Base)² + (Height)².
  - The line joining the mid-point of a side of a triangle to the positive vertex is called the median.
  - The point where the three medians of a triangle meet is called centroid. The centroid divides each of the medians in the ratio 2 : 1.
  - In an isosceles triangle, the altitude from the vertex bisects the base.
  - The median of a triangle divides it into two triangles of the same area.
  - The area of the triangle formed by joining the mid-points of the sides of a given triangle is one-fourth of the area of the given triangle.

- **Results on Quadrilaterals**
  - The diagonals of a parallelogram bisect each other.
  - Each diagonal of a parallelogram divides it into triangles of the same area.
  - The diagonals of a rectangle are equal and bisect each other.
  - The diagonals of a square are equal and bisect each other at right angles.
  - The diagonals of a rhombus are unequal and bisect each other at right angles.
  - A parallelogram and a rectangle on the same base and between the same parallels are equal in area.
  - Of all the parallelograms of given sides, the parallelogram which is a rectangle has the greatest area.
  - Area of a rectangle = (Length × Breadth)
  - Perimeter of a rectangle = 2(Length + Breadth)
  - Area of a square = (side)² = $\frac{1}{2}$ (diagonal)²
  - Area of 4 walls of a room = 2 (Length + Breadth) × Height.
  - Area of a triangle = $\frac{1}{2}$ × Base × Height

- Area of a triangle
  $= \sqrt{s(s-a)(s-b)(s-c)}$
  where a, b, c are the sides of the triangle and $s = \frac{1}{2}(a + b + c)$

- Area of an equilateral triangle = $\frac{\sqrt{3}}{4}$ × (side)².

- Radius of incircle of an equilateral triangle of side a = $\frac{a}{2\sqrt{3}}$

- Radius of circumcircle of an equilateral triangle of side a = $\frac{a}{\sqrt{3}}$

- Radius of incircle of a triangle of area Δ and semi-perimeter $s = \frac{\Delta}{s}$

- Area of parallelogram = (Base × Height)

- Area of a rhombus = $\frac{1}{2}$ × (Product of diagonals)

- Area of a trapezium = $\frac{2\pi r\theta}{360}$ × (sum of parallel sides) × distance between them

- Area of a circle = πr^2, where r is the radius.

- Circumference of a circle = $2\pi r$

- Length of an arc = $\frac{2\pi r\theta}{360}$, where θ is the central angle

- Area of a sector = $\frac{1}{2}$ (arc × r) = $\frac{\pi r^2 \theta}{360}$

- Circumference of a semi-circle = πr

- Area of semi-circle = $\frac{\pi r^2}{2}$

- **Formulae on Surface Area and Volume**
  - **Cuboid**
    Let length = l, breadth = b and height = h units. Then
    (i) Volume = ($l \times b \times h$) cubic units

Mensuration

- (ii) Surface area = $2(lb + bh + lh)$ sq. units
- (iii) Diagonal = $\sqrt{l^2 + b^2 + h^2}$ units

• **Cube**

Let each edge of a cube be of length a. Then,
- (i) Volume = a^3 cubic units
- (ii) Surface area = $6a^2$ sq. units
- (iii) Diagonal = $\sqrt{3}a$ units

• **Cylinder**

Let radius of base = r and Height (or length) = h. Then,
- (i) Volume = $(\pi r^2 h)$ cubic units
- (ii) Curved surface area = $(2\pi rh)$ sq. units
- (iii) Total surface area = $2\pi r(h + r)$ sq. units

• **Cone**

Let radius of base = r and Height = h. Then,
- (i) Slant height, $l = \sqrt{h^2 + r^2}$ units
- (ii) Volume = $\frac{1}{3}\pi r^2 h$ cubic units
- (iii) Curved surface area = (πrl) sq. units
- (iv) Total surface area = $(\pi rl + \pi r^2)$ sq. units

• **Sphere**

Let the radius of the sphere be r. Then,
- (i) Volume = $\frac{4}{3}\pi r^3$ cubic units
- (ii) Surface area = $(4\pi r^2)$ sq. units

• **Hemisphere**

Let the radius of a hemisphere be r. Then,
- (i) Volume = $\frac{2}{3}\pi r^3$ cubic units
- (ii) Curved surface area = $(2\pi r^2)$ sq. units
- (iii) Total surface area = $(3\pi r^2)$ sq. units

Note: 1 litre = 1000 cm³.

■ **Formulae on Pipes and Cistern**

• **Inlet:**

A pipe connected with a tank or a cistern or a reservoir, that fills it, is known as an inlet

• **Outlet:**

A pipe connected with a tank or cistern or reservoir, emptying it, is known as an outlet

  ➤ If a pipe can fill a tank in x hours, then:
  Part filled in 1 hour = $\frac{1}{x}$

  ➤ If a pipe can empty a tank in y hours, then:
  Part emptied in 1 hour = $\frac{1}{y}$

  ➤ If a pipe can fill a tank in x hours and another pipe can empty the full tank in y hours (where $y > x$), then on opening both the pipes
  Net part filled in 1 hour = $\left(\frac{1}{x} - \frac{1}{y}\right)$

  ➤ If a pipe can fill a tank in x hours and another pipe can empty the full tank in y hours (where $y > x$), then on opening both the pipes
  Net part emptied in 1 hour = $\left(\frac{1}{y} - \frac{1}{x}\right)$

Solved Examples

1. A rectangular block 6 cm by 12 cm by 15 cm is cut into exact number of equal cubes. The least possible number of cubes will be:
   (a) 6   (b) 11
   (c) 33 (d) 40
   Solution: Option (d) is correct.
   Explanation:
   Volume of block = $6 \times 12 \times 15 = 1080$ cm³
   The side of largest cube = $(3 \times 3 \times 3)$ cm³
   = 27 cm³
   Number of cubes = 1080/27 = 40

2. The percentage increase in the surface area of a cube when each side is doubled is:
   (a) 25%   (b) 50%
   (c) 150% (d) 300%
   Solution: Option (d) is correct.
   Explanation:
   Let the side of the cube be a,
   Then surface area = $6a^2$
   If side is 2a, then surface area = $6(2a)^2 = 24a^2$

   So % increase in surface area
   $= \left(\frac{24a^2 - 6a^2}{6a^2}\right) \times 100\% = 300\%$

3. A circular track is 14 cm wide and its inner circumference is 440 cm. The diameter of the outer circle of the track:
   (a) 84 cm   (b) 77 cm
   (c) 168 cm (d) 336 cm
   Solution: Option (c) is correct.
   Explanation:
   Let radius of the inner track = r
   Then, $2\pi r = 440$ cm
   $\Rightarrow r = \frac{440 \times 70}{22 \times 2} = 70$ cm
   Track is 14 cm wide; so radius of outer circle of the track is 70 + 14 = 84 cm
   So diameter = $2 \times 84 = 168$ cm

4. The volume of a cube is V. The total length of its edges is:
   (a) $6V^{2/3}$ (b) $8\sqrt{V}$
   (c) $12V^{2/3}$ (d) $12V^{1/3}$
   Solution: Option (d) is correct.
   Explanation:
   Let the edge of a cube be a
   Then, $a^3 = V$, $a = \sqrt[3]{V}$
   Total length of edge = $12 \times (V)^{1/3}$ as there are 12 edges.

5. The area of a square increased by............ , if its side increases by 30%.
   (a) 71% (b) 60%
   (c) 69% (d) 30%
   Solution: Option (c) is correct.
   Explanation:
   Let the side of the square be 10
   Then area = $(10)^2$ = 100
   New side = 10×1.3 = 13
   New area = $(13)^2$ = 169
   % increase in area = 69%

Multiple Choice Questions

1. The ratio between the length and the breadth of a rectangular park is 3 : 2. If a man cycling along the boundary of the park at the speed of 12 km/hr completes one round in 8 minutes, then the area of the park (in sq. m) is:
   (a) 15360 (b) 153600
   (c) 30720 (d) 307200

2. An error 2% in excess is made while measuring the side of a square. The percentage of error in the calculated area of the square is:
   (a) 2% (b) 2.02%
   (c) 4% (d) 4.04%

3. The ratio between the perimeter and the breadth of a rectangle is 5 : 1. If the area of the rectangle is 216 sq. cm, what is the length of the rectangle?
   (a) 16 cm (b) 18 cm
   (c) 24 cm (d) Data inadequate

4. The percentage increase in the area of a rectangle, if each of its sides is increased by 20% is:
   (a) 40% (b) 42%
   (c) 44% (d) 46%

5. A rectangular park 60 m long and 40 m wide has two concrete crossroads running in the middle of the park and rest of the park has been used as a lawn. If the area of the lawn is 2109 sq. m, then what is the width of the road?
   (a) 2.91 m (b) 3 m
   (c) 5.82 m (d) None of these

6. The diagonal of the floor of a rectangular closet is 7.5 feet. The shorter side of the closet is 4.5 feet. What is the area of the closet in square feet?
   (a) 5 (b) 13
   (c) 27 (d) 37

7. A towel, when bleached, was found to have lost 20% of its length and 10% of its breadth. The percentage of decrease in area is:
   (a) 10% (b) 10.08%
   (c) 20% (d) 28%

8. A man walked diagonally across a square plot. Approximately, what was the percent saved by not walking along the edges?
   (a) 20 (b) 24
   (c) 30 (d) 33

9. The diagonal of a rectangle is 41 cm and its area is 20 sq. cm. The perimeter of the rectangle must be:
   (a) 9 cm (b) 18 cm
   (c) 20 cm (d) 41 cm

10. What is the least number of square tiles required to pave the floor of a room 15 m 17 cm long and 9 m 2 cm broad?
    (a) 814 (b) 820
    (c) 840 (d) 844

11. The difference between the length and breadth of a rectangle is 23 m. If its perimeter is 206 m, then its area is:
    (a) 1520 m² (b) 2420 m²
    (c) 2480 m² (d) 2520 m²

12. The length of a rectangle is halved, while its breadth is tripled. What is the percentage change in area?
    (a) 25% increase (b) 50% increase
    (c) 50% decrease (d) 75% decrease

13. The length of a rectangular plot is 20 metres more than its breadth. If the cost of fencing the plot @ 26.50 per metre is Rs. 5300, what is the length of the plot in metres?
    (a) 40 (b) 50
    (c) 120 (d) None of these

14. A rectangular field is to be fenced on three sides leaving a side of 20 feet uncovered. If the area of the field is 680 sq. feet, how many feet of fencing will be required?
    (a) 34 (b) 40
    (c) 68 (d) 88

15. A tank is 25 m long, 12 m wide and 6 m deep. The cost of plastering its walls and bottom at 75 paise per sq. m, is:
    (a) Rs. 456 (b) Rs. 458
    (c) Rs. 558 (d) Rs. 568

16. The area of a playground is 1600 m². What is the perimeter?
    I. It is a perfect square playground.
    II. It costs Rs. 3200 to put a fence around the playground at the rate of Rs. 20 per metre.
    (a) I alone is sufficient while II alone is not sufficient to answer
    (b) II alone is sufficient while I alone is not sufficient to answer
    (c) Either I or II alone is sufficient to answer
    (d) Both I and II are not sufficient to answer

17. The area of a rectangle is equal to the area of right-angle triangle. What is the length of the rectangle?
    I. The base of the triangle is 40 cm.
    II. The height of the triangle is 50 cm.
    (a) I alone is sufficient while II alone is not sufficient to answer
    (b) II alone is sufficient while I alone is not sufficient to answer
    (c) Either I or II alone is sufficient is answer
    (d) Both I and II are not sufficient to answer

18. What is the height of the triangle?
    I. The area of the triangle is 20 times its base.
    II. The perimeter of the triangle is equal to the perimeter of a square of side 10 cm.
    (a) I alone is sufficient while II alone is not sufficient to answer
    (b) II alone is sufficient while I alone is not sufficient to answer
    (c) Either I or II alone is sufficient to answer
    (d) Both I and II are not sufficient to answer

19. What will be the cost of painting the inner walls of a room if the rate of painting is Rs. 20 per square foot?
    I. Circumference of the floor is 44 feet.
    II. The height of the wall of the room is 12 feet.
    (a) I alone is sufficient while II alone is not sufficient to answer
    (b) II alone is sufficient while I alone is not sufficient to answer
    (c) Either I or II alone is sufficient to answer
    (d) Both I and II are necessary to answer

20. What is the area of the hall?
    I. Material cost of flooring per square metre is Rs. 2.50
    II. Labour cost of flooring the hall is Rs. 3500
    III. Total cost of flooring the hall is Rs. 14,500.
    (a) I and II only   (b) II and III only
    (c) All I, II and III   (d) Any two of the three

21. What is the area of a right-angled triangle?
    I. The perimeter of the triangle is 30 cm.
    II. The ratio between the base and the height of the triangle is 5 : 12.
    III. The area of the triangle is equal to the area of a rectangle of length 10 cm.
    (a) I and II only
    (b) II and III only
    (c) I and III only
    (d) III and either I or II only

22. What is the area of rectangular field?
    I. The perimeter of the field is 110 metres.
    II. The length is 5 metres more than the width.
    III. The ratio between length and width is 6 : 5 respectively.
    (a) I and II only
    (b) Any two of the three
    (c) All I, II and III
    (d) I and either II or III only

23. What is the area of the given rectangle?
    I. Perimeter of the rectangle is 60 cm.
    II. Breadth of the rectangle is 12 cm.
    III. Sum of two adjacent sides is 30 cm.
    (a) I only   (b) II only
    (c) I and II only   (d) II and either I or III

24. What is the cost of painting the two adjacent walls of a hall at Rs. 5 per m² which has no windows or doors?
    I. The area of the hall is 24 sq. m.
    II. The breadth, length and height of the hall are in the ratio of 4 : 6 : 5 respectively.
    III. Area of one wall is 30 sq. m.
    (a) I only   (b) II only
    (c) III only   (d) Either I or III

25. Find the area of the largest circle that can be drawn in a square of side 14 cm.
    (a) 154 cm²   (b) 144 cm²
    (c) 136 cm²   (d) 121 cm²

26. In a quadrilateral, the length of one of its diagonal is 23 cm and the perpendiculars drawn on this diagonal from other two vertices measure 17 cm and 7 cm respectively. Find the area of the quadrilateral.
    (a) 225 cm²   (b) 149 cm²
    (c) 276 cm²   (d) 136 cm²

27. The circumference of a circle is 100 cm. Find the side of the square inscribed in the circle.
    (a) $\sqrt{2} \times \dfrac{50}{\pi}$ (b) $\sqrt{2} \times \dfrac{60}{\pi}$
    (c) $\sqrt{3} \times \dfrac{60}{\pi}$ (d) $\sqrt{3} \times \dfrac{30}{\pi}$

28. If the radius of a circle is increased by 5%, find the percentage increase in its area.
    (a) 10%   (b) 10.25%
    (c) 10.75%   (d) 11%

29. If all sides of a hexagon is increased by 2%, find the percentage increase in its area.
    (a) 6.06%   (b) 4.04%
    (c) 10.05%   (d) 5.80%

30. If diameter of a circle is increased by 12%, find the percentage increase in its circumference.
    (a) 6%   (b) 12%
    (c) 18%   (d) 9%

31. A right triangle with sides 3 cm, 4 cm and 5 cm is rotated the side of 3 cm to form a cone. The volume of the cone so formed is:
    (a) 12π cm^3 (b) 15π cm^3
    (c) 16π cm^3 (d) 20π cm^3

32. In a shower, 5 cm of rain falls. The volume of water that falls on 1.5 hectares of ground is:
    (a) 75 cu. m (b) 750 cu. m
    (c) 7500 cu. m (d) 75000 cu. m

33. A hall is 15 m long and 12 m broad. If the sum of the areas of the floor and the ceiling is equal to the sum of the areas of four walls, the volume of the hall is:
    (a) 720 m^3 (b) 900 m^3
    (c) 1200 m^3 (d) 1800 m^3

34. 66 cubic centimetres of silver is drawn into a wire 1 mm in diameter. The length of the wire in metres will be:
    (a) 84 (b) 90
    (c) 168 (d) 336

35. A hollow iron pipe is 21 cm long and its external diameter is 8 cm. If the thickness of the pipe is 1 cm and iron weighs 8 g/cm^3, then the weight of the pipe is:
    (a) 3.6 kg (b) 3.696 kg
    (c) 36 kg (d) 36.9 kg

36. A boat having a length 3 m and breadth 2 m is floating on a lake. The boat sinks by 1 cm when a man gets on it. The mass of the man is:
    (a) 12 kg (b) 60 kg
    (c) 72 kg (d) 96 kg

37. 50 men took a dip in a water tank 40 m long and 20 m broad on a religious day. If the average displacement of water by a man is 4 m^3, then the rise in the water level in the tank will be:
    (a) 20 cm (b) 25 cm
    (c) 35 cm (d) 50 cm

38. The slant height of a right circular cone is 10 m and its height is 8 m. Find the area of its curved surface.
    (a) 30 π m^2 (b) 40 π m^2
    (c) 60 π m^2 (d) 80 π m^2

39. A cistern 6m long and 4 m wide contains water up to a depth of 1 m 25 cm. The total area of the wet surface is:
    (a) 49 m^2 (b) 50 m^2
    (c) 53.5 m^2 (d) 55 m^2

40. A metallic sheet is of rectangular shape with dimensions 48 m × 36 m. From each of its corners, a square is cut off so as to make an open box. If the length of the square is 8 m, the volume of the box (in m^3) is:
    (a) 4830 (b) 5120
    (c) 6420 (d) 8960

41. The curved surface area of a cylindrical pillar is 264 m^2 and its volume is 924 m^3. Find the ratio of its diameter to its height.
    (a) 3 : 7 (b) 7 : 3
    (c) 6 : 7 (d) 7 : 6

42. A cistern of capacity 8000 litres measures externally 3.3 m by 2.6 m by 1.1 m and its walls are 5 cm thick. The thickness of the bottom is:
    (a) 90 cm (b) 1 dm
    (c) 1 m (d) 1.1 cm

43. What is the total surface area of a right circular cone of height 14 cm and base radius 7 cm?
    (a) 344.35 cm^2 (b) 462 cm^2
    (c) 498.35 cm^2 (d) None of these

44. A large cube is formed from the material obtained by melting three smaller cubes of 3, 4 and 5 cm side. What is the ratio of the total surface areas of the smaller cubes and the large cube?
    (a) 2 : 1 (b) 3 : 2
    (c) 25 : 18 (d) 27 : 20

45. How many bricks, each measuring 25 cm × 11.25 cm × 6 cm, will be needed to build a wall of 8 m × 6 m × 22.5 cm?
    (a) 5600 (b) 6000
    (c) 6400 (d) 7200

46. What is the volume of 32 metres high cylindrical tank?
    I. The area of its base is 154 m^2
    II. The diameter of the base is 14 m
    (a) I alone is sufficient while II alone is not sufficient to answer
    (b) II alone is sufficient while I alone is not sufficient to answer
    (c) Either I or II alone is sufficient to answer
    (d) Both I and II are not sufficient to answer

47. Is the given rectangular block a cube?
    I. At least 2 faces of the rectangular block are squares.
    II. The volume of the block is 64.
    (a) I alone is sufficient while II alone is not sufficient to answer
    (b) II alone is sufficient while I alone is not sufficient to answer
    (c) Either I or II alone is sufficient to answer
    (d) Both I and II are not sufficient to answer

48. What is the capacity of a cylindrical tank?
    I. Radius of the base is half of its height which is 28 metres.
    II. Area of the base is 616 sq. metres and its height is 28 metres.
    (a) I alone is sufficient while II alone is not sufficient to answer
    (b) II alone is sufficient while I alone is not sufficient to answer
    (c) Either I or II alone is sufficient to answer
    (d) Both I and II are not sufficient to answer

49. What is the height of a circular cone?
    I. The area of that cone is equal to the area of a rectangle whose length is 33 cm.
    II. The area of the base of that cone is 154 sq. cm.
    (a) I alone sufficient while II alone is not sufficient to answer

(b) II alone is sufficient while I alone is not sufficient to answer
(c) Either I or II alone is sufficient to answer
(d) Both I and II are not sufficient to answer

50. What is the volume of a cube?
   I. The area of each face of the cube is 64 square metres.
   II. The length of one side of the cube is 8 metres.
   (a) I alone is sufficient while II alone is not sufficient to answer
   (b) II alone is sufficient while I alone is not sufficient to answer
   (c) Either I or II alone is sufficient to answer
   (d) Both I and II are not sufficient to answer

51. What is the capacity of the cylindrical tank?
   I. The area of the base is 61,600 sq. cm.
   II. The height of the tank is 1.5 times the radius.
   III. The circumference of base is 880 cm.
   (a) Only I and II
   (b) Only II and III
   (c) Only I and III
   (d) Only II and either I or III

52. Three pipes A, B and C can fill a tank from empty to full in 30 minutes, 20 minutes, and 10 minutes respectively. When the tank is empty, all the three pipes are opened. A, B and C discharge chemical solutions P, Q and R respectively. What is the proportion of the solution R in the liquid in the tank after 3 minutes?
   (a) 5/11   (b) 6/11
   (c) 7/11   (d) 8/11

53. Pipes A and B can fill a tank in 5 and 6 hours respectively. Pipe C can empty it in 12 hours. If all the three pipes are opened together, then the tank will be filled in:
   (a) $1\frac{13}{17}$ hours   (b) $2\frac{8}{11}$ hours
   (c) $1\frac{13}{17}$ hours   (d) $4\frac{1}{2}$ hours

54. A pump can fill a tank with water in 2 hours. Because of a leak, it took 2⅓ hours to fill the tank. The leak can drain all the water of the tank in:
   (a) 4 hours   (b) 7 hours
   (c) 8 hours   (d) 14 hours

55. Two pipes A and B can fill a cistern in 37.5 minutes and 45 minutes respectively. Both pipes are opened. The cistern will be filled in just half an hour, if the B is turned off after:
   (a) 5 min.   (b) 9 min.
   (c) 10 min.   (d) 15 min.

56. A tank is filled by three pipes with uniform flow. The first two pipes operating simultaneously fill the tank in the same time during which the tank is filled by the third pipe alone. The second pipe fills the tank 5 hours faster than the first pipe and 4 hours slower than the third pipe. The time required by the first pipe is:
   (a) 6 hours   (b) 10 hours
   (c) 15 hours   (d) 30 hours

57. Two pipes can fill a tank in 20 and 24 minutes respectively and a waste pipe can empty 3 gallons per minute. All the three pipes working together can fill the tank in 15 minutes. The capacity of the tank is:
   (a) 60 gallons   (b) 100 gallons
   (c) 120 gallons   (d) 180 gallons

58. A tank is filled in 5 hours by three pipes A, B and C. The pipe C is twice as fast as B and B is twice as fast as A. How much time will pipe A alone take to fill the tank?
   (a) 20 hours
   (b) 25 hours
   (c) 35 hours
   (d) Cannot be determined

59. Two pipes A and B together can fill a cistern in 4 hours. Had they been opened separately, then B would have taken 6 hours more than A to fill the cistern. How much time will be taken by A to fill the cistern separately?
   (a) 1 hour   (b) 2 hours
   (c) 6 hours   (d) 8 hours

60. Two pipes A and B can fill a tank in 20 and 30 minutes respectively. If both the pipes are used together, then how long will it take to fill the tank?
   (a) 12 min   (b) 15 min
   (c) 25 min   (d) 50 min

61. Two pipes A and B can fill a tank in 15 minutes and 20 minutes respectively. Both the pipes are opened together but after 4 minutes, pipe A is turned off. What is the total time required to fill the tank?
   (a) 10 min. 20 sec   (b) 11 min. 45 sec
   (c) 12 min. 30 sec   (d) 14 min. 40 sec

62. One pipe can fill a tank three times as fast as another pipe. If together the two pipes can fill the tank in 36 minutes, then the slower pipe alone will be able to fill the tank in:
   (a) 81 min.   (b) 108 min.
   (c) 144 min.   (d) 192 min.

63. A large tanker can be filled by two pipes A and B in 60 minutes and 40 minutes respectively. How many minutes will it take to fill the tanker from empty state if B is used for half the time and A and B fill it together for the other half?
   (a) 15 min   (b) 20 min
   (c) 27.5 min   (d) 30 min

64. A tap can fill a tank in 6 hours. After half the tank is filled, three more similar taps are opened. What is the total time taken to fill the tank completely?
   (a) 3 hrs 15 min   (b) 3 hrs 45 min
   (c) 4 hrs   (d) 4 hrs 15 min

65. Three taps A, B and C can fill a tank in 12, 15 and 20 hours respectively. If A is open all the time and B and C are open for one hour each alternately, the tank will be full in:
   (a) 6 hours   (b) 6.5 hours
   (c) 7 hours   (d) 7.5 hours

66. Three pipes A, B and C can fill a tank in 6 hours. After working at it together for 2 hours, C is closed and A and B can fill the remaining part in 7 hours. The number of hours taken by C alone to fill the tank is:
    (a) 10 (b) 12
    (c) 14 (d) 16

67. How much time will the leak take to empty the full cistern?
    I. The cistern is normally filled in 9 hours.
    II. It takes one hour more than the usual time to fill the cistern because of the leak in the bottom.
    (a) I alone is sufficient while II alone is not sufficient to answer
    (b) II alone is sufficient while I alone is not sufficient to answer
    (c) Either I or II alone is sufficient to answer
    (d) Both I and II are necessary to answer

68. How long will it take to empty the tank if both the inlet pipe A and the outlet pipe B are opened simultaneously?
    I. A can fill the tank in 16 minutes.
    II. B can empty the full tank in 8 minutes.
    (a) I alone is sufficient while II alone is not sufficient to answer
    (b) II alone is sufficient while I alone is not sufficient to answer
    (c) Either I or II alone is sufficient to answer
    (d) Both I and II are necessary to answer

69. If both the pipes are opened, how many hours will be taken to fill the tank?
    I. The capacity of the tank is 400 litres.
    II. The pipe A fills the tank in 4 hours.
    III. The pipe B fills the tank in 6 hours.
    (a) Only I and II (b) Only II and III
    (c) All I, II and III (d) Any two of the three

70. Find the number of lead balls of diameter 1 cm each that can be made from a sphere of diameter 16 m.
    (a) 4096 (b) 2050
    (c) 3016 (d) 5024

Mensuration

Answer Key

1. (b)	2. (d)	3. (b)	4. (c)	5. (b)	6. (c)	7. (d)	8. (c)	9. (b)	10. (a)
11. (d)	12. (b)	13. (d)	14. (d)	15. (c)	16. (c)	17. (d)	18. (a)	19. (d)	20. (c)
21. (a)	22. (b)	23. (d)	24. (c)	25. (a)	26. (c)	27. (a)	28. (b)	29. (b)	30. (b)
31. (a)	32. (b)	33. (c)	34. (a)	35. (b)	36. (b)	37. (b)	38. (c)	39. (a)	40. (b)
41. (b)	42. (b)	43. (c)	44. (c)	45. (c)	46. (c)	47. (d)	48. (c)	49. (d)	50. (c)
51. (d)	52. (b)	53. (c)	54. (d)	55. (b)	56. (c)	57. (c)	58. (c)	59. (c)	60. (a)
61. (d)	62. (c)	63. (d)	64. (b)	65. (c)	66. (c)	67. (d)	68. (d)	69. (b)	70. (a)

Explanatory Notes

1. (b)
   Perimeter = Distance covered in 8 min.
   = (12000/60 × 8) = 160 m
   Let length = $3x$ metres and breadth
   = $2x$ metres
   Then, $2(3x + 2x)$ = 1600 or x = 160
   ∴ Length = 480 m and Breadth = 320 m
   ∴ Area = (480 × 320) m² = 153600 m²

2. (d)
   100 cm is read as 10^2 cm.
   ∴ A_1 = (100 × 100) cm² and
   A_2 (102 × 102) cm².
   $(A_2 - A_1)$ = $[(102)^2 - (100)^2]$
   = (102 + 100) × (102 – 100)
   = 404 cm²
   ∴ Percentage error
   = [404/(100 × 100) × 100]%
   = 4.04%

3. (b)
   $2(l + b)/b$ = 5/1
   ⇒ $2l + 2b$ = $5b$
   ⇒ $3b$ = $2l$
   $b = 2l/3$
   Then, Area = 216 cm²
   ⇒ $l × b$ = 216
   ⇒ $l × 2l/3$ = 216
   ⇒ l^2 = 324
   ⇒ l = 18 cm

4. (c)
   Let original length
   = x metres and original breadth
   = y metres
   Original area = (xy) m²
   New length = $(120/100) x$ m = $(6/5) x$ m
   New breadth = $(120/100) y$ m = $(6/5) y$ m
   New Area = $(6/5) x$ m × $(6/5) y$ m
   = $(36/25)xy$ m²
   The difference between the original area
   = xy and new area $36/25\ xy$ is
   = $(36/25)xy - xy$
   = $xy(36/25 - 1)$
   = $xy(11/25)$ or $(11/25)xy$
   ∴ Increase % = $[(11/25)xy × 1/xy × 100]$%
   = 44%

5. (b)
   Area of the park = (60 × 40) m²
   = 2400 m²
   Area of the lawn = 2109 m²
   Area of the crossroads = (2400 – 2109) m²
   = 291 m²
   Let the width of the road be x metres. Then,
   $60x + 40x - x^2$ = 291
   ⇒ $x^2 - 100x + 291$ = 0
   ⇒ $(x - 97)(x - 3)$ = 0
   ⇒ x = 3

6. (c)
   Other side = $\sqrt{(7.5)^2 - (4.5)^2}$ ft
   = $\sqrt{\dfrac{144}{4}}$ = 6 ft
   Area of closet = (6 × 4.5) sq. ft
   = 27 sq. ft.

7. (d)
   Let original length = x and original breadth
   = y
   Decrease in area = $xy - [(80/100)x × (90/100)y]$
   = $(7/25)xy$
   ∴ Decrease % = $[(7/25)xy × 1/xy × 100]$%
   = 28%

8. (c)
Let the side of the square (ABCD) be x metres.

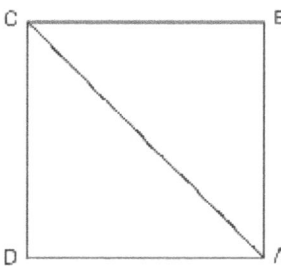

Then, $\quad$ AB + BC = $2x$ metres
$\quad\quad\quad$ AC = $\sqrt{2}x$ = $(1.41x)$ m
Saving on $2x$ metres = $(0.59x)$ m
$\quad\quad$ Saving % = $(0.59x/2x) \times 100\%$
$\quad\quad\quad\quad\quad$ = 30 %(approx)

9. (b)
$\quad\quad\quad \sqrt{l^2 + b^2} = \sqrt{41}$
Also, $\quad\quad lb = 20$
$\quad\quad (l + b)^2 = (l^2 + b^2) + 2lb$
$\quad\quad\quad\quad\quad = 41 + 40 = 81$
$\Rightarrow \quad\quad (l + b) = 9$
$\therefore \quad$ Perimeter = $2(l + b)$ = 18 cm.

10. (a)
Length of largest tile = H.C.F. of 1517 cm and $\quad\quad$ 902 cm = 41 cm
$\quad\quad$ Area of each tile = (41×41) cm^2
$\therefore$ Required number of tiles
$\quad\quad\quad\quad\quad = (1517 \times 902)/(41 \times 41)$
$\quad\quad\quad\quad\quad = 814$

11. (d)
We have: $\quad (l - b) = 23$ and $2(l + b)$
$\quad\quad\quad\quad\quad = 206$ or $(l + b) = 103$
Solving the two equations, we get:
$\quad\quad\quad l = 63$ and $b = 40$
$\therefore \quad\quad$ Area = $(l \times b) = (63 \times 40)$ m^2
$\quad\quad\quad\quad\quad = 2520$ m^2

12. (b)
Let original length = x and original breadth
$\quad\quad\quad\quad = y$
$\quad\quad$ Original area = xy
$\quad\quad$ New length = $x/2$
$\quad\quad$ New breadth = $3y$
$\quad\quad$ New area = $(x/2 \times 3y) = (3/2)xy$
$\therefore \quad$ Increase % = $(1/2)xy \times (1/xy) \times 100\%$
$\quad\quad\quad\quad = 50\%$

13. (d)
$\quad\quad$ Let breadth = x metres

Then, length = $(x + 20)$ metres
$\quad$ Perimeter = $(5300/26.50)$ m
$\quad\quad\quad\quad = 200$ m
$\therefore \quad\quad 2[(x + 20) + x] = 200$
$\Rightarrow \quad\quad\quad 2x + 20 = 100$
$\Rightarrow \quad\quad\quad\quad 2x = 80$
$\Rightarrow \quad\quad\quad\quad x = 40$
Hence, $\quad\quad$ length = $x + 20 = 60$ m

14. (d)
We have: $\quad\quad l = 20$ ft and lb
$\quad\quad\quad\quad = 680$ sq. ft.
So, $\quad\quad\quad b = 34$ ft.
$\therefore \quad$ Length of fencing = $(l + 2b) = (20 + 68)$ ft
$\quad\quad\quad\quad = 88$ ft.

15. (c)
Area to be plastered = $[2(l + b) \times h] + (l \times b)$
$\quad\quad\quad\quad = \{[2(25 + 12) \times 6]$
$\quad\quad\quad\quad\quad + (25 \times 12)\}$ m^2
$\quad\quad\quad\quad = (444 + 300)$ m^2
$\quad\quad\quad\quad = 744$ m^2.
$\therefore \quad$ Cost of plastering = Rs. $(744 \times 75/100)$
$\quad\quad\quad\quad = $ Rs. 558

16. (c)
$\quad\quad\quad$ Area = 1600 m^2
I. Side = $\sqrt{1600}$ m = 40 m
So, perimeter = (40×4) m = 160 m
$\therefore$ I alone gives the answer.
II. Perimeter = Total cost = 3200m/160 m
Cost per metre = 20
$\therefore$ II alone gives the answer.
$\therefore$ Correct answer is (C).

17. (d)
Given: Area of rectangle = Area of a right-angle triangle.
$\Rightarrow \quad\quad l \times b = \frac{1}{2} \times B \times H$
I. gives, $\quad\quad B = 40$ cm
II. gives, $\quad\quad H = 50$ cm
Thus, to find l, we need b also, which is not given.
$\therefore$ Given data is not sufficient to give the answer.
$\therefore$ Correct answer is (D).

18. (a)
I. A = $20 \times B \Rightarrow \frac{1}{2} \times B \times H = 20 \times B \Rightarrow H = 40$
$\therefore$ I alone gives the answer.
II. gives the perimeter of the triangle = 40 cm
This does not give the height of the triangle
$\therefore$ Correct answer is (A)

19. (d)
I. gives = 44
II. gives H = 12
$\therefore$ A = $2\pi rh = (4 \times 12)$

Cost of painting = Rs. (44 × 12 × 20)
Thus, I and II together give the answer.
∴ Correct answer is (D).

20. (c)
   I.   Material cost = Rs. 2.50 per m²
   II. Labour cost = Rs. 3500
   III. Total cost = Rs. 14,500
   Let the area be A sq. metres
   ∴ Material cost = Rs. (14500 – 3500)
                   = Rs. 11,000
   ∴ 5A/2 = 11000
   A = (11000 × 2)/5 = 4400 m²
   Thus, all I, II and III are needed to get the answer.
   ∴ Correct answer is (C).

21. (a)
   From II base :
   height = 5 : 12
   Let base = $5x$ and height = $12x$
   Then, hypotenuse = $\sqrt{(5x)^2 + (12x)^2} = 13x$
   From I the perimeter of the triangle = 30 cm
   ∴ $5x + 12x + 13x = 30 \Leftrightarrow = 1$
   So, base = $5x$ = 5 cm
         height = $12x$ = 12 cm
   ∴ Area = (1/2 × 5 × 12) = 30 cm²
   Thus, I and II together give the answer.
   Clearly III is redundant, since the breadth of the rectangle is not given.
   ∴ Correct answer is (A)

22. (b)
   I. $2(l + b) = 110$ ⇒ $l + b = 55$
   II. $l = (b + 5)$ ⇒ $l – b = 5$
   III. $l/b = 6/5$ ⇒ $5l – 6b = 0$
   These are three equations in l and b. We may solve them pair-wise.
   ∴ Any two of the three will give the answer.
   ∴ Correct answer is (B).

23. (d)
   From I and II, we can find the length and breadth of the rectangle. Therefore, the area can be obtained.
   So, III is redundant.
   Also, from II and III, we can find the length and breadth.
   Therefore, the area can be obtained.
   So, I is redundant.
   ∴ Correct answer is II and either I or III.

24. (c)
   From II, let $l = 4x$, $b = 6x$ and $h = 5x$
   Then, area of the hall = $(24x^2)$ m²
   From I, Area of the hall = 24 m²

From II and I, we get
$24x^2 = 24 \Leftrightarrow x = 1$
∴ $l = 4$ m, $b = 6$ and $h = 5$ m
Thus, area of two adjacent walls
= $[(l \times h) + (b \times h)]$ m² can be found out and so the cost of painting two adjacent walls may be found out.
Thus, III is redundant.
∴ Correct answer is (C).

25. (a)
   By the formula:
   Required area = $\pi (14/2)^2 = 22/7 \times 7^2$
                 = 154 cm²

26. (c)
   Area of quadrilateral = $\frac{1}{2}$ × any diagonal × (sum of perpendiculars drawn on diagonal from two vertices)
   = $\frac{1}{2} \times D \times (P_1 + P_2)$
   = $\frac{1}{2} \times 23 \times (17 + 7)$
   = 12 × 23 = 276 cm²

27. (a)
   Circumference of the circle = $2\pi r$
   $r = \frac{50}{\pi}$
   ∴ Side of the inscribed square
   = $\sqrt{2} r = \sqrt{2} \times \frac{50}{\pi}$

28. (b)
   % increase in its area = $2 \times 5 + 5^2/100$
                         = 10 + 0.25 = 10.25%

29. (b)
   Required percentage increase
   = $2 \times 2 + 2^2/100$
   = 4 + 0.04 = 4.04%

30. (b)
   Diameter is rarely used as the measuring side of a circle.
   Thus % increase in circumference = 12%

31. (a)

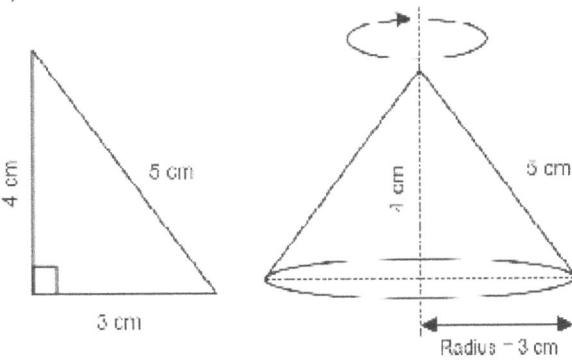

Clearly, we have r = 3 cm and h = 4 cm

∴ Volume = $\frac{1}{3}\pi r^2 h$
= (1/3 × π × 3² × 4) cm³
= 12π cm³

32. (b)
1 hectare = 10,000 m²
So, Area = (1.5 × 10000) m²
= 15000 m²
Depth = (5/100) m = (1/20) m
∴ Volume = (Area × Depth)
= (15000 × 1/20) m³
= 750 m³

33. (c)
2(15 + 12) × h = 2(15 × 12)
⇒ h = (180/27) m = (20/3) m
∴ Volume = (15 × 12 × 20/3) m³
= 1200 m³

34. (a)
Let the length of the wire be h
Radius = 1/2 mm
= 1/20 cm. Then
⇒ (22/7 × 1/20 × 1/20 × h)
= 66
⇒ h = (60 × 20 × 20 × 7)/22
= 8400 cm = 84 m

35. (b)
External radius = 4 cm
Internal radius = 3 cm
Volume of iron = (22/7 × [(4)² − (3)²] × 21) cm³
= (22/7 × 7 × 1 × 21) cm³
= 462 cm³
∴ Weight of iron = (462 × 8) gm = 3696 gm
= 3.696 kg.

36. (b)
Volume of water displaced
= (3 × 2 × 0.01) m³
= 0.06 m³
∴ Mass of man = Volume of water displaced × Density of water
= (0.06 × 1000) kg = 60 kg.

37. (b)
Total volume of water displaced
= (4 × 50) m³ = 200 m³.
Rise in water level = [200/(40 × 20)] m
= 0.25 m = 25 cm

38. (c)
l = 10 m
h = 8 m
So, r = $\sqrt{l^2 - h^2}$
= $\sqrt{10^2 - 8^2}$ = 6 m
∴ Curved surface area = πrl = (π × 6 × 10) m²
= 60 π m²

39. (a)
Area of the wet surface
= [2(lb + bh + lh) − lb]
= 2(bh + lh) + lb
= [2 (4 × 1.25 + 6 × 1.25) + 6 × 4] m²
= 49 m².

40. (b)
Clearly, l = (48 − 16) m = 32 m
b = (36 −16) m = 20 m
h = 8 m
∴ Volume of the box = (32 × 20 × 8) m³
= 5120 m³

41. (b)
(πr²h)/ (2πrh) = 924/264
r = [(924 /264) × 2] = 7 m
And, 2πrh = 264
h = (264 × 7/22 × 1/2 × 1/7)
= 6 m
∴ Required ratio = 2r/h =14/6 = 7 : 3

42. (b)
Let the thickness of the bottom be x cm.
Then, [(330 − 10) × (260 − 10) × (110 −x)]
= 8000 × 1000
⇒ 320 × 250 × (110 − x) = 8000 × 1000
⇒ (110 − x) = (8000 × 1000)/ (320 ×250)
= 100
x = 10 cm = 1 dm

43. (c)
h = 14 cm, r = 7 cm.
So, l = $\sqrt{7^2 + 14^2}$ = $\sqrt{245}$ = $7\sqrt{5}$ cm
∴ Total surface area
= πrl + πr²
= (22/7 × 7 + 22/7 × 7²) cm²
= [154(5 + 1)] cm²
= (154 × 3.236) cm²
= 498.35 cm²

44. (c)
Volume of the large cube
= (3³ + 4³ + 5³) = 216 cm³
Let the edge of the large cube be a.
So, a³ = 216 ⇒ a = 6 cm.
∴ Required ratio = [6 × (3² + 4² + 5²)]/(6 × 6²)
= 50/36 = 25 : 18

45. (c)
Number of bricks = Volume of the wall/Volume of 1 brick
= (800 × 600 × 22.5)/ (25 × 11.25 × 6)
= 6400

46. (c)
Given, height = 32 m
I. gives the area of the base = 154 m²

∴ Volume = (Area of the base × Height)
= (154 × 32) m³
Thus, I alone gives the answer.
II. gives the radius of the base = 7 m
∴ Volume = $\pi r^2 h$
= (22/7 × 7 × 7 × 32) m³
= 4928 m³
Thus, II alone gives the answer.
∴ Correct answer is (C).

47. (d)
I. gives that any two of l, b, h are equal.
II. gives that lbh = 64.
From I and II, the values of l, b, h may be
(1 ,1 , 64), (2 ,2 ,16), (4, 4, 4)
Thus, the block may be a cube or cuboid.
∴ Correct answer is (D).

48. (c)
I. gives, h = 28 m and r = 14
∴ Capacity = $\pi r^2 h$, which can be obtained.
Thus, I alone gives the answer.
II. gives, πr^2 = 616 m² and h = 28 m.
∴ Capacity = ($\pi r^2 \times h$) = (616 × 28) m³.
Thus, II alone gives the answer.
∴ Correct answer is (C).

49. (d)
II. gives the value of r.
But, in I, the breadth of rectangle is not given.
So, we cannot find the surface area of the cone.
Hence, the height of the cone cannot be determined.
∴ Correct answer is (D).

50. (c)
Let each edge be a metre. Then,
I. a^2 = 64
a = 8 m
Volume = (8 × 8 × 8) m³ = 512 m³
Thus, I alone gives the answer.
II. a = 8 m
Volume = (8 × 8 × 8) m³ = 512 m³
Thus, II alone gives the answer.
∴ Correct answer is (C).

51. (d)
Capacity = $\pi r^2 h$
I. gives, πr^2 = 61600. This gives r.
II. gives, h = 1.5 r.
Thus, I and II give the answer.
Again, III gives $2\pi r$ = 880. This gives r.
So, II and III also give the answer.
∴ Correct answer is (D).

52. (b)
Part filled by (A + B + C) in 3 minutes
= 3 (1/30 + 1/20 + 1/10)
= (3 × 11/60) = 11/20

Part filled by C in 3 minutes
= 3/10
∴ Required ratio = (3/10 × 20/11) = 6/11

53. (c)
Net part filled in 1 hour(1/5 + 1/6 −1/12) = 17/60
∴ The tank will be full in 60/17 hours
i.e., $3\dfrac{9}{17}$ hours

54. (d)
Work done by the leak in 1 hour
= (1/2 − 3/7) =1/14
∴ Leak will empty the tank in 14 hrs.

55. (b)
Let B be turned off after x minutes. Then,
Part filled by (A + B) in x min. + Part filled by A in
(30 − x) min. = 1.
∴ x(2/75 + 1/45) + (30 − x)2/75 = 1
⇒ 11x/225 + (60 − 2x)/75 = 1
⇒ 11x + 180 − 6x = 225
⇒ x = 9

56. (c)
Suppose, first pipe alone takes x hours to fill the tank .
Then, second and third pipes will take (x − 5) and
(x − 9) hours respectively to fill the tank.
1/x + 1/(x − 5) = 1/(x − 9)
(x −5 +x)/x(x − 5) = 1/(x − 9)
⇒ (2x − 5)(x − 9) = x(x − 5)
⇒ x^2 − 18x + 45 = 0
⇒ (x − 15)(x − 3) = 0
x = 15   [Neglecting x = 3]

57. (c)
Work done by the waste pipe in 1 minute
= 1/15 − (1/20 + 1/24)
= (1/15 − 11/20)
= − 1/40 [−ve sign means emptying]
∴ Volume of 1/40 part = 3 gallons
Volume of whole = (3 × 40) gallons = 120 gallons

58. (c)
Suppose pipe A alone takes x hours to fill the tank.
Then, pipes B and C will take x/2 and x/4 hours
respectively to fill the tank.
1/x + 2/x + 4/x = 1/5
7/x = 1/5
⇒ x = 35 hrs

59. (c)
Let the cistern be filled by pipe A alone in x hours.
Then, pipe B will fill it in (x + 6) hours.
1/x + 1/(x + 6) = 1/4
(x + 6 + x)/x (x + 6) = 1/4
⇒ x^2 − 2x − 24 = 0
⇒ (x − 6)(x + 4) = 0
⇒ x = 6
[Neglecting the negative value of x]

60. (a)
    Part filled by A in 1 min = 1/20
    Part filled by B in 1 min =1/30
    Part filled by (A + B) in 1 min
    = (1/20 + 1/30) = 1/12
    ∴ Both pipes can fill the tank in 12 minutes.
61. (d)
    Part filled in 4 minutes = 4(1/15 + 1/20) = 7/15
    Remaining part =(1 –7/15) = 8/15
    Part filled by B in 1 minute = 1/20
    ∴   1/20 : 8/15 : : 1: x
    $x = (8/15 \times 1 \times 20) = 10\frac{2}{3}$ min = 10 min. 40 sec.
    The tank will be full in (4 min. + 10 min. + 40 sec.) = 14 min. 40 sec.
62. (c)
    Let the slower pipe alone fills the tank in x minutes.
    Then, faster pipe will fill it in $x/3$ minutes.
    $1/x + 3/x = 1/36$
    $4/x = 1/36$
    ⇒ $x = 144$ min
63. (d)
    Part filled by (A + B) in 1 minute
    = (1/60 + 1/40) =1/24
    Suppose the tank is filled in x minutes.
    Then, $x/2(1/24 + 1/40) = 1$
    $x/2 \times x/15 = 1$
    $x = 30$ min.
64. (b)
    Time taken by one tap to fill half of the tank
    = 3 hrs.
    Part filled by the four taps in 1 hour
    = (4 x 1/6) = 2/3
    Remaining part = (1 – 1/2) =1/2
    ∴   2/3 : ½ :: 1 : x
    ⇒ $x = (1/2 \times 1 \times 3/2)$
    = 3/4 hours = 45 minutes
    So, total time taken = 3 hrs. 45 minutes
65. (c)
    (A + B)'s 1 hour's work = (1/12 + 1/15) = 3/20
    (A + C)'s hour's work = (1/12 + 1/20) = 2/15
    Part filled in 2 hrs = (3/20 + 2/15) = 17/60
    Part filled in 6 hrs = (3 × 17/60) = 17/20
    Remaining part = (1 – 17/20) = 3/20
    Now, it is the turn of A and B and 3/20 part is filled by A and B in 1 hour.
    ∴ Total time taken to fill the tank
    = (6 + 1) hrs = 7 hrs.

66. (c)
    Part filled in 2 hours = 2/6 = 1/3
    Remaining part = (1 – 1/3) = 2/3
    ∴ (A + B)'s 7 hour's work = 2/3
    (A + B)'s 1 hour's work = 2/21
    ∴   C's 1 hour's work = {(A + B + C)'s 1 hour's work} – {(A + B)'s 1 hour's work}
    = (1/6 – 2/21) =1/14
    ∴ C alone can fill the tank in 14 hours.
67. (d)
    I. Time taken to fill the cistern without leak
        = 9 hours.
        Part of cistern filled without leak in 1 hour
        = 1/9
    II. Time taken to fill the cistern in presence of leak = 10 hours.
        Net filling in 1 hour = 1/10
        Work done by leak in 1 hour
        = (1/9 – 1/10) = 1/90
    ∴ Leak will empty the full cistern in 90 hours.
    Clearly, both I and II are necessary to answer the question.
    ∴ Correct answer is (D).
68. (d)
    I. A's 1 minute's filling work = 1/16
    II. B's 1 minute's filling work = 1/8
        (A + B)'s 1 minute's emptying work
        = (1/8 – 1/16) =1/16
    Tank will be emptied in 16 minutes.
    Thus, both I and II are necessary to answer the question.
    ∴ Correct answer is (D).
69. (b)
    II. Part of the tank filled by A in 1 hour =1/4
    III. Part of the tank filled by B in 1 hour =1/6
         (A + B)'s 1 hour's work = (1/4 + 1/6) = 5/12
    ∴ A and B will fill the tank in 12/5 hrs
    = 2 hrs 24 min.
    So, II and III are needed.
    ∴ Correct answer is (B).
70. (a)
    Number of balls = Volume of big sphere / Volume of one small sphere
    = $(4\pi / 3 \times 8 \times 8 \times 8) / (4\pi / 3 \times 0.5 \times 0.5 \times 0.5)$
    = 4096

Mensuration

Previous Year Questions

1. The length of the diagonal of a cube is $6\sqrt{3}$. Its total surface area is:
   [NTSE 2001 – Jammu first stage paper]
   (a) 144 cm² (b) 216 cm²
   (c) 180 cm² (d) 108 cm²

2. The volume of a cube is 2744 cm³. Its surface area is:
   [NTSE 2003 – Haryana stage paper]
   (a) 196 cm² (b) 1176 cm²
   (c) 784 cm² (d) 588 cm²

3. The total surface area of a cube is 864 cm². Its volume is:
   [NTSE 2012 – Himachal Pradesh first stage paper]
   (a) 3456 cm³ (b) 432 cm³
   (c) 1728 cm³ (d) 3458 cm³

4. How many bricks each measuring (25 cm × 11.25 cm × 6 cm) will be required to construct a wall (8 m × 6 m × 22.5 m) :
   [NTSE 2012 – Delhi first stage paper]
   (a) 8000 (b) 6400
   (c) 4800 (d) 7200

5. The area of the base of a rectangular tank is 6500 cm² and the volume of water contained in it is 2.6 m³. The depth of the water in the tank is:
   [NTSE 2006 – Goa first stage paper]
   (a) 3.5 m (b) 4 m
   (c) 5 m   (d) 8 m

6. The volume of a wall 5 times at high as it is broad and 8 times as long as it is high, is 12.8 m³. The breath of the wall is:
   [NTSE 2004 – Kerala second stage paper]
   (a) 30 cm   (b) 40 cm
   (c) 22.5 cm (d) 25 cm

7. If each edge of a cube is increased by 50%, the percentage increased in the surface area is:
   [NTSE 2002 – Maharashtra second stage paper]
   (a) 50%   (b) 75%
   (c) 100% (d) 125%

8. How many bags of grain can be stored in a cuboidal granary (8m × 6m × 3m), if each bag occupies a space of 0.64 m³ ?
   [NTSE 2000 – Tripura first stage paper]
   (a) 8256 (b) 90
   (c) 212   (d) 225

9. A cube of side 6 cm is cut into a number of cubes each of side 2 cm. The number of cubes formed is:
   [NTSE 2005 – Rajasthan second stage paper]
   (a) 6   (b) 9
   (c) 12 (d) 27

10. During conversion of a solid from one shape to another, the volume of the new shape will:
    [NTSE 2001 – Gujrat second stage paper]
    (a) decrease
    (b) increase
    (c) remain unaltered
    (d) be doubled

National Talent Search Examination (NTSE)-X

Answer Key

| 1. (b) | 2. (b) | 3. (c) | 4. (b) | 5. (b) | 6. (b) | 7. (d) | 8. (d) | 9. (d) | 10. (c) |

Explanatory Notes

1. (b)
$$\sqrt{3}a = 6\sqrt{3} \Rightarrow a = 6$$
Total surface area $= 6a^2 = (6 \times 6 \times 6)$ cm^2
$= 216$ cm^2

2. (b)
$$a^3 = 2744 = (2^3 \times 7^3)$$
$\Rightarrow a (2 \times 7) = 14$ cm
$\therefore$ Surface area $= 6a^2 = (6 \times 14 \times 14)$ cm^2
$= 1176$ cm^2

3. (c)
$$6a^2 = 864 = 144$$
$\Rightarrow a = 12$ cm
$\therefore$ Volume $= (12 \times 12 \times 12)$ cm^3
$= 1728$ cm^3

4. (b)
Volume of wall $= (800 \times 600 \times 22.5)$ cm^3
Number of bricks $= \dfrac{\text{Volume of wall}}{\text{Volume of 1 brick}}$
$= \left(\dfrac{800 \times 600 \times 22.5}{25 \times 11.25 \times 6}\right)$

5. (b)
Area of the base $= \dfrac{6500}{100 \times 100}$ m$^2 = \dfrac{13}{20}$ m^2
Let the depth of the water be d meters. Then
$$\dfrac{13}{20} \times d = 2.6$$
$$d = \left(\dfrac{26}{10} \times \dfrac{20}{13}\right) \text{ m} = 4\text{m}$$

6. (b)
Let breadth $= x$ cm.
Then height $= 5x$ cm and
length $= 40x$ cm
$\therefore 40x \times x \times 5x = 12.8 \times 100 \times 100 \times 100$
$x^3 = 64000 = (40 \times 40 \times 40)$
$\Rightarrow x = 40$ cm

7. (d)
Let the original edge be an original surface area
$= 6a^2$
New edge $= 150\%$ of a
$= \dfrac{150a}{100} = \dfrac{3a}{2}$
New surface area $= 6 \times \left(\dfrac{3a}{2}\right)^2 = \dfrac{27a^2}{2}$
Increase in area $= \left(\dfrac{27a^2}{2} - 6a^2\right) = \dfrac{15a^2}{2}$
Increase % $= \left(\dfrac{15a^2}{2} \times \dfrac{1}{6a^2} \times 100\right)$
$= 125\%$

8. (d)
Number of bags $= \left(\dfrac{8 \times 6 \times 3}{0.64}\right) = 225$

9. (d)
Number of cubes formed
$= \dfrac{\text{Volume of given cube}}{\text{Volume of each small cube}}$
$= \left(\dfrac{6 \times 6 \times 6}{2 \times 2 \times 2}\right) = 27$

10. (c)
During conversion of a solid from one shape to another, the volume remains the same.

UNIT 12
Statistics

1. In continuous frequency distribution, the upper limit of a class is not included in that class while in discontinuous both the limits are included.
2. The height of rectangles corresponds to the numerical value of the data.
3. Frequency polygons are a graphical device for understanding the shapes of distribution.
4. Bar charts are used for comparing two or more values.
5. A histogram differs from a bar chart, since in the former the area of the bar denotes the value, not the height.
6. The height of the rectangle is the ratio of the frequency of the class to the width or size of the class.
7. Last cumulative frequency is always the sum total of all the frequencies.
8. If both a histogram and a frequency polygon are drawn on the same graph, then we should first draw the histogram and then join the mid-points of the tops of the adjacent rectangles in the histogram with line-segments to get the frequency polygon.
9. If classes are not of equal width, then the height of the rectangle is calculated by the ratio of the frequency of that class, to the width of that class.
10. A measure of central tendency tries to estimate the central value which represents the entire data.
11. The three measures of central tendency for ungrouped data are mean, mode and median.
12. The disadvantage of arithmetic mean is that it is affected by extreme values.
13. The median is to be calculated only after arranging the data in ascending order or descending order.
    (a) Average height is the modal value.
    (b) Disadvantage of the mode is that it is not uniquely defined in many cases.
    (c) The data is symmetric about the mean position when the three averages, mean median and mode are all equal.
    (d) The data is asymmetric when the three measures are unequal.
14. The variate corresponding to the highest frequency is taken as the mode and not as the frequency.

■ **Ogive Definition**

Ogive is a graph of a cumulative distribution, which shows data values on the horizontal axis and either the cumulative frequencies, the cumulative relative frequencies or cumulative percent frequencies on the vertical axis. The Ogive is constructed by plotting a point corresponding to the cumulative frequency of each class. The most commonly used graphs of frequency distribution are as follows:

1. Histogram
2. Frequency polygon
3. Frequency Curve
4. Ogives (Cumulative frequency curves)

■ **Ogive Chart**

An Ogive Chart is a curve of the cumulative frequency distribution or cumulative relative frequency distribution. To draw such a curve, first of all the simple frequency must be expressed as percentage of the total frequency. Then, such percentages are cumulated and plotted as in the case of an ogive.

■ **Frequency Ogive**

There are two ways of constructing an ogive or cumulative frequency curve. The steps for constructing less than Ogive chart and more than Ogive chart are given below:

■ **Steps for constructing a less than Ogive chart (less than Cumulative frequency curve):**

1. Draw and label the horizontal and vertical axes.
2. Take the cumulative frequencies along the y axis (vertical axis) and the upper class limits on the x axis (horizontal axis).
3. Plot the cumulative frequencies against each upper class limit.
4. Join the points with a smooth curve.

■ **Let us see with the help of a table how to construct a 'less than' Ogive chart:**

Class	c.f.
Less than 10	4
Less than 20	9
Less than 30	21
Less than 40	32
Less than 50	41

Class	c.f.	Frequency
0-10	Less than 10 - less than 0 = 4-0	4
10-20	Less than 20 - less than 10 = 9-4	5
20-30	Less than 30 - less than 20 = 21-9	12
30-40	Less than 40 - less than 30 = 32-21	11
40-50	Less than 50 - less than 40 = 40-32	8

When we write, 'less than 10 - less than 0', the difference gives the frequency 4 for the class interval (0 - 10) and so on.

■ **Let us see with the help of a table how to construct a 'more than' Ogive chart:**

Class	c.f.
More than 0	40
More than 10	36
More than 20	31
More than 30	19
More than 40	8
More than 50	0

Class	c.f.	Frequency
0-10	More than 0 - more than 10 = 40-36	4
10-20	More than 10 - more than 20 = 36-31	5
20-30	More than 20 - more than 30 = 31-19	12
30-40	More than 30 - more than 40 = 19-8	11
40-50	More than 40 - more than 50 = 8-0	8

When we write 'more than 0 - more than 10', the difference gives the frequency 4 for the class interval (0 - 10) and so on.

Solved Examples

1. Draw the more than cumulative frequency curve for the following data

Class	F
10-20	3
20-30	15
30-40	8
40-50	20
50-60	7
60-70	4
70-80	6
80-90	2

Solution:

First let's find the more than cumulative frequency corresponding to each class. For this the frequencies of the succeeding classes are added to the frequency of a class. The greater than cumulative **frequency table** is given below.

Lower limit	Frequency More than	Cumulative Frequency
10	3	65
20	15	65 - 3 = 62
30	8	62 - 15 = 47
40	20	47 - 8 = 41
50	7	41 - 20 = 19
60	4	19 - 7 = 12
70	6	12 - 4 = 8
80	2	8 - 6 = 2

Now we draw the horizontal and vertical axes and label them. Plot the cumulative frequencies corresponding to the lower limit of each class and join the points using a smooth curve.

The more than cumulative frequency curve is shown below.

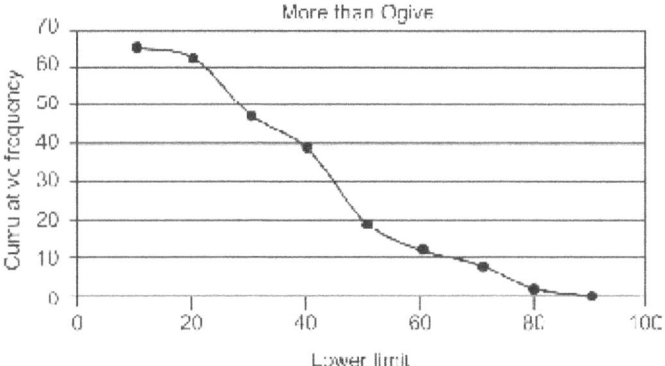

2. Draw a 'less than' ogive curve for the following data:

Marks	Frequency
0-10	2
10-20	8
20-30	12
30-40	18
40-50	28
50-60	22
60-70	6
70-80	4

Solution:
Frequency distribution of the data:

Marks	Frequency	Cumulative Frequency
0-10	2	2
10-20	8	10
20-30	12	22
30-40	18	40
40-50	28	68
50-60	22	90
60-70	6	96
70-80	4	100

To plot an Ogive

I. We plot the points with coordinates having abscissa as actual limits and ordinates as the cumulative frequencies, (10, 2), (20, 10), (30, 22), (40, 40), (50, 68), (60, 90), (70, 96) and (80, 100) are the coordinates of the points.

II. Join the points plotted by a smooth curve.

III. An Ogive is connected to a point on the X-axis representing the actual lower limit of the first class.

Scale:
X-axis 1 cm = 10 marks, Y-axis 1 cm = 10 c.f.

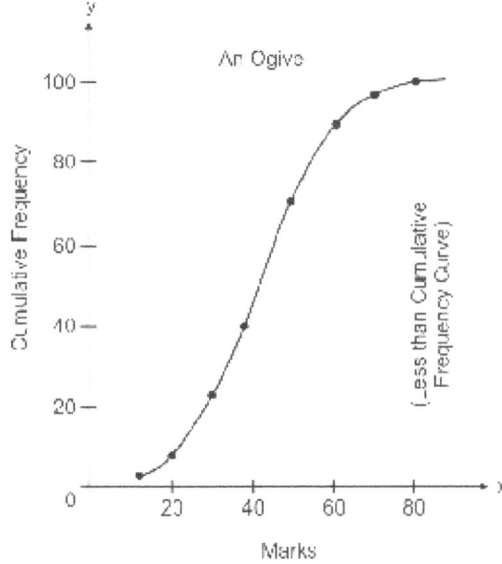

3. Using the data given below, construct a 'more than' cumulative frequency table and draw the Ogive.

Marks	Frequency
1 – 10	3
11 – 20	8
21 – 30	12
31 – 40	14
41 – 50	10
51 – 60	6
61 – 70	5
71 – 80	2

Solution:

Step 1: more than' cumulative frequency table for the given data:

Marks	Frequency	Cumulative Frequency
More than 1	3	60
More than 11	8	57
More than 21	12	49
More than 31	14	37
More than 41	10	23
More than 51	6	13
More than 61	5	7
More than 71	2	2

[115]

Step 2:
To plot an Ogive:
I. We plot the points with coordinates having abscissa as actual lower limits and ordinates as the cumulative frequencies, (70.5, 2), (60.5, 7), (50.5, 13),
(40.5, 23), (30.5, 37), (20.5, 49),(10.5, 57), (0.5, 60) are the coordinates of the points.
II. Join the points by a smooth curve.
III. An Ogive is connected to a point on the X-axis representing the actual upper limit of the last class in this case i.e., point (80.5, 0).

Scale:
X-axis 1 cm = 10 marks
Y-axis 2 cm = 10 c.f

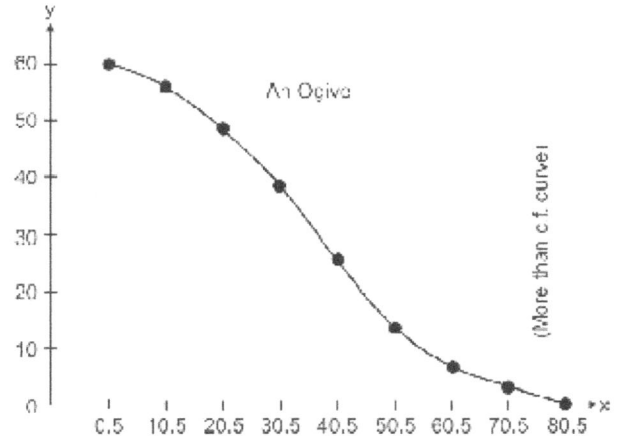

4. In a moderately skewed distribution, if the value of the mean is 5 and the median is 6, determine the value of the mode.

Solution:
Mean = 5, Median = 6
The formula is:
Mode = 3 Median – 2 Mean
Mode = 3(6) – 2(5) = 18 – 10 = 8 = 8

5. If median = 16, mode = 20. Find the mean.
Solution:
Mode = 20, Median = 16
The formula is:
Mean = 3/2 Median – 1/2 Mode
Mean = 3/2 (16) – 1/2 (20)
= 3(8) – 10 = 24 – 10 = 14

6. Find the mean deviation about the median for the following data: 2, 7, 5, 3, 10, 6, 9.
Solution:
Step 1: Arranging the data in ascending order, 2, 3, 5, 6, 7, 9, 10
Median is 4th observation.   M = 6
Step 2: The absolute values of the deviations from median are shown with the help of table:

Values (x)	$|x_i - M|$
2	4
3	3
5	1
6	0
7	1
9	3
10	4
Total	16

Here,   N = 7 (Number of terms)
Mean Deviation = $|xi–M|/N$
Mean Deviation (M) = 16/7 = 2.29

Multiple Choice Questions

1. While computing the mean of the grouped data, we assume that the frequencies are :
   (a) evenly distributed over the classes
   (b) centred at the class marks of the classes
   (c) centred at the lower limits of the classes
   (d) centred at the upper limits of the classes

2. The relation between mean, mode and median is :
   (a) mode = (3 × mean) – (2 × median)
   (b) mode = (3 × median) – (2 × mean)
   (c) median = (3 × mean) – (2 × mode)
   (d) mean = (3 × median) – (2 × mode)

3. Consider the frequency distribution of the heights of 60 students of a class.

Height (in cm)	No. of Students	Cumulative Frequency
150-155	16	16
155-160	12	28
160-165	9	37
165-170	7	44
170-175	10	54
175-180	6	60

Statistics

The sum of the lower limit of the modal class and the upper limit of the median class is:
(a) 310 (b) 315
(c) 320 (d) 330

4. Consider the following frequency distribution.

Class	Frequency
0 – 10	3
10 – 20	9
20 – 30	15
30 – 40	30
40 – 50	18
50 – 60	5

The modal class is
(a) 10–20 (b) 20–30
(c) 30–40 (d) 50–60

5. Mode = ?

(a) $x_k + h \cdot \left\{ \dfrac{(f_{k-1} - f_k)}{(2f_k - f_{k-1} - f_{k+1})} \right\}$

(b) $x_k + h \cdot \left\{ \dfrac{(f_k - f_{k-1})}{(2f_k - f_{k-1} - f_{k+1})} \right\}$

(c) $x_k + h \cdot \left\{ \dfrac{(f_k - f_{k-1})}{(f_k - 2f_{k-1} - f_{k+1})} \right\}$

(d) $x_k + h \cdot \left\{ \dfrac{(f_k - f_{k-1})}{(f_k - f_{k-1} - 2f_{k+1})} \right\}$

6. If the mean and median of a set of numbers are 8.9 and 9 respectively, then the mode will be:
(a) 7.2 (b) 8.2
(c) 9.2 (d) 10.2

7. Look at the frequency distribution table given below :

Class interval	Frequency
35–45	8
45–55	12
55–65	20
65–75	10

The median of the above distribution is :
(a) 56.5 (b) 57.5
(c) 58.5 (d) 59

8. Consider the the following table:

Class Interval	Frequency
10 – 13	5
14 – 18	11
18 – 22	16
22 – 26	25
26 – 30	19

The mode of the above data is:
(a) 23.5 (b) 24
(c) 24.4 (d) 25

9. The mean and mode of a frequency distribution are 28 and 16 respectively. The median is :
(a) 22 (b) 23.5
(c) 24 (d) 25.5

10. The median and mode of a frequency distribution are 26 and 29 repectively. Then the mean is:
(a) 27.5 (b) 24.5
(c) 28.4 (d) 25.8

11. For a symmetrical frequency distribution we have
(a) mean < mode < median
(b) mean > mode > median
(c) mean = mode = median
(d) mean = $\dfrac{1}{2}$ (mean + median)

12. Look at the cumulative frequency distribution table given below:

Monthly Income	Number of Families
More than Rs. 10000	100
More than Rs. 14000	85
More than Rs. 18000	69
More than Rs. 20000	50
More than Rs. 25000	37
More than Rs. 30000	15

Number of families having income range Rs. 20000 to Rs. 25000 is:
(a) 19 (b) 16
(c) 13 (d) 22

13. Which of the following is not a measure of central tendency ?
(a) mean (b) mode
(c) median (d) standard deviation

14. Which of following cannot be determined graphically ?
(a) mean (b) median
(c) mode (d) None of these

15. The mode of a frequency distribution is obtained graphically from:
(a) a frequency curve
(b) a frequency polygon
(c) a histogram
(d) an ogive

16. The median of a frequency distribution is found graphically with the help of:
    (a) a histrogram
    (b) a frequency curve
    (c) a frequency polygon
    (d) Ogives

17. The cumulative frequency table is useful in determining the:
    (a) mean   (b) median
    (c) mode   (d) All of these

18. The abscissa of the point of intersection of the Less Than Type and of the More Than Type cumulative frequency curves of a grouped data gives its:
    (a) mean   (b) median
    (c) mode   (d) None of these

19. In the formula, $\bar{x} = \left\{ A + \dfrac{\Sigma f_i d_i}{\Sigma f_i} \right\}$ for finding the mean of the grouped data, the d_i are the deviations from A of :
    (a) lower limits of the classes
    (b) upper limits of the classes
    (c) mid points of the classes
    (d) None of these

20. If $\Sigma x_i'$ are the mid points of the class intervals of a grouped data f_i' are the corresponding frequencies and $\bar{x}$ is the mean, then $\Sigma f_i (x_i - \bar{x}) = ?$
    (a) 1   (b) 0
    (c) -1 (d) 2

Statistics

Answer Key

1. (b)	2. (b)	3. (b)	4. (c)	5. (b)	6. (c)	7. (b)	8. (c)	9. (c)	10. (b)
11. (c)	12. (c)	13. (d)	14. (a)	15. (c)	16. (d)	17. (b)	18. (b)	19. (c)	20. (b)

Explanatory Notes

1. (b)
   In computing the mean of the grouped data, we assume that the frequencies are centred at the class marks of the classes.
   We know that BD : DC = AB : BC

2. (b)
   We have : mode = (3 × median) – (2 × mean)

3. (b)
   The class having maximum frequency is the modal class.
   So, the modal class is 150 – 155. Its lower limit is 150.
   Also N = 60 $\Rightarrow \frac{N}{2}$ = 30 and the cumulative frequency just more than 30 is 37. Its class is 160 – 165), whose upper limit it 165.
   Required sum = (150 + 165) = 315

4. (c)
   The class 30–40 has maximum frequency. So that modal class is 30–40.

5. (b)
   Clearly (b) is true.

6. (c)
   Mode = (3 × median) – (2 × mean)
   = (3 × 9) – (2 × 8.9)
   = 27 – 17.8 = 9.2

7. (b)
   We have

Class Interval	Frequency	Cumulative Frequency
35 – 45	8	8
45 – 55	12	20
55 – 65	20	40
65 – 75	10	50

   Here N = 50, $\Rightarrow \frac{N}{2}$ = 25, which lies in class interval 55 – 65

   Median = $l + \left\{ h \times \frac{N/2 - Cf}{f} \right\}$
   = $55 + \frac{(65-55)}{20} \times (25 - 20)$
   = 57.5

8. (c)
   The maximum frequency is 25 and the modal class is 22–26.

   $\therefore x_k = 22, f_k = 25, f_{k-1} = 16, f_{k+1} = 19$ and $h = 4$

   $\therefore$ Mode = $x_k + h \cdot \left\{ \frac{(f_k - f_{k-1})}{(2f_k - f_{k-1} - f_{k+1})} \right\}$

   = $\left\{ 22 + 4 \times \frac{(25-16)}{(50-16-19)} \right\}$

   = $\left(22 + 4 \times \frac{9}{15} \right) = \left(22 + \frac{12}{15} \right)$

   = (22 + 2.4) = 24.4

9. (c)
   3 × median = (mode + 2 mean)
   = (16 + 2 × 28) = 72
   $\Rightarrow$ median = $\frac{72}{3} = 24$

10. (b)
    Mode = (3 × median) – (2 × mean)
    2 × mean = (3 × median) – (mode)
    = (3 × 26) – 29
    = 49
    mean = $\frac{49}{2} = 24.5$

11. (c)
    We must have : mean = mode = median

12. (c)

13. (d)
    Standard deviation is not a meausre of central tendency.

14. (a)
    Mean cannot be determined graphically.

15. (c)
    Mode of a frequency distribution can not be obtained graphically from a histogram.

16. (d)
    The median of a frequency distribution is found graphically with the help of ogives.

17. (b)
    The cumulative frequency table is useful in determining the median.

18. (b)
    The abscissa of the point of intersection of the two ogives gives the median.

19. (c)
    d_i' are deviations from A of midpoints of the classes.

20. (b)
    Clearly we have $\Sigma f_i (x_i - \bar{x}) = 0$.

Previous Year Questions

1. Median = ?

   [NTSE 2003 – Kerala first stage paper]

   (a) $l + \left\{ h \times \dfrac{\left(\dfrac{N}{2} - cf\right)}{f} \right\}$ (b) $l + \left\{ h \times \dfrac{\left(cf - \dfrac{N}{2}\right)}{f} \right\}$

   (c) $l - \left\{ h \times \dfrac{\left(\dfrac{N}{2} - cf\right)}{f} \right\}$ (d) None of these

2. $\Sigma f_i = 15, \Sigma f_i x_i = 3p + 36$ and mean of any distri-bution is 3, then $p = ?$

   [NTSE 2005 – Jammu first stage paper]
   (a) 2 (b) 3
   (c) 4 (d) 5

3. For what value of x, the mode of the following data is 8 :

   4, 5, 6, 8, 5, 4, 8, 5, 6, x, 8

   [NTSE 2012 – Bihar first stage paper]
   (a) 5 (b) 6
   (c) 8 (d) 4

4. If the value of mean and mode 30 and 15 respectively, the median = ?

   [NTSE 2000 – Gujrat second stage paper]
   (a) 22.5 (b) 24.5
   (c) 25   (d) 26

5. The numbers 5, 7, 10, 12, $2x - 8$, $2x + 10$, 35, 41, 42, 50 are arranged in ascending order. If the median is 25, then $x = ?$

   [NTSE 2012 – Chandigarh first stage paper]
   (a) 10 (b) 11
   (c) 12 (d) 9

6. Which of the following is the median of first ten prime numbers.

   [NTSE 2000 – Assam first stage paper]
   (a) 10 (b) 11
   (c) 12 (d) 13

7. The median and mode of a distribution are 21.2 and 21.4 respectively. Find its mean

   [NTSE 2004 – Rajasthan second stage paper]
   (a) 21.2 (b) 21.4
   (c) 21.1 (d) 21.0

8. The sum of deviation of a set of values $x_1, x_2, x_3 \ldots x_n$ measured from 50 is -10 and the sum of observation is 990. Then = ?

   [NTSE 2002 – Goa first stage paper]
   (a) 15 (b) 18
   (c) 20 (d) 25

9. Which is true ? For the distribution

x	15	17	19	$20 + p$	23
f	2	3	4	$5p$	6

   Mean is 20, then $p = ?$

   [NTSE 2005 – Punjab first stage paper]
   (a) 1   (b) 2
   (c) 1.5 (d) 2.5

10. The median of the following frequency distribution is

x	6	7	5	2	10	9	3
f	9	12	8	13	11	14	7

    [NTSE 2001 – UP first stage paper]
    (a) 6 (b) 5
    (c) 4 (d) 7

Statistics

Answer Key

1. (a)	2. (b)	3. (c)	4. (c)	5. (c)	6. (c)	7. (c)	8. (c)	9. (a)	10. (a)

Explanatory Notes

1. (b) Clearly (a) is true.

2. (b)
$$\text{Mean} = \frac{\Sigma f_i x_i}{\Sigma f_i} \qquad 3 = \frac{3p + 36}{15}$$
$$45 = 3p + 36 \qquad \Rightarrow 3p = 9$$
$$\Rightarrow p = 3$$

3. (c)
   Number of 4's = 2
   Number of 5's = 3
   Number of 6's = 2
   Since mode = 8
   Number of 8's = 3 ∴ $x = 3$

4. (c)
$$\text{Median} = \text{mode} + \frac{2}{3}(\text{mean} - \text{mode})$$
$$= 15 + \frac{2}{3}(30 - 15)$$
$$= 15 + 10 = 25$$

5. (c)
Given observations are :
5, 7, 10, 12, $(2x - 8)$ $(2x + 10)$, 35, 41, 42, 50
Here N = 10, which is even
∴ Median = $\frac{1}{2}$ [5th observation + 6th observation]
$= \frac{1}{2}[2x - 8 + 2x + 10] = \frac{4x + 2}{2} = 2x + 1$
$25 = 2x + 1$
$24 = 2x \qquad \Rightarrow x = 12$

6. (c)
First ten prime numbers are :
2, 3, 5, 7, 11, 13, 17, 19, 23, 29
Here N = 10, which is even
∴ Median
$= \frac{1}{2}\left[\frac{N^{th}}{2}\text{ observation} + \left(\frac{N}{2} + 1\right)\text{observation}\right]$
$= \frac{1}{2}$ [5th observation + 6th observation]
$= \frac{1}{2}(11 + 13) = 12$

7. (c)
We know that mean = mode + $\frac{3}{2}$ (median-mode)
$= 21.4 + \frac{3}{2}(21.2 - 21.4)$
$= 21.4 + \frac{3}{2}(-0.2)$
$= 21.4 - 0.3 = 21.1$

8. (c)
Since $\sum_{i=1}^{n}(x_i - 50) = -10$
$\Rightarrow \sum_{i=1}^{n} x_i - \sum_{i=1}^{n} 50 = -10$
$\Rightarrow \sum_{i=1}^{n} x_i - 50n = -10$
But $\sum_{i=1}^{n} x_i = 990$
∴ $990 - 50n = -10$
$1000 = 50n$
$\Rightarrow n = 20$

9. (a)
Mean
$= \frac{15 \times 2 + 17 \times 3 + 19 \times 4 + (20 + p)5p + 23 \times 6}{2 + 3 + 4 + 5p + 6}$
$20 = \frac{30 + 51 + 76 + 100p + 5p^2 + 138}{15 + 5p}$
$\Rightarrow 300 + 100p = 295 + 100p + 5p^2$
$\Rightarrow 5p^2 = 5p^2$
$\Rightarrow p^2 = 1$
$\Rightarrow p = 1$
[∵ $5p > 0$, since this represents frequency]
[∴ $p > 0$]

10. (a)
Arranging x in the ascending order

x	f	c.f.
2	13	13
3	7	20
5	8	28
6	9	37 ← median class
7	12	49
9	14	63
10	11	74

Here
$\frac{N}{2} = \frac{74}{2} = 37$
∴ Median $n = 6$

UNIT 13
Probability

Probability is the measurement of uncertainty. In this chapter chances of happening of events are discussed.

Examples
1. In a toss of single coin, the chance of appearing head income sense.
2. In a toss of two coins the chance that at least one of the coins shows head.
3. In a throw of single dice, the chance of appea-ring an even number.
4. The chance of drawing a black ball from a bag containing two black and two red balls.

Terminology

- **Random Experiment**

    It is an experiment which, if conducted repeatedly under homogeneous conditions, does not give the same result. The result may be any one of the various possible 'outcomes'. For example, if an unbiased dice is thrown, it will not always fall with any particular number up. Any of the six numbers on the dice can come up.

- **Exhaustive Cases**

    All possible outcomes of an event are known as exhaustive cases. In the throw of a single dice the exhaustive cases are 6 as the dice has only six faces each marked with a different number. Similarly, the number of exhaustive cases in the throw of 2 coins would be four (2 × 2), i.e. HH, TT, HT and TH (where H stands for head and T for tail).

- **Favourable Cases**

    The numbers of outcomes which result in the happening of a desired event are called favourable cases. Thus in a single throw of a dice the number of favourable cases of getting an odd number is three, i.e. 1,3 and 5.

    Mutually Exclusive Events

    Two or more events are said to be mutually exclusive if the happening of any one of them excludes the happening of all others in a single (i.e. same) experiment.

- **Equally Likely Cases**

    Two or more events are said to be equally likely if the chances of their happening are equal, i.e. there is no preference of any one event to the other. Thus, in a throw of unbiased dice, the coming up of 1, 2, 2, 4, 5, or 6 is equally likely.

Independent and Dependent Events

An event is said to be independent if its happening is not affected by the happening of other events and if it does not affect the happening of other events.

If A and B are independent events associated with a random experiment, Then

$$P(A \cap B) = P(A)P(B)$$

1. A bag contains 3 red and 5 black balls and a second bag contains 6 red and 4 black balls. A ball is drawn from each bag. Find the probability that both are red.

Solution

Let A be the event that a red ball is drawn from first bag and B be the event that a red ball is drawn from the second bag.

Then A and B are independent events.

∴ Required probability

$$= P(A) \times P(B)$$
$$= \frac{3}{8} \times \frac{6}{10} = \frac{9}{40}$$

- **Sample Space**

    A set containing all possible outcomes of a random experiment is known as Sample Space.

Key Points

1. Probability of an event lies between 0 and 1.
2. Probability can never be negative.
3. A pack of playing cards consists of 52 cards which are divided into 4 suits of 13 cards each. Each suit consists of one ace, one king, one queen, one jack and 9 other cards numbered from 2 to 10. Four suits are named as spades, hearts, diamonds and clubs.
4. King, queen and jack are face cards.
5. The two possible outcomes of tossing a coin are head and tail.
6. The sum of probabilities of all elementary events of an experiment is 1.
7. If S be the sample space and A and B are the events of a random experiments. Then,

    (a) $0 \leq P < (A) \leq 1$

    (b) $P(S) = 1$

    (c) $P(\emptyset) = 0$

    (d) $P(A) + P(\overline{A}) = 1$

(e) $P(A \cup B) = P(A) + P(B) - P(A \cap B)$
$= P(A) + P(B)$
if A and B are mutually exclusive.

Conditional Probability

Let A and B be two events associated with a random experiment, then the probability of occurrence of A under the condition that B has already occurred and $P(B) \neq 0$, is called the conditional probability and it is denoted by P(A/B).

Thus, P (A/B) = Probability of occurrence of A given that B has already happened.

Similarly P (B/A) = Probability of occurrence of B given that A has already happened.

2. A bag contains 7 white and 5 red balls. Two balls are drawn from the bag after the other without replacement. Consider the following events.
A = Drawing a white ball in the first draw
B = Drawing a red ball in the second draw
Now, P (B/A) = Probability of drawing a red ball in the second draw given that a white ball has already been drawn in the first draw.
Since, 8 balls are left after drawing a white ball in first draw and out of these 8 balls 4 balls are red, therefore P(B/A) = 8/4 = 1/2

3. If A and B are two events associated with a random experiment such that P(A) = 0.3, P(B) = 0.4 and $P(A \cup B) = 0.5$. Find $P(A \cap B)$.
(a) 0.6 (b) 0.5
(c) 0.2 (d) 0.7
Solution: Option (c) is correct.

Explanation:
$P(A \cap B) = P(A) + P(B) - P(A \cup B)$
$= 0.3 + 0.4 - 0.5 = 0.2$

4. What is a probability that one is ace, one king and one queen?
(a) $\frac{19}{5525}$ (b) $\frac{21}{5525}$
(c) $\frac{17}{5525}$ (d) $\frac{16}{5525}$
Solution: Option (d) is correct.
Explanation:
$\frac{{}^4C_1 \times {}^4C_1 \times {}^4C_1}{{}^{52}C_3} = \frac{4 \times 4 \times 4}{22100} = \frac{16}{5525}$

5. Four boys and 3 girls stand in a queue for an interview. The probability that they will stand in alternate position is:
(a) 1/34 (b) 1/35
(c) 1/17 (d) 1/68
Solution: Option (b) is correct.
Explanation:
Total number of arrangement for 4 boys and 3 girls in a queue = 7!
When they occupy alternate position the arrangement would be like B G B G B G B
Thus, the total number of possible arrangements
$= \underbrace{4 \times 3 \times 2}_{\text{For Boys}} = \underbrace{3 \times 2}_{\text{For Girls}}$
Required Probability
$= \frac{4 \times 3 \times 2 \times 3 \times 2}{7!}$
$= \frac{4 \times 3 \times 2 \times 3 \times 2}{7 \times 6 \times 5 \times 4 \times 3 \times 2} = \frac{1}{35}$

Multiple Choice Questions

1. A card is drawn from a pack of 52 cards. The probability of getting a queen of club or a king of heart is:
(a) 1/13 (b) 2/13
(c) 1/26 (d) 1/52

2. A bag contains 4 white, 5 red and 6 blue balls. Three balls are drawn at random from the bag. The probability that all of them are red, is:
(a) 1/22 (b) 3/22
(c) 2/91 (d) 2/77

3. Two cards are drawn together from a pack of 52 cards. The probability that one is a spade and one is a heart, is:
(a) 3/20 (b) 29/34
(c) 47/100 (d) 13/102

4. One card is drawn at random from a pack of 52 cards. What is the probability that the card drawn is a face card (Jack, Queen and King only)?
(a) 1/13 (b) 3/13
(c) 1/4 (d) 9/52

5. A bag contains 6 black and 8 white balls. One ball is drawn at random. What is the probability that the ball drawn is white?
(a) 3/4 (b) 4/7
(c) 1/8 (d) 3/7

6. Two dice are thrown simultaneously. What is the probability of getting two numbers whose product is even?
(a) 1/2 (b) 3/4
(c) 3/8 (d) 5/16

7. In a class, there are 15 boys and 10 girls. Three students are selected at random. The probability that 1 girl and 2 boys are selected, is:
(a) 21/46 (b) 25/117
(c) 1/50 (d) 3/25

8. In a lottery, there are 10 prizes and 25 blanks. A lottery is drawn at random. What is the probability of getting a prize?
   (a) 1/10 (b) 2/5
   (c) 2/7 (d) 5/7

9. From a pack of 52 cards, two cards are drawn together at random. What is the probability of both the cards being kings?
   (a) 1/15 (b) 25/57
   (c) 35/256 (d) 1/221

10. Two dice are tosse(d) The probability that the total score is a prime number is:
    (a) 1/6 (b) 5/12
    (c) 1/2 (d) 7/9

11. Tickets numbered 1 to 20 are mixed up and then a ticket is drawn at random. What is the probability that the ticket drawn has a number which is a multiple of 3 or 5?
    (a) 1/2 (b) 2/5
    (c) 8/15 (d) 9/20

12. A bag contains 2 red, 3 green and 2 blue balls. Two balls are drawn at random. What is the probability that none of the balls drawn is blue?
    (a) 10/21 (b) 11/21
    (c) 2/7 (d) 5/7

13. In a box, there are 8 red, 7 blue and 6 green balls. One ball is picked up randomly. What is the probability that it is neither red nor green?
    (a) 1/3 (b) 3/4
    (c) 7/19 (d) 8/21

14. What is the probability of getting a sum 9 from two throws of a dice?
    (a) 1/6 (b) 1/8
    (c) 1/9 (d) 1/12

15. Three unbiased coins are tosse(d) What is the probability of getting at most two heads?
    (a) 3/4 (b) 1/4
    (c) 3/8 (d) 7/8

16. A dice is thrown once. What is the probability of getting a number less than 3 ?
    (a) 1/2 (b) 1/3
    (c) 1/6 (d) 1/4

17. A dice is thrown once. What is the probability of getting a number more than 4 ?
    (a) 1/3 (b) 1/6
    (c) 1/2 (d) 3/4

18. A dice is thrown one. What is the probability of getting a prime number ?
    (a) 1/3 (b) 1/2
    (c) 2/3 (d) None of these

19. In throw of dice, what is the probability of getting a 4 ?
    (a) 2/3 (b) 1/2
    (c) 31/4 (d) 1/3

20. Cards bearing number 3 to 20 are placed in a bag and mixed throughly. A card is taken out of the bag at random. What is the probability that the number on the card taken out is an even number?
    (a) 9/17 (b) 1/2
    (c) 5/9 (d) 7/18

Probability

Answer Key

1. (c)	2. (c)	3. (d)	4. (b)	5. (b)	6. (b)	7. (a)	8. (c)	9. (d)	10. (b)
11. (d)	12. (a)	13. (a)	14. (c)	15. (d)	16. (b)	17. (a)	18. (b)	19. (c)	20. (b)

Explanatory Notes

1. (c)
   Here, $n(S) = 52$
   Let E = event of getting a queen of club or a king of heart.
   Then, $n(E) = 2$
   ∴ $P(E) = n(E)/n(S) = 2/52 = 1/26$

2. (c)
   Let S be the sample space.
   Then, $n(S)$ = number of ways of drawing 3 balls out of 15
   = $^{15}C_3$
   = $(15 \times 14 \times 13)/(3 \times 2 \times 1)$
   = 455
   Let E = event of getting all the 3 red balls.
   ∴ $n(E) = {}^5C_3 = {}^5C_2$
   = $(5 \times 4)/(2 \times 1) = 10$.
   ∴ $P(E) = n(E)/n(S) = 10/455 = 2/91$

3. (d)
   Let S be the sample space.
   Then, $n(S) = {}^{52}C_2$
   = $(52 \times 51)/(2 \times 1) = 1326$
   Let E = event of getting 1 spade and 1 heart.
   ∴ $n(E)$ = number of ways of choosing 1 spade out of 13 and 1 heart out of 13
   = $({}^{13}C_1 \times {}^{13}C_1) = (13 \times 13)$
   = 169
   ∴ $P(E) = n(E)/n(S)$
   = 169/1326 = 13/102

4. (b)
   Clearly, there are 52 cards, out of which there are 12 face cards.
   ∴ P (getting a face card) = 12/52 = 3/13

5. (b)
   Let number of balls = (6 + 8) = 14
   Number of white balls = 8
   P (drawing a white ball) = 8/14 = 4/7

6. (b)
   In a simultaneous throw of two dice, we have n(S) = (6 × 6) = 36.
   Then, E = {(1, 2), (1, 4), (1, 6), (2, 1), (2, 2), (2, 3), (2, 4), (2, 5), (2, 6), (3, 2), (3, 4), (3, 6), (4, 1), (4, 2), (4, 3), (4, 4), (4, 5), (4, 6), (5, 2), (5, 4), (5, 6), (6, 1), (6, 2), (6, 3), (6, 4), (6, 5), (6, 6)}
   ∴ $n(E) = 27$
   ∴ $P(E) = n(E)/n(S) = 27/36 = 3/4$

7. (a)
   Let S be the sample space and E be the event of selecting 1 girl and 2 boys.
   Then, $n(S)$ = Number ways of selecting 3 students out of 25
   = $^{25}C_3$
   = $(25 \times 24 \times 23)/(3 \times 2 \times 1)$
   = 2300
   ∴ $n(E) = ({}^{10}C_1 \times {}^{15}C_2)$
   = $[10 \times (15 \times 14)/(2 \times 1)]$
   = 1050
   ∴ $P(E) = n(E)/n(S)$
   = 1050/2300
   = 21/46

8. (c)
   P (getting a prize) = 10/(10 + 25)
   = 10/35 = 2/7

9. (d)
   Let S be the sample space
   Then, $n(S) = {}^{52}C_2$
   = $(52 \times 51)/(2 \times 1)$
   = 1326
   Let E = event of getting 2 kings out of 4
   ∴ $n(E) = {}^4C_2 = (4 \times 3)/(2 \times 1) = 6$
   ∴ $P(E) = n(E)/n(S)$
   = 6/1326 = 1/221

10. (b)
    Clearly, $n(S) = (6 \times 6) = 36$
    Let E = Event that the sum is a prime number.
    Then E = {(1, 1), (1, 2), (1, 4), (1, 6), (2, 1), (2, 3), (2, 5), (3, 2), (3, 4), (4, 1), (4, 3), (5, 2), (5, 6), (6, 1), (6, 5)}
    ∴ $n(E) = 15$
    ∴ $P(E) = n(E)/n(S)$
    = 15/36 = 5/12

11. (d)
    Here, S = {1, 2, 3, 4, ..., 19, 20}
    Let E = event of getting a multiple of 3 or 5
    = {3, 6, 9, 12, 15, 18, 5, 10, 20}.
    ∴ $P(E) = n(E)/n(S) = 9/20$

12. (a)
    Total number of balls = (2 + 3 + 2) = 7
    Let S be the sample space
    Then, $n(S)$ = Number of ways of drawing 2 balls out of 7
    = $^{7}C_2 = (7 \times 6)/(2 \times 1) = 21$

Let E = Event of drawing 2 balls, none of which is blue.
∴ n(E) = Number of ways of drawing 2 balls out of (2 + 3) balls.
= $^5C_2$
= (5 × 4)/ (2 × 1)
= 10
∴ P(E) = n(E)/n(S)
= 10/21

13. (a)
Total number of balls
= (8 + 7 + 6) = 21
Let E = event that the ball drawn is neither red nor green
= event that the ball drawn is blue
∴ n(E) = 7
∴ P(E) = n(E)/n(S)
= 7/21 = 1/3

14. (c)
In two throws of a dice,
n(S) = (6 × 6) = 36
Let E = event of getting a sum
= {(3, 6), (4, 5), (5, 4), (6, 3)}
∴ P(E) = n(E)/n(S) = 4/36 = 1/9

15. (d)
Here S = {TTT, TTH, THT, HTT, THH, HTH, HHT, HHH}
Let E = Event of getting at most two heads
Then E = {TTT, TTH, THT, HTT, THH, HTH, HHT}
∴ P(E) = n(E)/n(S) = 7/8

16. (b)
Here S = {1, 2, 3, 4, 5, 6}
Let E = Event of getting a number less than 3
= {1, 2}
∴ P(E) = $\frac{2}{6} = \frac{1}{3}$

17. (a)
Here S = {1, 2, 3, 4, 5, 6}
Let E = Event of getting a number more than 4
= {5, 6}
∴ P(E) = $\frac{2}{6} = \frac{1}{3}$

18. (b)
Here S = {1, 2, 3, 4, 5, 6}
Let E = Event of getting a prime number
= {2, 3, 5}
∴ P(E) = $\frac{3}{6} = \frac{1}{2}$

19. (c)
Here S = {1, 2, 3, 4, 5, 6}
Let E = Event of getting a 4 = {4}
∴ P(E) = $\frac{1}{6}$

20. (b)
Total number of cards = 18
Let E = Event of getting an even number
4 = {4, 6, 8, 10, 12, 16, 18, 20}.
Their number is 9
∴ P(E) = $\frac{9}{8} = \frac{1}{2}$

Probability

Previous Year Questions

1. A bag contains 4 red and 6 black balls. A ball is taken out of the bag at random. What is the probability of getting a black ball?
   [NTSE 2003 – Bihar first stage paper]
   (a) 2/5 (b) 3/5
   (c) 1/10 (d) None of these

2. A bag contains 8 red and 2 black and 5 white balls. One ball is drawn at random. What is the probability that the ball drawn is not block?
   [NTSE 2004 – MP second stage paper]
   (a) 8/15 (b) 2/15
   (c) 13/15 (d) 1/3

3. A bag contains 3 white, 4 red and 5 black balls. One ball is drawn at random. what is the probability that the ball drawn is neither black nor white?
   [NTSE 2000 – Punjab first stage paper]
   (a) 1/4 (b) 1/2
   (c) 1/3 (d) 3/4

4. What is the probability of an impossible event?
   [NTSE 2012 – Tripura first stage paper]
   (a) 1/2 (b) 0
   (c) 1 (d) None of these

5. What is the probability of a sure event?
   [NTSE 2006 – WB second stage paper]
   (a) 0 (b) 1/2
   (c) 1 (d) None of these

6. A card is drawn at random from a well shuffled deck of 52 cards. What is the probability of getting a black king?
   [NTSE 2003 – Tamilnadu second stage paper]
   (a) 1/3 (b) 1/26
   (c) 2/39 (d) None of these

7. From a well shuffled deck of 52 cards, one card is drawn at random. What is the probability of getting a queen?
   [NTSE 2006 – Jammu first stage paper]
   (a) 1/13 (b) 1/26
   (c) 4/39 (d) None of these

8. One card is drawn at random from a well shuffled deck of 52 cards. What is the probability of getting of face card? *[NTSE 2000 – Rajasthan first stage paper]*
   (a) 1/26 (b) 3/26
   (c) 3/13 (d) 4/13

9. One card is drawn at random from a well shuffled deck of 52 cards. What is the probability of getting of black face card? *[NTSE 2012 – Gujrat first stage paper]*
   (a) 1/26 (b) 3/26
   (c) 3/13 (d) 4/13

10. Wha is the probability that an ordinary year has 53 mondays? *[NTSE 2002 – UP second stage paper]*
    (a) 2/7 (b) 1/7
    (c) 7/52 (d) 7/53

Answer Key

| 1. (b) | 2. (c) | 3. (c) | 4. (b) | 5. (c) | 6. (b) | 7. (a) | 8. (c) | 9. (b) | 10. (b) |

Explanatory Notes

1. (b)
   Total number of balls = (4 + 6) = 10
   Number of black balls = 6
   $$P \text{ (getting of black ball)} = \frac{6}{10} = \frac{3}{5}$$

2. (c)
   Total number of balls = (8 + 2 + 5) = 15
   Number of non-black balls = 13
   $$P \text{ (getting a non-black ball)} = \frac{13}{15}$$

3. (c)
   Total number of balls = (3 + 4 + 5) = 12
   Number of balls each of which is neither black nor white = 4
   ∴ P (getting a ball which is neither black nor white)
   $$= \frac{4}{12} = \frac{1}{3}$$

4. (b)
   The probability of an impossible event is zero.

5. (c)
   The probability of a sure event is 1.

6. (b)
   Total number of cards = 52
   Number of black kings = 2
   $$P\text{(getting a black king)} = \frac{2}{52} = \frac{1}{26}$$

7. (a)
   Total number of cards = 52
   Number of queens = 4
   $$P\text{(getting a queen)} = \frac{4}{52} = \frac{1}{13}$$

8. (c)
   Total number of cards = 52
   Number of face cards = (4 jacks + 4 queens + 4 kings
   = 12
   $$P\text{(getting a face card)} = \frac{12}{52} = \frac{3}{13}$$

9. (b)
   Total number of cards = 52
   Number of black face cards = 2 + 2 + 2) = 6
   $$P\text{(getting a face card)} = \frac{6}{52} = \frac{3}{26}$$

10. (b)
    An ordinary year has 365 days is 52 weeks and 1 day. This day can be any one of the 7 days of the week.
    $$P \text{ (this day to be Monday)} = \frac{1}{2}$$

UNIT 14
Logarithm

■ Logarithm
If a is a positive real number, other than 1 and $a^m = x$, then we write:

$m = \log_a x$ and we say that the value of $\log x$ to the base a is m.

Examples:
- $10^3 = 1000 \Rightarrow \log_{10} 1000 = 3$
- $3^4 = 81 \Rightarrow \log_3 81 = 4$
- $2^{-3} = 1/8 \Rightarrow \log_2(1/8) = -3$
- $(0.1)^2 = 0.01 \log_{(0.1)} 0.01 = 2$

■ Properties of Logarithms
1. $\log_a(xy) = \log_a x + \log_a y$
2. $\log_a\left(\dfrac{x}{y}\right) = \log_a x - \log_a y$
3. $\log_x x = 1$
4. $\log_a 1 = 0$
5. $\log_a(x^n) = n(\log_a x)$
6. $\log_a x = -\dfrac{1}{\log_x a}$
7. $\log_a x = \dfrac{\log_b x}{\log_b a} = \dfrac{\log x}{\log a}$

■ Common Logarithms
Logarithms to the base 10 are known as common logarithms.

The logarithm of a number contains two parts, namely 'characteristic' and 'mantissa'.

■ Characteristic
The internal part of the logarithm of a number is called its characteristic.

Case I: When the number is greater than 1.
In this case, the characteristic is one less than the number of digits in the left of the decimal point in the given number.

Case II: When the number is less than 1.
In this case, the characteristic is one more than the number of zeros between the decimal point and the first significant digit of the number and it is negative.
Instead of -1, -2 etc. we write (one bar), (two bar), etc.

Examples:

Number	Characteristic	Number	Characteristic
654.24	2	0.6453	1
26.649	1	0.06134	2
8.3547	0	0.00123	3

■ Mantissa:
The decimal part of the logarithm of a number is known is its **mantissa**. For mantissa, we look through log table.

Example 1:
Find the value of $\log_2(\log_3)81$.

(a) 0   (b) 1
(c) 2   (d) $\dfrac{1}{2}$

Solution: Option (c) is correct.

Explanation:
$\log_2(\log_3)81 = \log_2(\log_3 3^4) = \log_2(4)$
$= \log_2(2^2) = 2$

Example 2:
Find the simplest value of

$$\log_7 \sqrt{7\sqrt{7\sqrt{7\ldots\infty}}}$$

(a) 0   (b) 3
(c) $\dfrac{1}{2}$ (d) 1

Solution: Option (d) is correct.

Explanation:

Let $x = \log_7 \sqrt{7\sqrt{7\sqrt{7\ldots\infty}}}$

$\Rightarrow x^2 = 7x$

$\Rightarrow x = 7$ or 0

$\therefore \log_7 \sqrt{7\sqrt{7\sqrt{7\ldots\infty}}} = \log_7 x = \log_7 7 = 1$

Example 3:
If $\log_{10} 3 = 0.4771$ and $\log_{10} 7 = 0.8451$, find the value of $\log_{10} 2\dfrac{1}{3}$.

(a) 0.368   (b) 0.548
(c) 0.221   (d) 0.478

Solution: Option (a) is correct.

Explanation:

$\log_{10} 2\dfrac{1}{3} = \log_{10} \dfrac{7}{3}$

$= \log_{10} 7 - \log_{10} 3$
$= 0.8451 - 04771$
$= 0.368$

Multiple Choice Questions

1. Which of the following statements is not correct?
   (a) $\log_{10} 10 = 1$
   (b) $\log(2 + 3) = \log(2 \times 3)$
   (c) $\log_{10} 1 = 0$
   (d) $\log(1 + 2 + 3) = \log 1 + \log 2 + \log 3$

2. If $\log 2 = 0.3010$ and $\log 3 = 0.4771$, the value of $\log_5 512$ is:
   (a) 2.870
   (b) 2.967
   (c) 3.876
   (d) 3.912

3. $\dfrac{\log \sqrt{8}}{\log 8}$ is equal to:
   (a) $\dfrac{1}{\sqrt{8}}$
   (b) $\dfrac{1}{4}$
   (c) $\dfrac{1}{2}$
   (d) $\dfrac{1}{8}$

4. If $\log 27 = 1.431$, then the value of $\log 9$ is:
   (a) 0.934
   (b) 0.945
   (c) 0.954
   (d) 0.958

5. If $\log\dfrac{a}{b} + \log\dfrac{b}{a} = \log(a+b)$, then,
   (a) $a + b = 1$
   (b) $a - b = 1$
   (c) $a = b$
   (d) $a^2 - b^2 = 1$

6. If $\log_{10} 7 = a$, then $\log_{10}\left(\dfrac{1}{70}\right)$ is equal to:
   (a) $-(1 + a)$
   (b) $(1 + a)^{-1}$
   (c) $\dfrac{a}{10}$
   (d) $\dfrac{1}{10a}$

7. If $\log_{10} 2 = 0.3010$, then $\log_2 10$ is equal to:
   (a) $\dfrac{699}{301}$
   (b) $\dfrac{1000}{301}$
   (c) 0.3010
   (d) 0.6990

8. If $\log_{10} 2 = 0.3010$, the value of $\log_{10} 80$ is:
   (a) 1.6020
   (b) 1.9030
   (c) 3.9030
   (d) None of these

9. If $\log_{10} 5 + \log_{10}(5x + 1) = \log_{10}(x + 5) + 1$, then x is equal to:
   (a) 1
   (b) 3
   (c) 5
   (d) 10

10. The value of $\left(\dfrac{1}{\log_3 60} + \dfrac{1}{\log_4 60} + \dfrac{1}{\log_5 60}\right)$ is:
    (a) 0
    (b) 1
    (c) 5
    (d) 60

11. If $\log 2 = 0.30103$, the number of digits in 2^{64} is:
    (a) 18
    (b) 19
    (c) 20
    (d) 21

12. If $\log_x \dfrac{9}{16} = -\dfrac{1}{2}$, then x is equal to:
    (a) $-\dfrac{3}{4}$
    (b) $\dfrac{3}{4}$
    (c) $\dfrac{81}{256}$
    (d) $\dfrac{256}{81}$

13. If $a^x = b^y$, then:
    (a) $\log\dfrac{a}{b} = \dfrac{x}{y}$
    (b) $\dfrac{\log a}{\log b} = \dfrac{x}{y}$
    (c) $\dfrac{\log a}{\log b} = \dfrac{y}{x}$
    (d) None of these

14. If $\log_x y = 100$ and $\log_2 x = 10$, then the value of y is:
    (a) 2^{10}
    (b) 2^{100}
    (c) 2^{1000}
    (d) 2^{10000}

15. The value of $\log_2 16$ is:
    (a) 1/8
    (b) 4
    (c) 8
    (d) 16

Logarithm

Answer Key

1. (b)	2. (c)	3. (c)	4. (c)	5. (a)	6. (a)	7. (b)	8. (b)	9. (b)	10. (b)
11. (c)	12. (d)	13. (c)	14. (c)	15. (b)					

Explanatory Notes

1. (b)
   (a) Since $\log_a a = 1$, so $\log_{10} 10 = 1$.
   (b) $\log(2+3) = \log 5$ and $\log(2 \times 3)$
   $= \log 6 = \log 2 + \log 3$
   $\therefore \log(2+3) \neq \log(2 \times 3)$
   (c) Since $\log_a 1 = 0$, so $\log_{10} 1 = 0$.
   (d) $\log(1+2+3) = \log 6$
   $= \log(1 \times 2 \times 3)$
   $= \log 1 + \log 2 + \log 3$.
   So, (b) is incorrect.

2. (c)
   $\log_5 512 = \dfrac{\log 512}{\log 5}$
   $= \dfrac{\log 2^9}{\log(10/2)} = \dfrac{9 \log 2}{\log 10 - \log 2}$
   $= \dfrac{9 \times 0.3010}{1 - 0.3010} = \dfrac{2.709}{0.699} = \dfrac{2709}{699} = 3.876$

3. (c)
   $\dfrac{\log \sqrt{8}}{\log 8} = \dfrac{\log 8^{1/2}}{\log 8} = \dfrac{\frac{1}{2}\log 8}{\log 8} = \dfrac{1}{2}$

4. (c)
   $\log 27 = 1.431$
   $\Rightarrow \log(3^3) = 1.431$
   $\Rightarrow 3 \log 3 = 1.431$
   $\Rightarrow \log 3 = 0.477$
   $\therefore \log 9 = \log(3^2)$
   $= 2 \log 3 = (2 \times 0.477) = 0.954$.

5. (a)
   $\log \dfrac{a}{b} + \log \dfrac{b}{a} = \log(a+b)$
   $\Rightarrow \log(a+b) = \log\left(\dfrac{a}{b} \times \dfrac{b}{a}\right) = \log 1$
   So, $a + b = 1$

6. (a)
   $\log_{10}\left(\dfrac{1}{70}\right) = \log_{10} 1 - \log_{10} 70$
   $= -\log_{10}(7 \times 10)$
   $= -(\log_{10} 7 + \log_{10} 10)$
   $= -(a + 1)$

7. (b)
   $\log_2 10 = \dfrac{1}{\log_{10} 2} = \dfrac{1}{0.3010}$
   $= \dfrac{10000}{3010} = \dfrac{1000}{301}$

8. (b)
   $\log_{10} 80 = \log_{10}(8 \times 10)$
   $= \log_{10} 8 + \log_{10} 10$
   $= \log_{10}(2^3) + 1$
   $= 3 \log_{10} 2 + 1$
   $= (3 \times 0.3010) + 1$
   $= 1.9030$

9. (b)
   $\log_{10} 5 + \log_{10}(5x+1) = \log_{10}(x+5) + 1$
   $\Rightarrow \log_{10} 5 + \log_{10}(5x+1) = \log_{10}(x+5) + \log_{10} 10$
   $\Rightarrow \log_{10}[5(5x+1)] = \log_{10}[10(x+5)]$
   $\Rightarrow 5(5x+1) = 10(x+5)$
   $\Rightarrow 5x + 1 = 2x + 10$
   $\Rightarrow 3x = 9$
   $\Rightarrow x = 3$

10. (b)
    Given expression $= \log_{60} 3 + \log_{60} 4 + \log_{60} 5$
    $= \log_{60}(3 \times 4 \times 5)$
    $= \log_{60} 60 = 1$

11. (c)
    $\log(2^{64}) = 64 \times \log 2$
    $= (64 \times 0.30103)$
    $= 19.26592$
    Its characteristic is 19
    Hence, the number of digits in 2^{64} is 20.

12. (d)
    $\log_x \dfrac{9}{16} = -\dfrac{1}{2}$
    $\Rightarrow x^{-1/2} = \dfrac{9}{16} \Rightarrow x^{-1/2} = \dfrac{9}{16}$
    $\Rightarrow \sqrt{x} = \dfrac{16}{9} \Rightarrow x = \left(\dfrac{16}{9}\right)^2 \Rightarrow x = \dfrac{256}{81}$

13. (c)
    $a^x = b^y$
    $\log a^x = \log b^y$
    $x \log a = y \log b$
    $\dfrac{\log a}{\log b} = \dfrac{y}{x}$

14. (c)
    $\log_2 x = 10 \Rightarrow x = 2^{10}$
    $\therefore \log_x y = 100$
    $\Rightarrow y = x^{100}$
    $\Rightarrow y = (2^{10})^{100}$ [put value of x]
    $\Rightarrow y = 2^{1000}$

15. (b)
    Let $\log_2 16 = n$
    Then, $2^n = 16 = 2^4$
    $\Rightarrow n = 4$
    $\therefore \log_2 16 = 4$

National Talent Search Examination (NTSE)-X

Previous Year Questions

1. Evaluate log [(tan 2) (tan 4) (tan 6) ... (tan 88)]
   [NTSE 2012– Goa first stage paper]
   (a) 0   (b) 2
   (c) 1   (d) Infinity

2. $\log_a 1$ is equal to:
   [NTSE 2006 – Bihar first stage paper]
   (a) 1   (b) 0
   (c) ∞   (d) None of these

3. $\log_{25} 25$ is equal to :
   [NTSE 2001 – Haryana first stage paper]
   (a) 1   (b) 0
   (c) ∞   (d) None of these

4. If $\log (1 + x) + \log (x - 1) = \log 8$, then x is equal to
   [NTSE 2003 – UP second stage paper]
   (a) 2   (b) 3
   (c) –3   (d) –2

5. If $\log_8 m + \log_8 \frac{1}{6} = \frac{2}{3}$, then m is equal to:
   [NTSE 2002 – Punjab first stage paper]
   (a) 12   (b) 48
   (c) 18   (d) 24

6. Given $\log_6$ and $\log_8$, then the only logarithm that cannot be obtained without using the table is
   [NTSE 2006 – Karnataka first stage paper]
   (a) $\log_{64}$ (b) $\log_{21}$
   (c) $\log \frac{8}{3}$ (d) $\log 9$

7. Solution of $\log_7 \log_5 \left(\sqrt{x+5} + \sqrt{x}\right) = 0$ is:
   [NTSE 2001 – Jammu first stage paper]
   (a) $x = 2$ (b) $x = 5$
   (c) $x = -5$ (d) $x = 4$

8. If $\log_{30} 3 = a$ and $\log_{30} 5 = b$, then the value of $\log_{30} 8$ is:
   [NTSE 2012 – Delhi first stage paper]
   (a) ab (b) $3(1 - a - b)$
   (c) $a + b$ (d) $\frac{1}{a+b}$

9. If $\log_a (ab) = x$, then $\log_b (ab)$ is:
   [NTSE 2005–Gujrat second stage paper]
   (a) $\frac{x}{(1+x)}$ (b) $\frac{1}{x}$
   (c) $\frac{x+1}{x-1}$ (d) $\frac{x}{x-1}$

10. If $\log (x + 1) + \log (x - 1) = \log_3$, then the value of x is:
    [NTSE 2000–Rajasthan second stage paper]
    (a) 3   (b) 2
    (c) 1   (d) None of these

Answer Key

1. (a)	2. (b)	3. (a)	4. (b)	5. (d)	6. (b)	7. (d)	8. (b)	9. (d)	10. (b)

UNIT 15
Surds and Indices

■ Indices
Indices are used to describe the general term for 2 i.e. x^2. There are a few laws to manipulate the expressions involving indices.

Laws of Indices
- $a^m \times a^n = a^{m+n}$
- $a^m \div a^n = a^{m-n}$
- $(a^m)^n = a^{mn}$
- $a^{\frac{1}{m}} = \sqrt[m]{a}$
- $a^{-m} = \frac{1}{a^m}$
- $a^{\frac{m}{n}} = (\sqrt[n]{a})^m$
- $a^0 = 1$

■ Surds
The roots of those quantities which cannot be exactly obtained are called **surds** e.g. $\sqrt{2}, 4\sqrt{8}$ etc. Let 'a' be a rational number and n be a positive integer such that $a^{1/n} = \sqrt[n]{a}$ is irrational. Then, $\sqrt[n]{a}$ is called a surd of order n. Surds are basically an expression involving a root, squared or cubed etc.

There are some basic rules when dealing with surds
- $\sqrt{a} + \sqrt{a} = 2\sqrt{a}$
- $6\sqrt{a} - 2\sqrt{a} = 4\sqrt{a}$
- $\sqrt{a} \times \sqrt{b} = \sqrt{ab}$
- $\sqrt{\frac{a}{b}} = \frac{\sqrt{a}}{\sqrt{b}}$

Also, notice the special case
$$\sqrt{a} \times \sqrt{a} = a^{\frac{1}{2}} \times a^{\frac{1}{2}} = a$$

Difference of Two Squares
$x^2 - y^2 = (x + y)(x - y)$. This is called the difference of two squares

■ Rationalising Surds
In general
- Fractions in the form $\sqrt{\frac{1}{a}}$ multiply top and bottom by $\sqrt{a}$
- Fractions in the form $\frac{1}{a+\sqrt{b}}$ multiply the top and bottom by $a-\sqrt{b}$
- Fractions in the form $\frac{1}{a-\sqrt{b}}$ multiply the top and bottom by $a+\sqrt{b}$

Solved Examples

1. Evaluate the following:
$$\frac{4+\sqrt{2}}{\sqrt{2}+1}$$
Solution:
$$\frac{4+\sqrt{2}}{\sqrt{2}+1} = \frac{(4+\sqrt{2})(\sqrt{2}-1)}{(\sqrt{2}+1)(\sqrt{2}-1)}$$
$$= 4\sqrt{2}+2-4-\sqrt{2}$$
$$= 3\sqrt{2}-2$$
$$= 2.2426$$

2. Evaluate the following:
$$\sqrt{\frac{\sqrt{5}+1}{\sqrt{5}-1}}$$
Solution:
$$\sqrt{\frac{\sqrt{5}+1}{\sqrt{5}-1}} = \sqrt{\frac{(\sqrt{5}+1)\times(\sqrt{5}+1)}{(\sqrt{5}-1)\times(\sqrt{5}+1)}}$$
$$= \sqrt{\frac{(\sqrt{5}+1)^2}{5-1}} = \sqrt{\frac{(\sqrt{5}+1)^2}{4}}$$
$$= \frac{\sqrt{5}+1}{2} = 1.168$$

3. Solve: $\dfrac{1}{\sqrt{5}}+\sqrt{20}+\sqrt{125}$

   Solution:
   $$\dfrac{1}{\sqrt{5}}+\sqrt{20}+\sqrt{125} = \dfrac{1}{\sqrt{5}}\times\dfrac{\sqrt{5}}{\sqrt{5}}+\sqrt{2\times 2\times 5}+\sqrt{5\times 5\times 5}$$
   $$= \dfrac{\sqrt{5}}{5}+2\sqrt{5}+5\sqrt{5}$$
   $$= \sqrt{5}\left(\dfrac{1}{5}+2+5\right) = 7\dfrac{1}{5}\sqrt{5}$$

4. Simplify and express in the form $a+b\sqrt{c}$: $(\sqrt{5}-2)^2$

   Solution:
   $$(\sqrt{5}-2)^2 = (\sqrt{5})^2 + 2^2 - 2\times\sqrt{5}\times 2$$
   $$= 5+4-4\sqrt{5} = 9-4\sqrt{5}$$

5. If $2^{x-1}+2^{x+1} = 1280$, then find the value of x.

   Solution:
   $$2^{x-1}+2^{x+1} = 1280 \Leftrightarrow 2^{x-1}(1+2^2) = 1280$$
   $$\Leftrightarrow 2^{x-1} = \dfrac{1280}{5} = 256 = 2^8$$
   $$\Leftrightarrow 2^{x-1} = 2^8$$
   $$\Leftrightarrow x-1 = 8$$
   $$x = 9$$
   Hence $x = 9$

Practice Exercise

1. If $x = 3+2\sqrt{2}$, then the value of $\sqrt{x}-\dfrac{1}{\sqrt{x}}$ is:
   a. 1
   b. 2
   c. $2\sqrt{2}$
   d. $3\sqrt{3}$

2. $\left(\dfrac{x^b}{x^c}\right)^{(b+c-a)} + \left(\dfrac{x^c}{x^a}\right)^{(c+a-b)} + \left(\dfrac{x^a}{x^b}\right)^{(a+b-c)}$
   a. x^{abc}
   b. 1
   c. $x^{ab+bc+ca}$
   d. x^{a+b+c}

3. If m and n are whole numbers such that $m^n = 121$, the value of $(m-1)^{n+1}$ is:
   a. 1
   b. 10
   c. 121
   d. 1000

4. $(256)^{0.16} \times (256)^{0.09} = $?
   a. 4
   b. 16
   c. 64
   d. 256.25

5. $(25)^{7.5} \times (5)^{2.5} \div (125)^{1.5} = 5^?$
   a. 8.5
   b. 13
   c. 16
   d. 17.5

6. Given that $10^{0.48} = x$, $10^{0.70} = y$ and $x^z = y^2$, then the value of z is close to:
   a. 1.45
   b. 1.88
   c. 2.9
   d. 3.7

7. Evaluate: $\sqrt{75}+\sqrt{147}$
   a. 20.7846
   b. 22.3698
   c. 18.336
   d. 21.7586

8. Find the value of: $\sqrt{80}+3\sqrt{245}-\sqrt{125} = $?
   a. 38.6395
   b. 44.7214
   c. 50.2136
   d. 3.2365

9. Find $\sqrt{242} \div \sqrt{72}$
   a. 1.2
   b. 2
   c. $\dfrac{4}{5}$
   d. $1\dfrac{5}{6}$

10. $(18a^8 b^6) \div (3a^2 b^2)$ simplifies to
    a. $6a^4 b^3$
    b. $6a^{10} b^8$
    c. $6a^6 b^4$
    d. $15a^6 b^3$

11. Replace the question mark with the suitable answer.
    $56 - 45 - \sqrt{?} = \sqrt{36}$
    a. 25
    b. 35
    c. 15
    d. 5

12. Replace question mark with the suitable answer:
    $(?)^2 = \dfrac{4}{25}$
    a. 1
    b. 1.5
    c. 2/5
    d. 3

13. Find: $\sqrt{210\dfrac{1}{4}} = $?
    a. $13\dfrac{1}{2}$
    b. $15\dfrac{1}{2}$
    c. $14\dfrac{1}{2}$
    d. $17\dfrac{1}{2}$

14. If $x = 5+2\sqrt{6}$, then $\dfrac{(x-1)}{\sqrt{x}}$ is equal to:
    a. $\sqrt{2}$
    b. $2\sqrt{2}$
    c. $\sqrt{3}$
    d. $2\sqrt{3}$

15. If $5^a = 3125$, then the value of $5^{(a-3)}$ is:
    a. 25
    b. 125
    c. 625
    d. 1625

Surds and Indices

Answer Key

1. (b)	2. (b)	3. (d)	4. (a)	5. (b)	6. (c)	7. (a)	8. (b)	9. (d)	10. (c)
11. (a)	12. (c)	13. (c)	14. (b)	15. (a)					

Explanatory Notes

1. (b)
$$\left(\sqrt{x} - \frac{1}{\sqrt{x}}\right)^2 = x + \frac{1}{x} - 2$$
$$= (3 + 2\sqrt{2}) + \left(\frac{1}{3 + 2\sqrt{2}}\right) - 2$$
$$= (3 + 2\sqrt{2}) + \left(\frac{1}{3 + 2\sqrt{2}}\right) \times \frac{(3 - 2\sqrt{2})}{(3 - 2\sqrt{2})} - 2$$
$$= (3 + 2\sqrt{2}) + (3 - 2\sqrt{2}) - 2 = 4$$
$$\therefore \sqrt{x} - \frac{1}{\sqrt{x}} = 2$$

2. (b)
Given Expression
$= x^{(b-c)(b+c-a)} \cdot x^{(c-a)(c+a-b)} \cdot x^{(a-b)(a+b-c)}$
$= x^{(b-c)(b+c)-a(b-c)} \cdot x^{(c-a)(c+a)-b(c-a)} \cdot x^{(a-b)(a+b)-c(a-b)}$
$= x^{(b^2-c^2+c^2-a^2+a^2-b^2)} \cdot x^{-a(b-c)-b(c-a)-c(a-b)}$
$= (x^0 \times x^0)$
$= (1 \times 1) = 1$

3. (d)
We know that $11^2 = 121$
Putting $m = 11$ and $n = 2$, we get:
$(m-1)^{n+1} = (11-1)^{(2+1)} = 10^3 = 1000$

4. (a)
$(256)^{0.16} \times (256)^{0.09} = (256)^{(0.16 + 0.09)}$
$= (256)^{0.25}$
$= (256)^{(25/100)}$
$= (256)^{(1/4)}$
$= (4^4)^{(1/4)}$
$= 4^{4(1/4)}$
$= 4^1$
$= 4$

5. (b)
Let $(25)^{7.5} \times (5)^{2.5} \div (125)^{1.5} = 5^x$
Then, $(5^2)^{7.5} \times (5)^{2.5} \div (5^3)^{1.5} = 5^x$
$\Rightarrow 5^{(2 \times 7.5)} \times 5^{2.5} \div 5^{(3 \times 1.5)} = 5^x$
$5^{15} \times 5^{2.5} \div 5^{4.5} = 5^x$
$5^x = 5^{(15 + 2.5 - 4.5)}$
$5^x = 5^{13}$
$x = 13$

6. (c)
$x^z = y^2 \Leftrightarrow 10^{(0.48z)} = 10^{(2 \times 0.70)} = 10^{1.40}$
$\Rightarrow 0.48z = 1.40$
$\Rightarrow z = 140/48 = 35/12 = 2.9$ (approx.)

7. (a)
$\sqrt{75} + \sqrt{147} = \sqrt{5 \times 5 \times 3} + \sqrt{7 \times 7 \times 3}$
$= 5\sqrt{3} + 7\sqrt{3}$
$= 12\sqrt{3} = 12 \times 1.732 = 20.7846$

8. (b)
$\sqrt{80} + 3\sqrt{245} - \sqrt{125} = \sqrt{4 \times 4 \times 5} + 3\sqrt{7 \times 7 \times 5} - \sqrt{5 \times 5 \times 5}$
$= 4\sqrt{5} + 21\sqrt{5} - 5\sqrt{5}$
$= 20\sqrt{5} = 44.7214$

9. (d)
$\sqrt{242} \div \sqrt{72} = \frac{\sqrt{121 \times 2}}{\sqrt{36 \times 2}} = \frac{11\sqrt{2}}{6\sqrt{2}} = \frac{11}{6} = 1\frac{5}{6}$

10. (c)
$(18a^8b^6) \div (3a^2b^2) = 18/3 \times a^{8-2} \times b^{6-2}$
$= 6a^6b^4$

11. (a)
$56 - 45 - \sqrt{?} = \sqrt{36}$
$11 - \sqrt{36} = \sqrt{?}$
$11 - 6 = \sqrt{?}$
$\therefore ? = 25$

12. (c)
$?^2 = \frac{4}{25}$
$? = \sqrt{\frac{4}{25}} = \frac{2}{5}$

13. (c)
$\sqrt{210\frac{1}{4}} = \sqrt{\frac{841}{4}} = \sqrt{\frac{29 \times 29}{4}} = \frac{29}{2} = 14\frac{1}{2}$

14. (b)
$x = 5 + 2\sqrt{6} = 3 + 2 + 2\sqrt{6}$
$= (\sqrt{3})^2 + (\sqrt{2})^2 + 2 \times \sqrt{2} \times \sqrt{3}$
$= (\sqrt{2} + \sqrt{3})^2$
Also, $(x - 1) = 4 + 2\sqrt{6} = 2(2 + \sqrt{6}) = 2\sqrt{2}(\sqrt{2} + \sqrt{3})$

15. (a)
$5^a = 3125 \Leftrightarrow 5^a = 5^5 \Leftrightarrow a = 5$
$\therefore 5^{(a-3)} = 5^{(5-3)} \Leftrightarrow 5^2 = 25$

UNIT 16: Simplification

In simplification of an expression, there are certain rules which should be strictly followed. These rules are as follows:
- BODMAS Rule
- Modulus of a Real Number
- Virnaculum (Bar)

Rule 1: 'BODMAS' Rule

This rule depicts the correct sequence in which the operations are to be executed so as to find out the value of the given expression. The BODMAS means

B - Bracket
O - of
D - Division
M - Multiplication
A - Addition
S - Subtraction

Thus, in simplifying an expression, first of all the brackets must be removed, strictly in the order (), {} and [ ].

After removing the brackets, we must use the following operations strictly in the order:
- Of
- Division
- Multiplication
- Addition
- Subtraction

Rule 2: Modulus of a Real Number

The modulus of a real number 'a' is defined as

$$|a| = \begin{cases} a, \text{if } a > 0 \\ -a, \text{if } a < 0 \end{cases}$$

Thus, $|5| = 5$ and $|-5| = -(-5) = 5$

Rule 3: Virnaculum (Bar)

When an expression contains virnaculum, before applying the 'BODMAS' rule, we simplify the expression under the virnaculum.

Solved Examples

1. A man has some hens and cows. If the number of heads is 48 and the number of feet equals 140, then the number of hens will be:
   a. 22   b. 23
   c. 24   d. 26

   Solution: Option (d) is correct.

   Explanation:
   Let the number of hens be x and the number of cows be y.
   Then, $x + y = 48$ ... (i)
   and $2x + 4y = 140 \Rightarrow x + 2y = 70$ ... (ii)
   Solving (i) and (ii) we get: x = 26, y = 22
   The required answer = **26**

2. Village X has a population of 68000, which is decreasing at the rate of 1200 per year. Village Y has a population of 42000, which is increasing at the rate of 800 per year. In how years will the population of the two villages be equal?
   a. 22 years   b. 16 years
   c. 13 years   d. 7 years

   Solution: Option (c) is correct.

   Explanation:
   Let the population of villages X and Y be equal after p years.
   Then, 68000 - 1200p = 42000 + 800p
   $\Rightarrow$ 2000p = 26000
   $\Rightarrow$ p = 13
   So, their population will be equal after 13 years.

3. A man has Rs. 480 in the denominations of one-rupee notes, five-rupee notes and ten-rupee notes. The number of notes of each denomination is equal. What is the total number of notes that he has?
   a. 45   b. 60
   c. 75   d. 90

   Solution: Option (d) is correct.

   Explanation:
   Let number of notes of each denomination be x.
   Then $x + 5x + 10x = 480$
            $16x = 480$
   $\therefore$ $x = 30$
   Hence, total number of notes = $3x$ = **90**

Simplification

Multiple Choice Questions

1. David gets on the elevator at the 11th floor of a building and rides up at the rate of 57 floors per minute. At the same time, Albert gets on an elevator at the 51st floor of the same building and rides down at the rate of 63 floors per minute. If they continue travelling at these rates, then at which floor will their paths cross?
   a. 19 b. 28
   c. 30 d. 37

2. $\dfrac{(469+174)^2 - (469-174)^2}{(469 \times 174)} = ?$
   a. 2 b. 4
   c. 295 d. 643

3. Free notebooks were distributed equally among children of a class. The number of notebooks each child got was one-eighth of the number of children. Had the number of children been half, each child would have got 16 notebooks. Total how many notebooks were distributed?
   a. 256 b. 432
   c. 512 d. 640

4. In a regular week, there are 5 working days and for each day, the working hours are 8. A man gets Rs. 2.40 per hour for regular work and Rs. 3.20 per hours for overtime. If he earns Rs. 432 in 4 weeks, then how many hours does he work for?
   a. 160 b. 175
   c. 180 d. 195

5. To fill a tank, 25 buckets of water is required. How many buckets of water will be required to fill the same tank if the capacity of the bucket is reduced to two-fifth of its present?
   a. 10 b. 35
   c. 62.5 d. Cannot be determined

6. Eight people are planning to share equally the cost of a rental car. If one person withdraws from the arrangement and the others share equally the entire cost of the car, then the share of each of the remaining persons increased by:
   a. 1/7 b. 1/8
   c. 1/9 d. 7/8

7. 'A' fires 5 shots to B's 3 but A kills only once in 3 shots while 'B' kills once in 2 shots. When 'B' has missed 27 times, A has killed:
   a. 30 birds b. 60 birds
   c. 72 birds d. 90 birds

8. One-third of Rahul's savings in National Savings Certificate is equal to one-half of his savings in Public Provident Fund. If he has Rs. 1, 50,000 as total savings, how much has he saved in Public Provident Fund?
   a. Rs. 30,000 b. Rs. 50,000
   c. Rs. 60,000 d. Rs. 90,000

9. A sum of Rs. 1360 has been divided among A, B and C such that A gets 2/3 of what B gets and B gets 1/4 of what C gets. B's share is:
   a. Rs. 120 b. Rs. 160
   c. Rs. 240 d. Rs. 300

10. There are two examinations rooms A and B. If 10 students are sent from A to B, then the number of students in each room is the same. If 20 candidates are sent from B to A, then the number of students in A is double the number of students in B. The number of students in room A is:
    a. 20 b. 80
    c. 100 d. 200

11. The price of 10 chairs is equal to that of 4 tables. The price of 15 chairs and 2 tables together is Rs. 4000. The total price of 12 chairs and 3 tables is:
    a. Rs. 3500 b. Rs. 3750
    c. Rs. 3840 d. Rs. 3900

12. If $a - b = 3$ and $a^2 + b^2 = 29$, find the value of ab
    a. 10 b. 12
    c. 15 d. 18

13. The price of 2 saris and 4 shirts is Rs. 1600. With the same money one can buy 1 sari and 6 shirts. If one wants to buy 12 shirts, how much shall he have to pay?
    a. Rs. 1200 b. Rs. 2400
    c. Rs. 4800 d. Cannot be determined

National Talent Search Examination (NTSE)-X

Answer Key

1. (c)	2. (b)	3. (c)	4. (b)	5. (c)	6. (a)	7. (a)	8. (c)	9. (c)	10. (c)
11. (d)	12. (a)	13. (b)							

Explanatory Notes

1. (c)
   Suppose their paths cross after x minutes.
   Then, $11 + 57x = 51 - 63x$
   $120x = 40$
   $x = 1/3$
   The number of floors covered by David in (1/3) min.
   = 1/3 × 57 = 19
   So, their paths cross at (11 + 19) i.e., 30th floor.

2. (b)
   Given expression = $\dfrac{(a+b)^2 - (a-b)^2}{ab}$
   = $4ab/ab$
   = 4 (where $a = 469$, $b = 174$)

3. (c)
   Let total number of children be x.
   Then, $x \times (1/8)x = x^2/8$ $\Leftrightarrow$ $x = 64$.
   ∴ The number of notebooks = $x^2/8 = 1/8 \times 64 \times 64 = 512$

4. (b)
   Suppose the man works overtime for x hours.
   Now, working hours in 4 weeks = (5 × 8 × 4) = 160
   $160 \times 2.40 + x \times 3.20 = 432$
   $3.20x = 432 - 384 = 48$
   $x = 15$
   Hence, total hours of work = (160 + 15) = 175

5. (c)
   Let the capacity of 1 bucket = x
   Then, the capacity of tank = $25x$
   New capacity of bucket = $2x/5$
   Required number of buckets = $25x/(2x/5) = 125/2 = 62.5$

6. (a)
   Original share of 1 person = 1/8
   New share of 1 person = 1/7
   Increase = 1/7 − 1/8 = 1/56
   Required fraction = (1/56) / (1/8) = 1/7

7. (a)
   Let the total number of shots be x. Then,
   Shots fired by A = $5x/8$
   Shots fired by B = $3x/8$
   Killing shots by A = 1/3 of $5x/8 = 5x/24$
   Shots missed by B = 1/2 of $3x/8 = 3x/16$
   $3x/16 = 27$ or $x = 144$
   Birds killed by A = $5x/24 = (5 \times 144)/24 = 30$

8. (c)
   Let savings in N.S.C and P.P.F. be Rs. x and
   Rs. $(150000 - x)$ respectively. Then,
   $1/3 x = 1/2(150000 - x)$
   $x/3 + x/2 = 75000$
   $5x/6 = 75000$
   $x = (75000 \times 6)/5 = 90000$
   Savings in Public Provident Fund
   = Rs. (150000 − 90000)
   = Rs. 60000

9. (c)
   Let C's share = Rs. x
   Then, B's share = Rs. $x/4$
   A's share = Rs. $2/3 \times x/4$ = Rs. $x/6$
   $\Rightarrow$ $17x/12 = 1360$
   $x = (1360 \times 12)/17$ = Rs. 960
   Hence, B's share = Rs. 960/4 = Rs. 240

10. (c)
    Let the number of students in rooms A and B
    be x and y respectively.
    Then, $x - 10 = y + 10$ $\Rightarrow x - y = 20$ ...(i)
    and $x + 20 = 2(y - 20)$ $\Rightarrow x - 2y = -60$ ... (ii)
    Solving (i) and (ii) we get: $x = 100$, $y = 80$.
    The required answer A = 100.

11. (d)
    Let the cost of a chair and that of a table be Rs. x and
    Rs. y respectively.
    Then, $10x = 4y$ or $y = 5x/2$.
    ∴ $15x + 2y = 4000$
    $\Rightarrow 15x + 2 \times 5x/2 = 4000$
    $\Rightarrow 20x = 4000$
    ∴ $x = 200$
    So, $y = 5/2 \times 200 = 500$
    Hence, the cost of 12 chairs and 3 tables = $12x + 3y$
    = Rs. (2400 + 1500) = Rs. 3900

12. (a)
    $2ab = (a^2 + b^2) - (a - b)^2 = 29 - 9 = 20 \Rightarrow ab = 10$

13. (b)
    Let the price of a sari and a shirt be Rs. x and Rs. y
    respectively.
    Then, $2x + 4y = 1600$ ... (i)
    and $x + 6y = 1600$ . ... (ii)
    Divide equation (i) by 2, we get the below equation.
    $x + 2y = 800$ ... (iii)
    Now, subtract (iii) from (ii)
    $4y = 800$
    Therefore, y = 200
    Now, apply the value of y in (iii)
    $x + 2 \times 200 = 800$
    $x + 400 = 800$
    Therefore x = 400
    Solving (i) and (ii) we get x = 400, y = 200
    The cost of 12 shirts = Rs. (12 × 200) = Rs. 2400.

UNIT 17
Commercial Mathematics

- **Commercial Mathematics**

  In mathematics, a percentage is a number or ratio as a fraction of 100. It is often denoted using the percent sign, '%', or the abbreviation 'pct.'

  For example, 45% (read as 'forty-five percent') is equal to 45/100, or 0.45. Percentages are used to express how large/small one quantity is, relative to another quantity. The first quantity usually represents a part of, or a change in the second quantity which should be greater than zero.

  For example, an increase of Rs 0.15 on a price of Rs 2.50 is an increase by a fraction of 0.15/2.50 = 0.06. Expressed as a percentage, this is therefore a 6% increase. The word 'percent' means 'out of 100' or 'per 100'.

- **Concept of Percentage**

  By a certain percent, we mean that many hundredths. Thus, x percent means x hundredths, written as $x\%$.

  To express $x\%$ as a fraction: We have,
  $$x\% = \frac{x}{100}$$

  To express $\frac{a}{b}$ as a percent :

  We have,
  $$\frac{a}{b} = \left(\frac{a}{b} \times 100\right)\%$$

- **Percentage Increase/Decrease**

  Sometimes due to inconsistent usage, it is not always clear from the context what a percentage is relative to. When speaking of a "10% rise" or a "10% fall" in a quantity, the usual interpretation is that this is relative to the initial value of that quantity. For example, if an item is initially priced at Rs. 200 and the price rises 10% (an increase of Rs. 20), the new price will be Rs. 220. Note that this final price is 110% of the initial price (100% + 10% = 110%).

- **Examples of Percent Changes**
  - An increase of 100% in a quantity means that the final amount is 200% of the initial amount (100% of initial + 100% of increase = 200% of initial); in other words, the quantity has doubled.
  - An increase of 800% means the final amount is 9 times the original (100% + 800% = 900% = 9 times as large).
  - A decrease of 60% means the final amount is 40% of the original (100% − 60% = 40%).
  - A decrease of 100% means the final amount is zero (100% − 100% = 0%).
  - If the price of a commodity increases by R%, then the reduction in consumption so as not to increase the expenditure is:
  $$\left[\frac{R}{(100+R)} \times 100\right]\%$$
  - If the price of a commodity decreases by R%, then the increase in consumption so as not to decrease the expenditure is:
  $$\left[\frac{R}{(100-R)} \times 100\right]\%$$

- **Successive Increase/ Decrease**

  All successive changes in %(increase or decrease) can be represented as a single percentage which is given by $\left(a + b + \frac{ab}{100}\right)\%$, where a and b show the first and second percentage changes.

- **Concept of True Discount**

  Suppose a man has to pay Rs. 156 after 4 years and the rate of interest is 14% per annum. Clearly, Rs. 100 at 14% will amount to R. 156 in 4 years. So, the payment of Rs. 156 now will clear off the debt of Rs. 156 due 4 years hence. We say that:

  Sum due = Rs. 156 due 4 years hence;
  Present Worth (P.W.) = Rs. 100;
  True Discount (T.D.) = Rs. (156 − 100) = Rs. 56
  = (Sum due) − (P.W.)

  We define:

  T.D. = Interest on P.W.;
  Amount = (P.W.) + (T.D.)

  Interest is reckoned on P.W. and true discount is reckoned on the amount.

Important Formulae

Let rate = R% per annum and Time = T years. Then,

- $\dfrac{100 \times \text{Amount}}{100 + (R \times T)} = \dfrac{100 \times T.D.}{R \times T}$

- $T.D. = \dfrac{(P.W.) \times R \times T}{100} = \dfrac{\text{Amount} \times R \times T}{100 + (R \times T)}$

- $\text{Sum} = \dfrac{(S.I.) \times (T.D.)}{(S.I.) - (T.D.)}$

- $(S.I.) - (T.D.) = S.I.$ on $T.D.$

- When the sum is put at compound interest, then P.W.

$$= \dfrac{\text{Amount}}{\left(1 + \dfrac{R}{100}\right)^T}$$

Note:

In general, a change of 'x' percent in a quantity results in a final amount that is 100 + 'x' percent of the original amount (equivalent to, 1 + 0.01x times the original amount).

Solved Examples

1. The population of the city is estimated to be 4, 32,000 after 2 years if the population growth is 20% per annum. What is the current population?
   (a) 3, 10,000 (b) 2, 85,000
   (c) 3, 80,000 (d) 3, 00,000
   Solution: Option (d) is correct.
   Explanation: Single percentage change
   $$\left(20 + 20 + \dfrac{20 \times 20}{100}\right)\% = 44\%$$
   Population after 2 years = Present population × 1.44
   $\therefore$ Present population $= \dfrac{4,32,000}{1.44} = 3,00,000$

2. Two successive discounts of 8% and 12% are equal to a single discount of:
   (a) 20% (b) 19.04%
   (c) 20.96% (d) 22%
   Solution: Option (b) is correct.
   Explanation:
   Single discount $= \left(a + b + \dfrac{ab}{100}\right)\%$
   $= \left(-8 - 12 + \dfrac{(-8) \times (-12)}{100}\right)\%$
   $= (-20 + 0.96)\% = -19.04\%$
   (–ve) sign is used because discount refers to the decrease in values.

3. If the height of a triangle is decreased by 40% and its base is increased by 40%, what will be the effect on its area?
   (a) No Change (b) 8% decrease
   (c) 16% decrease (d) 16% increase
   Solution: Option (c) is correct.
   Explanation: Let the height of the triangle be 'h' and the base be 'b'.
   Area $= \dfrac{1}{2}bh$
   Decreased height $= \dfrac{6}{10}h$

   Increased base $= \dfrac{14}{10}b$
   Area $= \dfrac{1}{2} \times \dfrac{6}{10}h \times \dfrac{14}{10}b$
   $= \dfrac{1}{2} \times \dfrac{84}{100}bh$
   Decrease in area $= \dfrac{1}{2}bh\left(1 - \dfrac{84}{100}\right)$
   $= \dfrac{1}{2}bh \times \dfrac{16}{100}$
   Percentage decrease $= \dfrac{1}{2}bh \times \dfrac{16}{100} \times \dfrac{2}{bh} \times 100$
   $= 16\%$

4. Fresh grapes contain 80 percent water while dry grapes contain 10 percent water. If the weight of dry grapes is 250 kg what was its total weight when it was fresh?
   (a) 1000kg (b) 1125 kg
   (c) 1225 kg (d) 1100kg
   Solution: Option b) is correct.
   Explanation: In 250 kg, there is 225 kg grape powder and 25 kg water. Now 225 = 20%, since 80% is water in fresh grapes. So total weight of fresh grapes = 225 kg × 5 = 1125 kg

5. $x\%$ of y is $y\%$ of:
   (a) x (b) $\dfrac{y}{100}$
   (c) $\dfrac{x}{100}$ (d) $100x$
   Solution: Option (a) is correct.
   Explanation:
   $$\dfrac{x}{100} \times y = y \times \dfrac{x}{100}$$
   $\therefore x\%$ of y is $y\%$ of x

6. If the length and width of a rectangular garden plot were each increased by 20 percent, then what would be the percent increase in the area of the plot?
   (a) 20% (b) 24%
   (c) 36% (d) 44%

Solution: Option (d) is correct.

Explanation:
Let the length and breadth be 10 unit each. Then original area = 100 sq. unit.
New length = 12 and new width = 12
New area = 12 × 12 = 144 sq. unit.
% increase in area = 44%

■ **Simple and Compound Interest**

Simple Interest (S.I): It is the interest that is calculated uniformly on the original principal throughout the loan period.

When we need a large sum of money for buying house, car, etc we borrow money either from bank or by some agency. The money borrowed is called **loan** and we become **borrower.**

When we borrow money in the form of loan that we have to return in a specified period of time by giving them extra fees. This extra fee is called **Interest** (S.I).

■ **Important Definitions**

Principal: Money borrowed

Rate: It is the percentage of the principal charged as interest each year. The rate is expressed as a decimal fraction, so percentages must be divided by 100.

Example: 5% = 5/100 = 0.05

Amount: The total money which the borrower pays back to the lender at the end of the specified period is called the amount.

Time: Time in years of the loan.

➢ The simple interest formula is often abbre-viated in this form:
   Interest = P × R × T

➢ If the time is given in month, divide the given formula by 12.
   Interest = (P × R × T) / 12

➢ If the time is given in days, divide the given formula by 365.
   Interest = (P × R × T) / 365
   Amount (A) = Principal (P) + Interest (S.I)

■ **Note:** The difference in amount for two different time periods is equal to the simple interest for the difference in two different times.

Example 1:
At a certain rate of simple interest Rs. 900 amounted to Rs. 1260 in 4 years. If the rate of interest be decreased by 2%, what will be the amount after 4 years?
(a) Rs. 1338 (b) Rs. 1188
(c) Rs. 1378 (d) Rs. 1128

Solution: Option (b) is correct.

Explanation:
$$SI = (1260 - 900) = 360$$
$$360 = \frac{900 \times R \times 4}{100} \therefore R = 10\%$$
New rate = (10 – 2) = 8%
$$\therefore I = \frac{900 \times 8 \times 4}{100} = 288$$
Amount after 4 years = (900 + 288) = Rs. 1188

Example 2:
The difference between the interests received from two different banks on Rs. 750 for two years is Rs. 90. The difference between their rates is:
(a) 4% (b) 6%
(c) 8% (d) None of these

Solution: Option b) is correct.

Explanation:
$$\frac{750 \times 2}{100}(R_1 - R_2) = 90$$
$$\Rightarrow (R_1 - R_2) = \frac{90 \times 100}{750 \times 2} = 6\%$$

Example 3:
If x is the simple interest on y and y is the simple interest on z, the rate % and the time being the same in both cases, what is the relation between x, y, and z?
(a) $x^2 = yz$ (b) $y^2 = xz$
(c) $z^2 = xy$ (d) $xyz = 1$

Solution: Option (b) is correct.

Explanation:
$$x = \frac{y \times R \times T}{100}$$
$$\therefore RT = \frac{100x}{y} \quad \ldots(i)$$
and
$$y = \frac{z \times R \times T}{100} \quad \ldots(ii)$$

From equations (i) and (ii)
$$\frac{100x}{y} = \frac{100y}{z}$$
$$\Rightarrow y^2 = xz$$

Example 4:
A sum of money becomes five times at simple rate of 8% per annum. At what rate percent will it become seven fold?
(a) 6% (b) 8%
(c) 12% (d) 14%

Solution: Option (c) is correct.

Explanation:

$$4 = \frac{8 \times T}{100}$$

or $\quad T = 50$ years

Now, to become seven fold

$$6 = \frac{R \times 50}{100}$$

or $\quad R = 12\%$

■ **Compound Interest**

It is the interest calculated on a sum of money which includes principal and interest calculated for previous year. The SI (Simple Interest) and CI (Compound Interest) for first year is same and for second and subsequent years differ by an amount which is arrived by calculating interest on interests for previous years.

In other words, compound interest can be defined as the investment rate that grows exponentially and not linearly as in the case of simple interest.

The following table will illustrate the conceptual working of simple interest and compound interest.

Rate of interest per annum is 10%.

For the year	Simple Interest		Compound Interest	
	Principal	SI	Principal	CI
1	1000	100	1000	100
2	1000	100	1000 + 100 = 1100	110
3	1000	100	1100 + 110 = 1210	121

On the basis of above calculation, it is clear that:
(i) Simple interest for each year is constant
(ii) Compound interest calculated for each year is interest on interest calculated for previous year.

■ **Important Formulas:**

Let $\quad$ Principal = P,
$\quad\quad$ Rate = r % per annum,
$\quad\quad$ Time = n years

1. When interest is compounded annually:

$$\text{Amount } A = P\left(1 + \frac{r}{100}\right)^n$$

2. When interest is compounded half-yearly:

$$\text{Amount } A = P\left(1 + \frac{r/2}{100}\right)^{2n}$$

3. When interest is compounded quarterly:

$$\text{Amount } A = P\left(1 + \frac{r/4}{100}\right)^{4n}$$

4. When interest is compounded annually but time is in fraction, i.e. years.

$$\text{Amount} = A = P\left(1 + \frac{r}{100}\right)^3 \times P\left(1 + \frac{\frac{2}{5}r}{100}\right)$$

5. When rates are different for different years, say r_1%, r_2%, r_3% for 1st, 2nd and 3rd year respectively.
Then, Amount

$$A = P\left(1 + \frac{r_1}{100}\right)P\left(1 + \frac{r_2}{100}\right)P\left(1 + \frac{r_3}{100}\right)$$

6. Present worth of Rs. x due n years hence is given by:

$$\text{Present Worth} = \frac{x}{\left(1 + \frac{r}{100}\right)}$$

■ **Note:**

- On a certain sum of money, the difference between compound interest and simple interest for 2 years at r% rate is given by sum

$$\left(\frac{r}{100}\right)^2$$

- On a certain sum of money, the difference between compound interest and simple interest for 3 years at r% per annum is given by:

$$\text{Difference} = \frac{\text{Sum} \times R^2 \times (300 + R)}{(100)^3}$$

Example 5:
Find the difference between CI and SI on Rs. 8000 for 3 years at 2.5% per annum.
(a) 15.125 $\quad$ (b) 17.225
(c) 19.125 $\quad$ (d) 18.250
Solution: Option (a) is correct.
Explanation:
By Formula

$$\text{Difference} = \frac{\text{Sum} \times R^2 \times (300 + R)}{(100)^3}$$

$$\text{Difference} = \frac{8000 \times (2.5)^2 \times (300 + 2.5)}{(100)^3}$$

$$= 15.125$$

Example 6:
There is 60% increase in an amount in 6 years at simple interest. What will be the compound interest of Rs. 12,000 after 3 years at the same rate?
(a) Rs. 2160 $\quad$ (b) Rs. 3120
(c) Rs. 3972 $\quad$ (d) Rs. 6240
Solution: Option (c) is correct.

Commercial Mathematics

Explanation:
Let   P = Rs. 100
Then, S.I. Rs. 60 and T
           = 6 years
∴   R = 100 × 60 / 100 × 6
           = 10% p.a.
Now,   P = Rs. 12000.
         T = 3 years and
         R = 10% p.a.
∴   (C)I. = Rs.[12000 × (1 + 10/100)^3 –1]
               = 3972

Example 7:
A bank offers 5% compound interest calculated on half-yearly basis. A customer deposits Rs. 1600 each on 1st January and 1st July of a year. At the end of the year, the amount he would have gained by way of interest is:
(a) Rs. 120   (b) Rs. 121
(c) Rs. 122   (d) Rs. 123
Solution: Option b) is correct.
Explanation:
     Amount = [Rs.1600 × (1 +5/2 × 100)^2
                                   + Rs.1600 × (1 +5/2 x100)]
              = Rs. 3321.
∴   C.I. = Rs. (3321 – 3200)
              = Rs. 121

Multiple Choice Questions

1. A batsman scored 110 runs which included 3 boundaries and 8 sixes. What percent of his total score did he make by running between the wickets?
   (a) 45%   (b) $45\frac{5}{11}\%$
   (c) 54%   (d) 55%

2. If A = x% of y and B = y% of x, then which of the following is true?
   a. A is smaller than B
   (b) A is greater than B
   (c) Relationship between A and B cannot be determined.
   (d) None of these

3. If 20% of $a = b$, then b% of 20 is the same as:
   (a) 4% of a   (b) 5% of a
   (c) 20% of a   (d) None of these

4. In a certain school, 20% of students are below 8 years of age. The number of students above 8 years of age is 2/3 of the number of students of 8 years of age which is 48. What is the total number of students in the school?
   (a) 72   (b) 80
   (c) 120   (d) 100

5. Two numbers A and B are such that the sum of 5% of A and 4% of B is two-third of the sum of 6% of A and 8% of B. Find the ratio of A : B.
   (a) 2 : 3   (b) 1 : 1
   (c) 3 : 4   (d) 4 : 3

6. A student multiplied a number by 3/5 instead of 5/3. What is the percentage error in the calculation?
   (a) 34%   (b) 44%
   (c) 54%   (d) 64%

7. In an election between two candidates, one got 55% of the total valid votes, 20% of the votes were invalid. If the total number of votes was 7500, the number of valid votes that the other candidate got, was:
   (a) 2700   (b) 2900
   (c) 3000   (d) 3100

8. Three candidates contested an election and received 1136, 7636 and 11628 votes respectively. What percentage of the total votes did the winning candidate get?
   (a) 57%   (b) 60%
   (c) 65%   (d) 90%

9. Two tailors X and Y are paid a total of Rs. 550 per week by their employer. If X is paid 120 percent of the sum paid to Y, how much is Y paid per week?
   (a) Rs. 200   (b) Rs. 250
   (c) Rs. 300   (d) None of these

10. Gauri went to the stationers and bought things worth Rs. 25, out of which 30 paise went on sales tax on taxable purchases. If the tax rate was 6%, then what was the cost of the tax free items?
    (a) Rs. 15   (b) Rs. 15.70
    (c) Rs. 19.70   (d) Rs. 20

11. A man purchased a cow for Rs. 3000 and sold it the same day for Rs. 3600, allowing the buyer a credit of 2 years. If the rate of interest be 10% per annum, then the man has a gain of:
    (a) 0%   (b) 5%
    (c) 7.5%   (d) 10%

12. A trader owes a merchant Rs. 10,028 due 1 year hence. The trader wants to settle the account after 3 months. If the rate of interest is 12% per annum, how much cash should he pay?
    (a) Rs. 9025.20   (b) Rs. 9200
    (c) Rs. 9600   (d) Rs. 9560

13. A man wants to sell his scooter. There are two offers, one at Rs. 12,000 cash and the other a credit of Rs. 12,880 to be paid after 8 months, money being at 18% per annum. Which is the better offer?
    (a) Rs. 12,000 in cash
    (b) Rs. 12,880 at credit
    (c) Both are equally good
    (d) None of the above

14. If Rs. 10 be allowed as true discount on a bill of Rs. 110 due at the end of a certain time, then the discount allowed on the same sum due at the end of double the time is:
    (a) Rs. 20   (b) Rs. 21.81
    (c) Rs. 22   (d) Rs. 18.33

15. Goods were bought for Rs. 600 and sold the same for Rs. 688.50 at a credit of 9 months and thus gaining 2%. The rate of interest per annum is:
    (a) $16\frac{2}{3}\%$ (b) 15%
    (c) 14%   (d) 13%

16. The true discount on a bill due 9 months hence at 16% per annum is Rs. 189. The amount of the bill is:
    (a) Rs. 1386   (b) Rs. 1764
    (c) Rs. 1575   (d) Rs. 2268

17. A man buys a watch for Rs. 1950 in cash and sells it for Rs. 2200 at a credit of 1 year. If the rate of interest is 10% per annum, the man:
    (a) gains Rs. 55   (b) gains Rs. 50
    (c) loses Rs. 30   (d) gains Rs. 30

18. The true discount on Rs. 1760 due after a certain time at 12% per annum is Rs. 160. The time after which it is due is:
    (a) 6 months   (b) 8 months
    (c) 9 months   (d) 10 months

19. The present worth of Rs. 2310 due 2.5 years hence, the rate of interest being 15% per annum, is:
    (a) Rs. 1750   (b) Rs. 1680
    (c) Rs. 1840   (d) Rs. 1443.75

20. Rs. 20 is the true discount on Rs. 260 due after a certain time. What will be the true discount on the same sum due after half of the former time, the rate of interest being the same?
    (a) Rs. 10   (b) Rs. 10.40
    (c) Rs. 15.20   (d) Rs. 13

21. The interest on Rs. 750 for 2 years is the same as the true discount on Rs. 960 due 2 years hence. If the rate of interest is the same in both cases, it is:
    (a) 12%   (b) 14%
    (c) 15%   (d) 16%

22. The simple interest and the true discount on a certain sum for a given time and at a given rate are Rs. 85 and Rs. 80 respectively. The sum is:
    (a) Rs. 1800   (b) Rs. 1450
    (c) Rs. 1360   (d) Rs. 6800

23. The present worth of Rs. 1404 due in two equal half-yearly instalments at 8% per annum simple interest is:
    (a) Rs. 1325   (b) Rs. 1300
    (c) Rs. 1350   (d) Rs. 1500

24. If the true discount on a sum due 2 years hence at 14% per annum be Rs. 168, the sum due is:
    (a) Rs. 768   (b) Rs. 968
    (c) Rs. 1960   (d) Rs. 2400

25. In an election of two candidates, the candidate who gets 41% is rejected by a majority of 2412 votes. Find the total number of votes polled.
    (a) 12600   (b) 11300
    (c) 13400   (d) 15600

26. A man loses 12.5% of his money and after spending 70% of the remainder he left with Rs. 210. How much did he lose at first?
    (a) Rs. 800   (b) Rs. 950
    (c) Rs. 1200   (d) Rs. 1050

27. 3.5% of income is taken as tax and 12.5% of the remaining is saved. This leaves Rs. 4,053 to spend. What is the income?
    (a) Rs. 6000   (b) Rs. 7200
    (c) Rs. 5600   (d) Rs. 4800

28. If 2 litres of water is evaporated on boiling from 8 litres of sugar solution containing 5% sugar, find the percentage of sugar in the remaining solution.
    (a) $6\frac{2}{3}\%$ (b) $8\frac{1}{3}\%$
    (c) $7\frac{1}{2}\%$ (d) $9\frac{2}{3}\%$

29. Due to fall in manpower, the production in a factory decreases by 25%. By what percent should the working hour be increased to restore the original production?
    (a) $9\frac{2}{3}\%$ (b) $34\frac{1}{3}\%$
    (c) $33\frac{1}{3}\%$ (d) $26\frac{2}{5}\%$

30. 12% of a certain sum of money is Rs. 43.5. Find the sum.
    (a) Rs. 340.50   (b) Rs. 362.50
    (c) Rs. 421.75   (d) Rs. 263.30

31. A person borrows Rs. 5000 for 2 years at 4% p.a. simple interest. He immediately lends it to another person at 6.25% p.a for 2 years. Find his gain in the transaction per year.
    (a) Rs. 112.50   (b) Rs. 125
    (c) Rs. 150   (d) Rs. 167.50

32. A certain amount earns simple interest of Rs. 1750 after 7 years. Had the interest been 2% more, how much more interest would it have earned?
    (a) Rs. 35   (b) Rs. 245
    (c) Rs. 350   (d) data inadequate

33. What will be the ratio of simple interest earned by certain amount at the same rate of interest for 6 years and that for 9 years?
    (a) 1 : 3   (b) 1 : 4
    (c) 2 : 3   (d) Data inadequate

34. A sum of Rs. 12,500 amounts to Rs. 15,500 in 4 years at the rate of simple interest. What is the rate of interest?
    (a) 3%   (b) 4%
    (c) 5%   (d) 6%

35. An automobile financier claims to be lending money at simple interest, but he includes the interest every six months for calculating the principal. If he is charging an interest of 10%, the effective rate of interest becomes:
    (a) 10%   (b) 10.25%
    (c) 10.5%   (d) None of these

36. A lent Rs. 5000 to B for 2 years and Rs. 3000 to C for 4 years on simple interest at the same rate of interest and received Rs. 2200 in all from both of them as interest. The rate of interest per annum is:
    (a) 5% (b) 7%
    (c) 7.5% (d) 10%
37. A sum of Rs. 725 is lent in the beginning of a year at a certain rate of interest. After 8 months, a sum of Rs. 362.50 more is lent but at the rate twice the former. At the end of the year, Rs. 33.50 is earned as interest from both the loans. What was the original rate of interest?
    (a) 3.6% (b) 4.5%
    (c) 5% (d) None of these
38. A man took loan from a bank at the rate of 12% p.a. simple interest. After 3 years he had to pay Rs. 5400 interest only for the period. The principal amount borrowed by him was:
    (a) Rs. 2000 (b) Rs. 10,000
    (c) Rs. 15,000 (d) Rs. 20,000
39. A sum of money amounts to Rs. 9800 after 5 years and Rs. 12005 after 8 years at the same rate of simple interest. The rate of interest per annum is:
    (a) 5% (b) 8%
    (c) 12% (d) 15%
40. A sum of money at simple interest amounts to Rs. 815 in 3 years and to Rs. 854 in 4 years. The sum is:
    (a) Rs. 650 (b) Rs. 690
    (c) Rs. 698 (d) Rs. 700
41. Mr. Thomas invested an amount of Rs. 13,900 divided in two different schemes A and B at the simple interest rate of 14% p.a. and 11% p.a. respectively. If the total amount of simple interest earned in 2 years be Rs. 3508, what was the amount invested in Scheme B?
    (a) Rs. 6400 (b) Rs. 6500
    (c) Rs. 7200 (d) Rs. 7500
42. A sum fetched a total simple interest of Rs. 4016.25 at the rate of 9% p.a. in 5 years. What is the sum?
    (a) Rs. 4462.50 (b) Rs. 8032.50
    (c) Rs. 8900 (d) Rs. 8925
43. How much time will it take for an amount of Rs. 450 to yield Rs. 81 as interest at 4.5% per annum of simple interest?
    (a) 3.5 years (b) 4 years
    (c) 4.5 years (d) 5 years
44. Reena took a loan of Rs. 1200 with simple interest for as many years as the rate of interest. If she paid Rs. 432 as interest at the end of the loan period, what was the rate of interest?
    (a) 3.6 (b) 6
    (c) 18 (d) Cannot be determined
45. Anita borrowed Rs. 800 for 2 years at the rate of 12% per annum. Find the interest. Also find the amount paid by her.
    (a) Rs. 192, Rs. 992 (b) Rs. 992, Rs. 192
    (c) Rs. 692, Rs. 200 (d) Rs. 962, Rs. 129
46. Deepak takes a loan of Rs. 8,000 to buy a used truck at the rate of 9 % Simple Interest. Calculate the annual interest to be paid for the loan amount.
    (a) Rs. 900 (b) Rs. 700
    (c) Rs. 720 (d) Rs. 780
47. Steve invested $ 10,000 in a savings bank account that earned 2% Simple Interest. Find the interest earned if the amount was kept in the bank for 4 years.
    (a) $ 500 (b) $650
    (c) $775 (d) $800
48. Ryan bought $ 15,000 from a bank to buy a car at 10% Simple Interest. If he paid $ 9,000 as interest while clearing the loan, find the time for which the loan was given.
    (a) 5.5 years (b) 6 years
    (c) 8.5 years (d) 9 years
49. In how much time will the simple interest on $3,500 at the rate of 9% p.a be the same as simple interest on $4,000 at 10.5% p.a for 4 years?
    (a) 5 years (b) 6 years
    (c) 5.33 years (d) 6.25 years
50. In what time will Rs. 8500 amount to Rs. 15767.50 at 4.5% per annum?
    (a) 16 years (b) 19 years
    (c) 17 years (d) 21 years
51. What sum of the money will produce Rs. 143 interest in $3\frac{1}{4}$ years at 2.5% simple interest?
    (a) Rs. 1700 (b) Rs. 1830
    (c) Rs. 1760 (d) Rs. 1950
52. A sum of money doubles itself in 10 years at simple interest. What is the rate of interest?
    (a) 10% (b) 20%
    (c) 30% (d) 15%
53. A sum of money trebles itself in 20 years at SI. Find the rate of interest.
    (a) 5% (b) 10%
    (c) 15% (d) 20%
54. In what time does a sum of money become four times at the simple interest rate of 5% per annum?
    (a) 40 years (b) 45 years
    (c) 60 years (d) 80 years
55. A sum was put at SI at a certain rate for 2 years. Had it been put at 3% higher rate, it would have fetched Rs. 300 more. Find the sum.
    (a) Rs. 12000 (b) Rs. 10000
    (c) Rs. 7000 (d) Rs. 5000
56. A sum of money doubles itself in 7 years. In how many years will it become fourfold?
    (a) 35 years (b) 45 years
    (c) 19 years (d) 21 years
57. The simple interest on Rs. 1650 will be less than the interest on Rs. 1800 at 4% simple interest by Rs. 30. Find the time.
    (a) 3 years (b) 5 years
    (c) 7 years (d) 9 years

58. Bobby invested a certain sum of money at 8% p.a. simple interest for 'n' years. At the end of 'n' years, Bobby got back 4 times his original investment. What is the value of n?
    (a) 50 years
    (b) 25 years
    (c) 12 years 6 months
    (d) 37 years 6 months

59. Anita invested a certain sum of money in a bank that paid simple interest. The amount grew to Rs. 240 at the end of 2 years. She waited for another 3 years and got a final amount of Rs. 300. What was the principal amount that she invested at the beginning?
    (a) Rs. 200
    (b) Rs. 150
    (c) Rs. 210
    (d) Rs. 175

60. Pratap invested a certain sum of money in a simple interest bond whose value grew to Rs.300 at the end of 3 years and to Rs. 400 at the end of another 5 years. What was the rate of interest in which he invested his sum?
    (a) 12.5%
    (b) 6.67%
    (c) 6.25%
    (d) 8.33%

61. Find compound interest on Rs. 7500 at 4% per annum for 2 Years, compounded annually.
    (a) Rs.512
    (b) Rs.552
    (c) Rs.612
    (d) Rs.622

62. Find the compound interest on Rs.16, 000 at 20% per annum for 9 months, compounded quarterly.
    (a) Rs. 2552
    (b) Rs. 2512
    (c) Rs. 2592
    (d) Rs. 2572

63. Simple interest on a certain sum of money for 3 years at 8% per annum is half the compound interest on Rs. 4000 for 2 years at 10% per annum. The sum placed on simple interest is:
    (a) Rs. 1550
    (b) Rs. 1650
    (c) Rs. 1750
    (d) Rs. 2000

64. Anil invested an amount of Rs.8000 in a fixed deposit scheme for 2 years at compound interest rate 5% per annum. How much amount will Anil get on maturity of the fixed deposit?
    (a) Rs. 8600
    (b) Rs. 8620
    (c) Rs. 8840
    (d) Rs. 8820

65. The present worth of Rs.169 due in 2 years at 4% per annum compound interest is:
    (a) Rs.150.50
    (b) Rs.154.75
    (c) Rs.156.25
    (d) Rs.158

66. On a sum of money, the simple interest for 2 years is Rs. 660, while the compound interest is Rs.696.30, the rate of interest being the same in both the cases. The rate of interest is:
    (a) 10%
    (b) 11%
    (c) 12%
    (d) 10.5%

67. The difference between simple interest and compound interest on Rs. 1200 for one year at 10% per annum reckoned half yearly is
    (a) Rs.2.50
    (b) Rs. 3
    (c) Rs. 4
    (d) Rs. 3.75

68. A sum of money invested at compound interest amounts to Rs. 800 in 3 years and to Rs. 840 in 4 years. The rate of interest per annum is
    (a) 4%
    (b) 5%
    (c) 6%
    (d) 2%

69. If the simple interest on a sum of money for 2 years at 5% per annum is Rs. 50, what is the compound interest on the same at the same rate and for the same time?
    (a) Rs. 51.25
    (b) Rs. 52
    (c) Rs. 54.25
    (d) Rs. 60

70. In what time will Rs.1000 become Rs.1331 at 10% per annum compounded annually?
    (a) 2 years
    (b) 3 years
    (c) 4 years
    (d) 7 years

Commercial Mathematics

Answer Key

1. (b)	2. (d)	3. (a)	4. (d)	5. (d)	6. (d)	7. (a)	8. (a)	9. (b)	10. (c)	11. (a)
12. (b)	13. (a)	14. (d)	15. (a)	16. (b)	17. (b)	18. (d)	19. (b)	20. (b)	21. (b)	22. (c)
23. (a)	24. (a)	25. (c)	26. (a)	27. (d)	28. (a)	29. (c)	30. (b)	31. (a)	32. (d)	33. (c)
34. (d)	35. (b)	36. (d)	37. (d)	38. (c)	39. (c)	40. (c)	41. (a)	42. (d)	43. (b)	44. (b)
45. (a)	46. (c)	47. (d)	48. (b)	49. (c)	50. (b)	51. (c)	52. (a)	53. (b)	54. (c)	55. (d)
56. (d)	57. (b)	58. (d)	59. (a)	60. (d)	61. (c)	62. (a)	63. (c)	64. (d)	65. (c)	66. (b)
67. (b)	68. (b)	69. (a)	70. (b)							

Explanatory Notes

1. (b)
   Number of runs made by running
   $= 110 - (3 \times 4 + 8 \times 6)$
   $= 110 - (60)$
   $= 50$
   $\therefore$ Required percentage $= (50/100 \times 100)\%$
   $= 45\frac{5}{11}\%$

2. (d)
   $x\%$ of $y = (x/100 \times y)$
   $= (y/100 \times x) = y\%$ of x
   Therefore, A = B

3. (a)
   20% of $a = b$
   $(20/100)a = b$
   $b\%$ of $20 = (b/100 \times 20)$
   $= [(20/100)a \times 1/100 \times 20]$
   $= (4/100)a = 4\%$ of a

4. (d)
   Let the number of students be x. Then,
   Number of students above 8 years of age
   $= (100 - 20)\%$ of x
   $= 80\%$ of x
   $\therefore \quad 80\%$ of $x = 48 + 2/3$ of 48
   $\Rightarrow (80/100) x = 80$
   $\Rightarrow x = 100$

5. (d)
   5% of A + 4% of B = $2/3$ (6% of A + 8% of B)
   $(5/100)A + (4/100)B = 2/3[(6/100)A + (8/100)B]$
   $(1/20)A + (1/25)B = (1/25)A + (4/75)B$
   $(1/20 - 1/25)A = (4/75 - 1/25)B$
   $(1/100)A = (1/75) B$
   $A/B = 100/75 = 4/3$
   $\therefore$ Required ratio = 4 : 3

6. (d)
   Let the number be x
   Then, error $= (5/3) x - (3/5) x$
   $= (16/15) x$
   Error% $= [(16x/15) \times (3/5x) \times 100]\%$
   $= 64\%$

7. (a)
   Number of valid votes
   $= 80\%$ of $7500 = 6000$
   $\therefore$ Valid votes polled by other candidate
   $= 45\%$ of 6000
   $= (45/100 \times 6000) = 2700$

8. (a)
   Total number of votes polled
   $= (1136 + 7636 + 11628)$
   $= 20400$
   $\therefore$ Required percentage
   $= [(11628/20400) \times 100]\%$
   $= 57\%$

9. (b)
   Let the sum paid to Y per week be Rs. z
   Then, $z + 120\%$ of $z = 550$
   $\Rightarrow z + (120/100) z = 550$
   $\Rightarrow (11/5) z = 550$
   $\Rightarrow z = (550 \times 5)/11 = 250$

10. (c)
    Let the amount taxable purchases be Rs. x.
    Then, 6% of $x = 30/100$
    $\Rightarrow x = [(30/100) \times (100/6)] = 5$
    $\therefore$ Cost of tax free items
    $=$ Rs. $[25 - (5 + 0.30)]$
    $=$ Rs. 19.70

11. (a)
    C.P. = Rs. 3000
    S.P. = Rs. $[(3600 \times 100)/ 100 + (10 \times 2)]$
    = Rs. 3000
    Gain = 0%

12. (b)
    Required money
    = P.W. of Rs. 10028 due 9 months hence
    = Rs. $[(10028 \times 100)/ (100 + 12 \times 9/12)]$
    = Rs. 9200

13. (a)
    P.W. of Rs. $12,880$ due 8 months hence
    = Rs. $[(12880 \times 100)/ (100 + 18 \times 8/12)]$
    = Rs. $(12880 \times 100)/112$
    = Rs. 11500

14. (d)
S.I. on Rs. (110 – 10) for a certain time = Rs. 10
S.I. on Rs. 100 for double the time = Rs. 20
T.D. on Rs. 120 = Rs. (120 – 100) = Rs. 20
T.D. on Rs. 110 = Rs.(20/120) × 110 = Rs. 18.33

15. (a)
$$S.P. = 102\% \text{ of Rs. } 600 = \text{Rs. } 612$$
Now, P.W. = Rs. 612 and sum = Rs. 688.50
∴ T.D. = Rs. (688.50 – 612) = Rs. 76.50
Thus, S.I. on Rs. 612 for 9 months is Rs. 76.50
∴ Rate = [(100 × 76.50)/ (612 × 3/4)] %
$$= 16\frac{2}{3}\%$$

16. (b)
Let P.W. be Rs. x
Then, S.I. on Rs. x at 16% for 9 months = Rs. 189
∴ $x \times 16 \times 9/12 \times 1/100 = 189$
or $x = 1575$
∴ P.W. = Rs. 1575
∴ Sum due = P.W. + T.D.
= Rs. (1575 + 189)
= Rs. 1764

17. (b)
S.P. = P.W. of Rs. 2200 due 1 year hence
= Rs. [(2200 × 100)/ 100 + (10 × 1)]
= Rs. 2000
∴ Gain = Rs. (2000 – 1950) = Rs. 50

18. (d)
P.W. = Rs. (1760 – 160) = Rs. 1600
∴ S.I. on Rs. 1600 at 12% is Rs. 160
∴ Time = (100 × 160)/(1600 × 12)
= 5/6 years
= (5/6 × 12 months)
= 10 months

19. (b)
P.W. = Rs. [(100 × 2310)/ (100 + 15 × 5/12)
= Rs. 1680

20. (b)
S.I. on Rs. (260 – 20) for a given time = Rs. 20
S.I. on Rs. 240 for half the time = Rs. 10
T.D. on Rs. 250 = Rs. 10
∴ T.D. on Rs. 260 = Rs. [(10/250) × 260]
= Rs. 10.40

21. (b)
S.I. on Rs. 750 = T.D. on Rs. 960
This means P.W. of Rs. 960 due 2 years hence is Rs. 750.
∴ T.D. = Rs. (960 – 750)
= Rs. 210
Thus, S.I. on Rs. 750 for 2 years is Rs. 210.
∴ Rate = [(100 × 210)/(750 × 2)] %
= 14%

22. (c)
Sum = (S.I. × T.D.)/(S.I.) – (T.D.)
= 85 × 80/ (85 – 80)
= Rs. 1360.

23. (a)
Required sum = P.W. of Rs. 702 due 6 months + P.W. of Rs. 702 due 1 year
Hence
= [(100 × 702)/(100 + 8 × 1/2) + (100 × 702)/(100 + 8 × 1)]
= Rs. (675 + 650)
= Rs. 1325

24. (a)
P.W. = (100 × T.D.)/ R × T
= (100 × 168)/14 × 2 = 600
∴ Sum = (P.W. + T.D.)
= Rs. (600 + 168) = Rs. 768

25. (c)
(59% – 41%) = 18% ≡ 2412
∴ 100% ≡ (2412/18) × 100
= 13400

26. (a)
$$\text{His initial money} = \frac{210 \times 100 \times 100}{(100 - 12.5)(100 - 70)}$$
$$= \frac{210 \times 100 \times 100}{87.5 \times 30}$$
= Rs. 800

27. (d)
$$\text{Income} = \frac{4053 \times 100 \times 100}{(100 - 3.5)(100 - 12.5)}$$
= Rs. 4,800

28. (a)
Sugar in the original solution
= 5% of 8 litres = 0.4 litres
After evaporation of 2 litres of water, the quantity of remaining solution
= 8 – 2 = 6 litres
∴ Required percentage of sugar
= (0.4/6) × 100%
$$= 6\frac{2}{3}\%$$

29. (c)
Required percentage increase in working hours
= [25/(100 – 25)] × 100
$$= 100/3 = 33\frac{1}{3}\%$$

30. (b)
$$\frac{12}{100} \text{ of a sum} = \text{Rs. } 43.50$$
∴ Sum $= \frac{87}{2} \times \frac{100}{12}$ = Rs. 362.50

Commercial Mathematics

31. (a)
Gain in 2 years
= Rs. [(5000 × 25/4 × 2/100) – {(5000 × 4 × 2)/100}]
= Rs. (625 – 400)
= Rs. 225
Gain in 1 year = Rs. 225/2 = 112.50

32. (d)
We need to know the S.I., principal and time to find the rate.
Since the principal is not given, so data is inadequate.

33. (c)
Let the principal be P and rate of interest be R%.

Required ratio = $\dfrac{\left(\dfrac{P \times R \times 6}{100}\right)}{\dfrac{(P \times R \times 9)}{100}} = \dfrac{6PR}{9PR}$

= $\dfrac{6}{9} = 2 : 3$

34. (d)
S.I. = Rs. (15500 – 12500)
= Rs. 3000

Rate = $\left(\dfrac{100 \times 3000}{12500 \times 4}\right)\% = 6\%$

35. (b)
Let the sum be Rs. 100. Then,

S.I. for first 6 months = Rs. $\left(\dfrac{100 \times 10 \times 1}{100 \times 2}\right)$ = Rs. 5

S.I. for last 6 months = Rs. $\left(\dfrac{105 \times 10 \times 1}{100 \times 2}\right)$
= Rs. 5.25

So, amount at the end of 1 year
= Rs. (100 + 5 + 5.25)
= Rs. 110.25
Effective rate = (110.25 – 100)
= 10.25%

36. (d)
Let the rate be R% p.a.

Then, $\left(\dfrac{5000 \times R \times 2}{100}\right) + \left(\dfrac{3000 \times R \times 4}{100}\right) = 2200$

⇒ 100 R + 120 R = 2200
⇒ R = 2200/220
Rate = 10%

37. (d)
Let the original rate be R%
Then, new rate = (2R)%
Note: Here, original rate is for 1 year(s); the new rate is for only 4 months i.e. $\dfrac{1}{3}$ year(s).

$\left(\dfrac{725 \times R \times 1}{100}\right) + \left(\dfrac{362.50 \times 2R \times 1}{3 \times 100}\right) = 33.50$

⇒ (2175 + 725) R = 33.50 × 100 × 3
⇒ (2175 + 725) R = 10050
⇒ (2900) R = 10050
⇒ R = 10050 / 2900 = 3.46
Original rate = 3.46%

38. (c)
Principal = Rs. $\left(\dfrac{100 \times 5400}{12 \times 3}\right)$
= Rs. 15000

39. (c)
S.I. for 3 years = Rs. (12005 – 9800)
= Rs. 2205

S.I. for 5 years = $\dfrac{2205}{3} \times 5$ = Rs. 3675

Principal = Rs. (9800 – 3675)
= Rs. 6125
Hence, rate = (100 × 3675)/(6125 × 5)
= 12%

40. (c)
S.I. for 1 year = Rs. (854 – 815) = Rs. 39
S.I. for 3 years = Rs. (39 × 3)
= Rs. 117
∴ Principal = Rs. (815 – 117)
= Rs. 698

41. (a)
Let the sum invested in Scheme A be Rs. x and that in Scheme B be Rs. (13900 – x)
Then, (x × 14 × 2)/100 + [(13900 – x) × 11 × 2]/100
= 3508
⇒ 28x – 22x = 350800 – (13900 × 22)
⇒ 6x = 45000
⇒ x = 7500
So, sum invested in Scheme B
= Rs. (13900 – 7500)
= Rs. 6400

42. (d)
Principal = Rs. (100 × 4016.25)/(9 × 5)
= Rs. 401625/45
= Rs. 8925

43. (b)
Time = (100 × 81)/(450 × 4.5) years
= 4 years

44. (b)
Let rate = R% and time
= R years
Then, (1200 × R × R)/100 = 432
⇒ 12 R² = 432
⇒ R² = 36
⇒ R = 6

45. (a)

Principal = 'P' = Rs. 800
Rate = R = 12% = 0.12
Time = 'T' = 2 years
Interest: I = P × R × T
I = 800 × 0.12 × 2
I = 192
Amount: A = P + I
A = 800 + 192 = Rs. 992

46. (c)
From the details given in the problem Principle = P = Rs. 8,000 and R = 9% or 0.09 expressed as a decimal.
As the annual interest is to be calculated, the time period T = 1
Plugging these values in the simple Interest formula,
I = P × T × R
= 8,000 × 1 × 0.09
= 720.00
Annual Interest to be paid = Rs. 720

47. (d)
Principle P = $ 10,000. Time Period T = 4 years and Rate of Interest = 2% = 0.02
Plugging these values in the simple Interest formula,
I = P × T × R
= 10,000 × 4 × 0.02
= $ 800
Interest earned for the investment = $ 800

48. (b)
Principle = $ 15,000; Rate of Interest R = 10% = 0.10 and the Interest paid = I = $ 9,000. And T is to be found.
T = I/(PR)
= 9000/(15,000 × 0.10)
= 6 years
The loan was given for 6 years

49. (c)
S.I on $4,000 at rate 10.5%
= 10.5/100
= 0.105 for 4 years
S.I = (P × R × T) /100
= 4000 × 0.105 × 4
S.I = $ 1,680
The interest of $1,680 is the same as that on $3,500 at 9% p.a. for supposed years.
Time = t = (S.I × 100)/(P × R)
= (1680 × 100)/ (3500 × 9)
Time = t = 5.33 years

50. (b)
Here interest = Rs. 15767.50 – 8500
= Rs. 7267.50
Therefore t = (7267.50 x 100)/(8500 x 4.5)
= 19 years

51. (c)
Let the required sum be Rs. P. Then,
Rs. P = (100 × 143)/3.25 × 2.5 = Rs. 1760

52. (a)
Let the sum be Rs. 100
After 10 years it becomes Rs. 200
Therefore Interest= Rs. 200 – Rs. 100 = Rs. 100
Then, Rate = (100 × I)/ (P × T)
= (100 × 100)/ (100 × 10)
= 10%

53. (b)
Rate = [100(3 – 1)]/20 = 10%

54. (c)
Time = [100(Multiple number of principle – 1)]/ Rate
= [100(4 – 1)]/5
= 60 years

55. (d)
Sum = (More Interest × 100)/ (Time × More Rate)
= (300 × 100)/ (2 × 3) = 5000

56. (d)
Rate = [100(2 – 1)]/7 =100/7
Therefore Time = [100(4 – 1)]/(100/7)
= 21 years

57. (b)
We may consider that Rs. (1800 – 1650) gives interest of Rs. 30 at 4% per annum.
Therefore,
Time = (30 × 100)/ (150 × 4) = 5 years

58. (d)
Let us say Bobby invested Rs.100
Then, at the end of 'n' years he would have got back Rs. 400
Therefore, the Simple Interest earned
= 400 – 100 = Rs. 300
Simple Interest = PRT/100
Substituting the values in the above equation we get
300 = (100 × n × 8)/100
8n = 300
n = 37.5 years

59. (a)
The sum grew to Rs. 240 at the end of 2 years.
At the end of another 3 years, the sum grew to Rs. 300
i.e. in 3 years, the sum grew by Rs. 60
Therefore, each year, it grew by Rs. 20
Sum at the end of 2 years = Rs. 240
Sum grew by Rs. 20 each year
Hence, in the first 2 years, the sum grew by
2 × 20 = Rs. 40
Therefore, sum at the beginning of the period
= Sum at the end of 2 years – Rs. 40
= Rs. 240 – Rs. 40 = Rs. 200

60. (d)
Initial amount invested = Rs. X
Therefore, the interest earned for the 5 year period between the 3rd year and 8th year
= Rs. 400 – Rs.300 = Rs.100

As the simple interest earned for a period of 5 years is Rs. 100, interest earned per year
= Rs. 20
Therefore, interest earned for 3 years
= 3 × 20 = Rs. 60
Hence, initial amount invested X = Amount after 3 years – interest for 3 years
= 300 – 60 = Rs. 240
Rate of interest = (interest per year principal invested) × 100
= (20/240) × 100 = 8.33%

61. (c)
Amount = Rs. [7500 × (1 + 4/100)^2]
= Rs. (7500 × 26/25 × 26/25)
= Rs.8112
C.I. = Rs. (8112 – 7500)
= Rs. 612

62. (a)
Principal = Rs.16, 000
Time = 9 months = 3 quarters
Amount = Rs. [16000 × (1 + 5/100)^3]
= [16000 × 21/20 × 21/20 × 21/20]
= Rs.18522
C.I = Rs. (18522 – 16000)
= Rs. 2522

63. (c)
C.I. = Rs. [4000 × (1 + 10/100)^2 – 4000]
= Rs. (4000 × 11/10 × 11/10 – 4000)
= Rs. 840
Sum = Rs. [420 × 100 /3 × 8]
= Rs.1750

64. (d)
Amount = Rs. [8000 × (1 + 5/100)^2]
= Rs. [8000 × 21/20 × 21/20]
= Rs. 8820

65. (c)
Present Worth = Rs. [169/(1 + 4/100)^2]
= Rs. (169 × 25/26 × 25/26)
= Rs.156.25

66. (b)
Difference in C.I and S.I for 2 years
= Rs. (696.30 – 660)
= Rs. 36.30
S.I for one year = Rs. 330
S.I on Rs.330 for 1 year
= Rs. 36.30
Rate = (100 × 36.30/330 × 1) %
= 11%

67. (b)
S.I = Rs. (1200 × 10 × 1/100)
= Rs.120
C.I = Rs. [1200 × (1+ 5/100)^2 –1200]
= Rs.123
Difference = Rs. [123 – 120]
= Rs. 3

68. (b)
S.I. on Rs.800 for 1 year
= Rs. [840 – 800]
= Rs. 40
Rate = (100 × 40/800 × 1) %
= 5%

69. (a)
Sum = Rs. (50 × 100/2 × 5)
= Rs. 500
Amount = [Rs. (500 × (1 + 5/100)^2]
= Rs. (500 × 21/20 × 21/20)
= Rs. 551.25
C.I = Rs. (551.25 – 500)
= Rs. 51.25

70. (b)
Principal = Rs.1000
Amount = Rs.1331
Rate = Rs. 10% p.a.
Let the time be n years. Then
[1000(1+10/100)^n] = 1331
(1+10/100)^n = (1331/1000)
(11/10)^n = (11/10)^3
Therefore n = 3 years

Previous Year Questions

1. Two numbers are respectively 20% and 50% more than the third. What percent is the first of the second?
   [NTSE 2012– Delhi first stage paper]
   (a) 60%   (b) 82%
   (c) 75%   (d) 80%

2. Two numbers are respectively 20% and 25% of a third number. What percent is the first of the second?
   [NTSE 2000– Jammu first stage paper]
   (a) 60%   (b) 45%
   (c) 80%   (d) 35%

3. In an examination, 35% of total students failed in Hindi, 45% failed in English and 20% in both. Find the percentage of those who passed in both the subjects.
   [NTSE 2003– Kerala first stage paper]
   (a) 60   (b) 40
   (c) 20   (d) 35

4. The price of a television includes the manufacturing cost, 10% sales tax and 10% profit. What is the manufacturing cost, if the price is Rs. 14,400? (Sales tax and profit are to be calculated on manufacturing cost.)
   [NTSE 2001– Tamilnadu first stage paper]
   (a) 10,000   (b) 12,000
   (c) 12,500   (d) 9,000

5. A man's income is increased by Rs. 1200 and at the same time, the rate of the tax to be paid is reduced from 12% to 10%. He now pays the same amount of tax as before. Calculate the man's increased income.
   [NTSE 2012– Maharashtra first stage paper]
   (a) Rs. 7000   (b) Rs. 6500
   (c) Rs. 7200   (d) Rs. 8000

6. If the simple interest on a sum of money at 5% per annum for 3 years is Rs. 1200, find the compound interest on the same sum for the same period at the same rate.
   [NTSE 2006 – Gujarat first stage paper]
   (a) 1251   (b) 1261
   (c) 1271   (d) 1281

7. What will be the compound interest on a sum of Rs. 25,000 after 3 years at the rate of 12% per annum?
   [NTSE 2005 – Assam first stage paper]
   (a) Rs. 9000.30   (b) Rs. 9720
   (c) Rs. 10123.20   (d) Rs. 10483.20

8. The compound interest on Rs. 30,000 at 7% per annum is Rs. 4347. The period (in years) is:
   [NTSE 2001 – Punjab first stage paper]
   (a) 2   (b) 5
   (c) 3   (d) 4

9. The difference between compound interest and simple interest on an amount of Rs. 15,000 for 2 years is Rs. 96. What is the rate of interest per annum?
   [NTSE 2003 – Karnataka first stage paper]
   (a) 8   (b) 10
   (c) 9   (d) Cannot be determined

10. The compound interest on a certain sum for 2 years at 10% per annum is Rs. 525. The simple interest on the same sum for double the time at half the rate percent per annum is:
    [NTSE 2004 – Himachal Pradesh first stage paper]
    (a) Rs. 400   (b) Rs. 500
    (c) Rs. 600   (d) Rs. 800

Commercial Mathematics

Answer Key

1. (d)	2. (c)	3. (b)	4. (b)	5. (c)	6. (b)	7. (c)	8. (a)	9. (a)	10. (b)

Explanatory Notes

1. (d)
   Required value = $\frac{120}{150} \times 100\% = 80\%$

2. (c)
   Required value = $\frac{20}{25} \times 100\% = 80\%$

3. (b)
   Let the total number of students in the class be 100.
   Number of students who failed in Hindi only
   = (35 – 20) = 15
   Number of students who failed in English only
   = (45 – 20) = 25
   Total number of students who either in Hindi or English or both = (15 + 20 + 25) = 60
   Therefore, total number of students who passed in both the subjects = (100 – 60) = 40

4. (b)
   Since sales tax and profit are to be calculated on manufacturing cost, therefore single percentage change = 20%
   Now, manufacturing cost x 1.2 = 14,400
   Therefore manufacturing cost
   = 14,400/1.2 = Rs. 12,000

5. (c)
   Let the original income of man be Rs. x
   Then, $x \times 12\% = (x + 1200) \times 10\%$
   $12x = 10x + 12000$
   $\Rightarrow 2x = 12000$
   $x = 6000$
   Original income = Rs. 6000
   ∴ Increased income = (6000 + 1200) = Rs. 7200

6. (b)
   Clearly, Rate = 5% p.a.
   Time = 3 years
   S.I = Rs. 1200
   So, Principal = Rs. (100 × 1200/3 × 5)
   = Rs. 8000
   Amount = Rs. [8000 × (1 + 5/100)³]
   = Rs. (8000 × 21/20 × 21/20 × 21/20)
   = Rs. 9261
   C.I = Rs. (9261 – 8000)
   = Rs. 1261

7. (c)
   Amount = Rs. (25000 × (1 + 12/100)³
   = Rs. (25000 × 28/25 × 28/25 × 28/25)
   = Rs. 35123.20
   C.I = Rs. (35123.20 – 25000)
   = Rs.10123.20

8. (a)
   Amount = Rs. (30000 + 4347)
   = Rs. 34347
   Let the time be n years
   Then, $30000(1 + 7/100)^n = 34347$
   $(1 + 7/100)^n = 34347/3000$
   $(107/100)^n = 11449/1000$
   $(107/100)^n = (107/100)^2$
   Therefore = 2 years

9. (a)
   $[15000 (1 + r/100)^2 - 15000] - (15000 \times r \times 2)/100$
   = 96
   By solving the above equation
   $r^2 = (96 \times 2)/3$
   = 64
   Therefore $r = 8\%$

10. (b)
    Let the sum be Rs. P.
    Then, $[P (1 + 10/100)^2 - P] = 525$
    $P = (11/10)^2 - 1$
    = 525
    P = (525 × 100)/21
    = 2500
    Therefore Sum = Rs. 2500
    S.I. (2500 × 5 × 4)/100 = Rs. 500

REGIONAL LANGUAGE TITLES

BANGLA LANGUAGE

   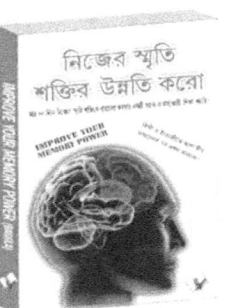

KANNADA LANGUAGE

 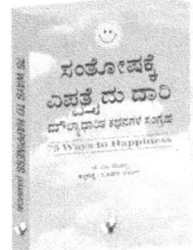

TAMIL LANGUAGE

GUJRATI LANGUAGE

Learn in Gujrati
1. Chanakya's ways of managing public administration
2. How to Sharpen Your Memory

MARATHI LANGUAGE

 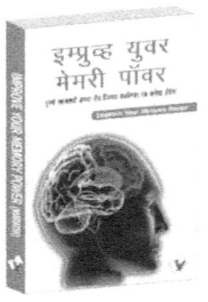

All books available at www.vspublishers.com

SCHOOL ATLAS

71 TRENDBLAZING SERIES OF PROJECTS & EXPERIMENTS

All books available at www.vspublishers.com

POPULAR SCIENCE

JOKES

CHILDREN'S ENCYCLOPEDIA

CHILDREN'S ENCYCLOPEDIA
THE WORLD OF KNOWLEDGE

FICTION

All books available at www.vspublishers.com

Quiz Books

MYSTERIES

DRAWING BOOKS

BIOGRAPHIES

QUOTES/SAYINGS

PUZZLES

ACTIVITIES BOOK

All books available at **www.vspublishers.com**

STUDENT DEVELOPMENT/LEARNING

CLASSIC SERIES

MAGIC & FACT

MUSIC

New

Graded Reader

Gift Pack

Save ₹ 300/-
Pay ₹ 1200/- instead of
₹ 1500/- for complete
Set of 10 books price
₹ 150/- each

All books available at www.vspublishers.com

CHILDREN TALES

TALES & STORIES

All Books Fully Coloured

HINDI LITERATURE

Save ₹ 150/- Pay ₹ 600/- instead of ₹ 750/- for complete Set of 5 books price ₹ 150/- each

Gift Pack

All books available at **www.vspublishers.com**

WOMEN ORIENTED

YOGA & FITNESS

BEAUTY CARE

ALTERNATIVE THERAPY

All books available at **www.vspublishers.com**

www.ingramcontent.com/pod-product-compliance
Lightning Source LLC
Chambersburg PA
CBHW080921180426
43192CB00040B/2610